Speaking in Hunger

Cultural Frames, Framing Culture
Robert Newman, Series Editor

Speaking in Hunger

Gender, Discourse, and Consumption in Clarissa

Donnalee Frega

UNIVERSITY OF SOUTH CAROLINA PRESS

Published in Columbia, South Carolina, by the
University of South Carolina Press

Manufactured in the United States of America

02 01 00 99 98 5 4 3 2 1

Library of Congress Cataloging-in-Publication Data

Frega, Donnalee, 1956–
    Speaking in hunger: gender, discourse, and consumption in
Clarissa / Donnalee Frega.
        p. cm. — (Cultural frames, framing culture)
    Includes bibliographical references and index.
    ISBN 1-57003-226-2. — ISBN 1-57003-275-0 (pbk.) ·
    1. Richardson, Samuel, 1689–1761. *Clarissa.* 2. Eating disorders
in literature. 3. Hunger in literature. 4. Women in literature.
5. Anorexia nervosa in literature. 6. Body, Human, in literature.
7. Power (Social sciences) in literature. 8. Discourse analysis,
Literary. 9. Epistolary fiction, English—History and criticism.
10. Women and literature—England—History—18th century.
I. Title. II. Series.
PR3664.C43F74   1998   97-21235
823'.6—DC21

The outline for this study appeared as "Speaking in Hunger: Conditional Consumption as Discourse in *Clarissa*," *Studies in the Literary Imagination* 28 (Spring 1995): 87–104. Permission to reprint from the Department of English at Georgia State University is gratefully acknowledged.

Contents

Series Editor's Preface

A commitment to relevance and to influence is the focus of this series of works on cultural studies. The series combines theoretical issues with practical applications so that abstract arguments are made accessible by framing them in terms of contemporary concerns of everyday life. The title of this series, "Cultural Frames, Framing Culture," indicates this intention. It highlights the mutual give-and-take between the way established culture frames our explanations and stories about contemporary affairs and the way these explanations and stories in turn produce the culture that frames them. The series will address a broad audience interested in reading contemporary culture—its images, messages, literature, and rhetoric—through fresh, provocative, and generally accessible approaches.

"Cultural Frames, Framing Culture" will encourage interdisciplinary studies. One of the potentially engaging facets of this series is that it offers books that combine a number of previously separated perspectives and also investigates why these separations have occurred. General topics for this series include pedagogical practices, representations of war, of the elderly or the infirm, religion and politics, constructions of race and gender, and the discourse of ecology.

Robert Newman

Acknowledgments

As this study developed through many years of research, work, conversation, and reflection, I am indebted to numerous friends and colleagues for their support and encouragement. I want to thank Marianna Torgovnick and Leigh DeNeef for an appointment as visiting scholar to the Department of English at Duke University which has allowed me to work in a dynamic intellectual community. Many friends at Duke have contributed to this study. I am forever indebted to Oliver Ferguson for insisting that I read *Clarissa* in its entirety and for embodying the qualities that he taught his students to appreciate in eighteenth-century texts: careful scholarship, gentle manners, and selfless integrity. George Gopen pored over initial drafts with the precision of a lawyer and a keen sense of humor. Jane Tompkins provided a helpful reading list of feminist scholarship. Marianna Torgovnick and Cathy Davidson offered practical support and personal encouragement when I most needed it. Words cannot acknowledge my gratitude for their generous friendship when my courage needed strengthening.

This book has benefited from many provocative discussions that stretched my thinking and led me to consider hard questions. Lilian Furst introduced me to Caroline Walker Bynum's superb work on consumption. Elizabeth Bergen Brophy read the manuscript with care and offered welcome reassurance and sound advice. Murray Brown gave the manuscript a painstaking and sympathetic reading and generally encouraged me through the project's final stages. Sue Lamb provided valuable suggestions for reading and was willing to talk about eating disorders over lunch. Psychologists Silvija Singh and Larry Newman reviewed my choice of scholarly and theoretical writings from their field and read the manuscript with the enthusiasm of good friends. Louise Jackson, reference librarian at UNC-Wilmington, spent many hours helping me verify citations of obscure eighteenth-century essays. Catherine Fry, my editor at the University of South Carolina Press, touched me with her confidence in the project and her enthusiasm for a topic close to my heart. Her interest in this study has refueled my enthusiasm for scholarly work and reminded me of the huge difference one woman can make simply by caring about another woman's work.

It is a special pleasure to thank those friends who have contributed to this study simply by being part of my life. With the sheer force of their unforgettable teaching, Grace Majewski and Calvin Smith propelled me toward this project before I could possibly have conceived of it. The hours I spent poring over Milton's lines with Calvin Smith are among the treasures of my life, and I became a teacher because of them.

This project has its roots in love. Paula Kamenish has sustained me with a courageous and cherished friendship. Fritzi Huber and Pat Coughlin have challenged my character and enriched my thinking more than I can acknowledge. My three children, Carl, Kurt, and Emma Lee, have hugged me at all the right times and have kept my work in perspective. My husband Alvin is my anchor, encouraging the joy I feel in my work and reminding me every day that feminism is not only about having a voice but about using it wisely and lovingly.

This book is dedicated to my parents, Donald and Georgetta Wells, who have helped in every way imaginable. They have brought me safely through storms and eased my passage, confirmed me in my hopes, and helped me to understand the complexity of love.

Speaking in Hunger

Introduction

Female hunger and eating habits have long been regarded as a form of discourse, a rich and complex metaphoric language of victimization, physicality, eroticism, and empowerment.[1] Feminist scholars acknowledge that women's ability to manipulate food distribution and their bodies (often the only resources in their power) can be a double-edged sword, a tool that allows women to repress their sexuality, to establish social rank, to engage in charitable activities, even while it forces them to accommodate physical victimization in order to empower themselves. I wish to argue that this seeming contradiction, often recognized as a mere displacement of power—a metaphoric equation of hunger with femininity, virginity, spiritualism, or class position—oversimplifies hunger as a language because it ignores the intricate ways in which this language is learned and shared.

As Maud Ellmann points out in *The Hunger Artists: Starving, Writing, and Imprisonment,* language depends on consensus, both public and private.[2] As a language, food-related behavior is multifaceted, uniting both the biological desire for food and the more complicated longing for less tangible "foods" that humans crave: acceptance, respect, love, support, security, self-determination.[3] Because biological, social, and religious forms of hunger are often superimposed on one another, women who use food as an analogue to self often find themselves unsure of their identities, unable to distinguish between powerful metaphors of suffering and desire. This tension has been particularly obvious in literary portrayals of heroines who use biological hunger to obtain the "authority" necessary to write their own stories.

While most literary studies of female fasting concentrate on Victorian novels,[4] I have chosen to frame my discussion around a reading of Richardson's *Clarissa,* an eighteenth-century classic, for several reasons. *Clarissa* is a novel about a heroine who writes while she starves, or fasts, to death in order to achieve self-determination. Its author has been called a "radical feminist," a social liberator, a "petticoat Puritan," and a hypocrite.[5] The conflicting and sometimes openly hostile debates that this novel has

1

evoked over a period of more than two centuries attest to the difficulties involved in approaching hunger as a language in any society. Clarissa's discursive choices can teach us a great deal about the rhetoric of consumption in our own time.

Much of my analysis of *Clarissa* draws on current profiles of disordered eating habits and on contemporary medical and psychological terminologies, particularly those of object-relations theories, psychodynamics and systems theories, and interpersonal and systemic family therapy (the most widely embraced approaches to studying narcissism and disordered eating patterns). While the term *anorexia nervosa* (AN) has become so familiar to contemporary readers that psychiatrist Vincenzo DiNicola calls it "a major preoccupation and a cultural icon in the West,"[6] historical accounts of fasting women suggest that self-starvation has existed in various forms throughout history and that a broader, more complex view of disordered eating may be imperative to understanding its many instances. Current clinical and diagnostic criteria define AN as characterized by a refusal to maintain body weight over a minimal normal weight for age and height, intense fear of gaining weight or becoming fat, and a distorted body image,[7] yet psychologists note that not all anorectic subjects in every context fit the neat patterns that researchers have mapped out for them. Psychiatrist Howard Steiger argues, "Anyone who works with large numbers of AN sufferers knows that this disorder is not uniformly about a desire to be thin." He explains, "Systematic cross-cultural research indicates that anorexia-like variants may be increasing, not only in unexpected sectors of Western society, but also in diverse non-Western contexts."[8]

This view of AN as a "medical chameleon," or as an umbrella term for variable instances of voluntary starvation, allows us to examine Clarissa's behavior as both historical and contemporary. When the disorder is considered in this way, psychiatrist W. L. Parry-Jones suggests, "It seems likely that present day anorexia nervosa has had varying counterparts during the last two centuries"; Mara Selvini Palazzoli argues, "It is quite possible that cases of anorexia nervosa have been known since time immemorial."[9] While some literary historians might object to approaching *Clarissa* through the terminology of the twentieth century, psychologists insist that revisioning historical and literary figures in this way provides fascinating new views of both behavior and meaning—and a uniquely valuable avenue to confronting the diversity and instability that inform cultural perspectives of illness.[10] As DiNicola explains:

A major problem in the history of self-starvation has been that we either take a continuum view where we look for historical and clinical analogues of anorexia nervosa that were missed or misunderstood in context (despite gaps in medical perception, this conforms to a gradualism view of self-starvation) or a caseness view which argues that anorexia nervosa is a modern disease which suddenly appeared under the requisite socio-cultural conditions. I propose that what is definitive about self-starvation is the changing socio-cultural blueprint: it determines whether fasting will be construed in religious terms as "holy anorexia," in medical terms as "chlorosis," in psychiatric terms as "anorexia nervosa," or in political terms such as "hunger strike." In this view, anorexia nervosa is a chameleon with protean clinical manifestations changing with the times, what we might call *anorexia multiforme.*[11]

While every age and society will have models that inform the meaning of starvation, research that records the developmental, familial, biological, and sociocultural factors (sociocultural factors are the norms, standards, and values of a society) which put young women at risk can help us to connect the experiences and voices of women of all times. Eating disorder specialist Jane White stresses that, while the mere presence of some risk factors does not ensure that a young woman will develop disordered eating patterns, profiles of particular family dynamics and personality traits have helped us to understand with increasing clarity how the developmental issues of autonomy and control can take the form of self-starvation.[12] It is essential that such struggles for autonomy be understood as a means both of self-expression and of communication. While starvation focuses attention on self, that self can only be expressed in a learned language shared by others—a language characterized by risk factors and behaviors as common today as they were in Richardson's age.

Most critical commentaries have argued that Clarissa's asceticism is a willful attempt to cast off her body, to deny herself socially and sexually, and to embrace spirituality at the expense of physical health.[13] Terry Castle asserts that the heroine's unwillingness to eat is not a language at all but, rather, a "repudiation of the world of signs and interpretation": "Having already misread, dreadfully, the signs of edibility, she now refrains from having to make any semantic decisions . . . she saves herself, in this . . .

3

perversely self-denying manner, from the task of deciphering. . . . she would rather starve herself . . . than trust her own readings."[14]

I wish to suggest that Clarissa's starvation is not a repudiation of language or a displacement of power, as Castle suggests, but, rather, a powerful and erotic (if dangerous) form of discourse. Clarissa becomes an authoritative voice as she suffers, chastising and reforming all around her, directing and managing her resources as she could not have done as a well-nourished, healthy woman. Moreover, I will argue that this language is not self-controlled but, instead, learned and interpersonal—a collaboration with, rather than a repudiation of, her family and society. Clarissa is able to starve herself to death only because the language we read as her hunger is one that her lover, Robert Lovelace, has also learned and shares with her. Critics have commonly attributed the interactions of Lovelace and Clarissa to historical, economic, sexual, or allegorical eighteenth-century conventions that demand that their roles be polarized, yet both Clarissa and Lovelace reject food, collaborating with each other in a language that is as empowering as it is personally destructive.[15]

Lovelace has often been cast as a stereotypical villain, a notorious "woman eater." While hunger is a particularly female language, it is part of a confrontational collaboration that harms all its participants grievously. If it is a double-edged sword for women, it is equally dangerous to men.[16] Lovelace has been killed by its razor-sharp blade long before he is run through by Morden's less metaphoric rapier. In order to interpret its fascination throughout the centuries, and to understand its social efficacy, we must consider the gender-specific nature of the language of hunger as both learned and collaborative.

This study is intended as an examination of several assumptions regarding food-related behavior: (1) hunger is a learned behavior, a behavior that is interpersonal rather than self-controlled; (2) because it is interpersonal, food-related behavior can be a particularly effective means of impressing and manipulating others; (3) food and hunger can be used as an analogue to oneself, as a means of establishing an identity; (4) hunger is a social metaphor that can interrogate authority structures, especially family dynamics.

A great deal of critical attention has been paid to the second and third of these assumptions, but few scholars have considered the important process by which the language of hunger is learned or can be unlearned. I will argue that the language of hunger is one of accommodation. It depends

4

on an internalized disposition toward oneself, a shared system of evaluation which forces men and women to interact in self-destructive ways. This study discusses the process by which both men and women become authorized to manipulate the discourse of hunger, possible collisions between "myths" of accommodation and aggression, and the efficacy of literary studies such as this one for social change. It is my particular hope that contemporary literary studies may serve to renew popular interest in novels such as *Clarissa*, literary portrayals of problems that continue to plague the nonfictive world. As Deborah Tannen suggests in a passage I admire, "What *is* required to effect change is an understanding of the patterns of human behavior . . . an appreciation of human beings—other researchers as well as the subjects of our research."[17]

Clarissa is a novel about two rich, handsome, brilliant, beloved children whose tragic deaths have provoked centuries of conflicting, passionate, ambiguous responses from researchers. It is a particularly poignant and frustrating novel because all of its characters suffer and all of its characters cause suffering. This blurring of oppressors and victims taunts those critics who hunt for motivations and incentives, who cast blame and contest injury; yet the last two decades have brought Richardson's tale of tragedy increasing popularity because its destructive relationships can be polarized to serve any theory. Theorists continue to view the ambiguities in this story of self-starvation as transgressions of a moral scheme, gloriously radical subversions of a patriarchal culture, proof of a psychological "split" in the author or the characters, or as reflections of the indeterminate nature of language itself.[18]

I wish to approach the novel from a nonpolarized viewpoint that understands that individuals may dominate and be dominated simultaneously. I accept Deborah Tannen's premise that "male dominance . . . is not sufficient to account for everything that happens to women and men. . . . The effect of dominance is not always the result of an intention to dominate."[19] In other words, domination can be created by interactions that are not necessarily intended to create power discrepancies but may be fueled by them.

Clarissa is also the story of a rape and has elicited strong emotional responses from both women and men. In attempting to understand the motivations of characters without casting blame, I may seem to be defending a rapist. To this charge I can only reply, with Dorothy Dinnerstein, that condemnation of destructive relationships is not enough; this inquiry attempts to undermine destructive relationships by uncovering their sources and perpetuating patterns. As Tannen warns, "There are those who believe that approaching gender differences in ways of speaking as 'cultural' differences implies that men do not dominate women, but only misunderstand them."[20] I will probably exasperate many critics by emphasizing that in Richardson's novel both children die and that both deaths are tragic.

I sympathize with those readers against whose anger Dinnerstein warns us, those readers who believe that "forgiveness of a kind *is*, as the proverb says, an inevitable by-product of understanding, . . . that the special rage which understanding dispels is the right and necessary fuel for energizing constructive struggle."[21] I can agonize with Jane Tompkins when, in her painfully personal article "Me and My Shadow," she worries: "If you're not angry, can you still act? Will you still care enough?"[22]

All of the characters in *Clarissa* are angry, in spite of the fact that they love one another. Most critical accounts of the novel have emphasized only the anger, concentrating on isolated incidents of oppression instead of examining the fascinating interpersonal relationships in which they occur. Many critics tend to avoid the duality that tortures these characters. As Brownstein explains, with keen insight, Clarissa and Lovelace "can make neither head nor tail of one another . . . it is hard to know what either of them is—hard for themselves to know . . . both are human."[23]

Although I rely on discussions of oppressive patterns of interaction and risk factors for much of my analysis,[24] I believe, with Nancy Chodorow, that "people, even within oppressive systems, can choose among a variety of actions; that although unreflected-upon feeling may determine action, it need not."[25] *Clarissa* is a story of starvation, betrayal, desertion, rape, revenge, murder. These acts cannot be defended or excused; they make us angry; however, the characters involved can be understood, and their contests can help us to negotiate the untenable boundaries between fictional suffering and a reader's response to it. I have drawn here on both historical and contemporary research to investigate the interactions and choices that fuel the language of hunger, both in life and in the literature that portrays it. This study is thus based on a premise stated by Maud Ellmann in her excellent study of both fictional and literary hunger: "The drama of starvation unsettles the dichotomy between the fictive and the real, between the world of language and the world of violence."[26]

1

Hunger at Home
Clarissa and the Harlowes

"I am extremely concerned, my dearest friend, for the disturbances that have happened in your family," begins Anna's letter and Richardson's novel.[1] Richardson's opening is masterful and far more complex than it seems. This first letter is purposefully inexplicit and frantic, full of dark hints and vague suggestions; it tells us very little about actual events. There has been a duel, it seems. There is a lover, whom nobody seems to like; and an irate brother, whom nobody seems to like; and a sister, whom the lover seems not to like; and several passionate uncles; and an admired, although ineffective, mother; and the lovely Clarissa. What the letter does manage to convey quite explicitly, however, is the sense that the disturbances Anna mentions have happened less to the family than in the family and that Clarissa has been caught up in the turmoil in spite of herself. We are left with the uneasy impression that the protagonist is somehow an unfortunate victim, inextricably bound in a web of domestic chaos and familial associations, a mere spectator, while the other family members are actors. When Anna suggests that Clarissa has inspired a duel between Lovelace and James, she refers to the incident as "an accident you could not help" (39).

Throughout this epistle Anna stresses Clarissa's passivity and detachment. In fact, Clarissa has apparently become the talk of the entire "world," the subject of the "public care," the object of "everyone's attention," precisely because she is completely uninterested in having a public reputation: "so steady, so uniform in your conduct; so desirous, as you always said, of sliding through life to the end of it unnoted; . . . not wishing to be observed even for your silent benevolence . . . though now pushed into blaze, as we see, to your regret" (40).

Anna's comments could easily apply to any number of suffering heroines in British fiction. Quiet, unobtrusive, seeking only the opportunity to be of service, little Jane (or Agnes, or Lucy, or Esther, or Tess) quietly carries out her duties. When she finally finds herself truly loved, usually by an older, kindly, somewhat humbled gentleman, it is for her unwavering diligence, her self-effacing gentility and stoicism in the face of life's demands—and for her ability to wait.

Like Esther Summerson or patient Agnes, Clarissa carries the keys to the house, cares for the poor, nurses in private her yearning to be loved. Unlike these sisters in stoicism, however, Clarissa need not wait for her virtues to be discovered; they are already amply publicized. We leave this first epistle with the disturbing impression that there is a contradiction in the exaggerated acclaim that Clarissa enjoys merely for wishing to remain anonymous. Aunt Harman, says Anna, is a complete stranger to Clarissa but is so charmed by her character that she assents to the fortune Clarissa has received by her grandfather's will, without even questioning his reasons for privileging his youngest grandchild over her two siblings. Young ladies who know the heroine, or perhaps have only heard of her, propose to abide by her example in all their conduct.

Clarissa has become a legend in her own time, and her identity as a legend seems to be strangely founded on her association with her family, on her ability to be useful and prudent in contradistinction to the naturally violent spirits with whom she must contend while "blamed at home for the faults of others." She is mysteriously implored to write the whole of her story (as opposed to "the" story) so that, "if anything unhappy should fall out from the violence of such spirits as you have to deal with, your account of all things previous to it will be your justification." The letter ends with Anna's lament, "I dread your directors and directresses . . . your sister and brother will certainly put you out of your course" (40).[2]

After this sinister beginning, one assumes that *Clarissa* will proceed like any other story of virtue in distress, with the virtuous characters and their antagonists set in clear and violent conflict; however, in her response to Anna's fervent request for details, Clarissa does not seem particularly distressed, merely unhappy. Her family is indeed in "TUMULTS," she relates with composure, but this is not their normal mode of living, nor have they been this way for long. We have been "strangely discomposed," she explains, "ever since the unhappy transaction":

> I have sometimes wished that it had pleased God to have taken me in my last fever, when I had everybody's love and good opinion; but oftener, that I had never been distinguished by my grandpapa as I was: which has estranged me, I doubt, my brother's and sister's affections; at least, has raised a jealousy, with regard to the apprehended favour of my two uncles, that now and then overshadows their love. (41)

"Now and then overshadows their love"? Anna's initial letter has led us to believe that Clarissa has always been a paragon of patience tossed upon stormy seas. Her identity has been established on her ability to survive quietly with her belligerent family. Clarissa's declaration implies rather the opposite—that she has always been the recipient of love and that she perceives as unusual the ill regards of her siblings. The discrepancy in tone between Clarissa's letter and Anna's is striking; is Clarissa oblivious to the spite and arrogance around her, or is she merely being loyal or kind?

Throughout the novel the protagonist will insist that her misfortunes are recent and that she has been indulged and beloved for most of her life. In fact, she will augment her distresses by measuring her pain against the weight of her remembered former happiness. Three months later, while locked in her room and threatened with a forced marriage to a despised suitor, she laments, "I am quite weary of my life—so happy, till within these few weeks!—so miserable now!" (191).

We are never allowed to accept these declarations unquestioned, however. Each time we relax the tension between the extremities in Richardson's creation, they are reinforced by another perspective. Each character protests that another is decidedly to blame for Clarissa's downfall. "I hate tyrants in every form and shape. But paternal and maternal tyrants are the worst of all; for they can have no bowels," rants Anna after Clarissa's elopement. "She had never been in the hands of this man, but for them" (583). Lovelace, too, continually insists that the Harlowes are evil and that Clarissa's angelic nature defines itself against their hateful ones. In fact, he excuses his role in Clarissa's betrayal, insisting that his deeds are merely responses to the more active contentions in the Harlowe household: "Don't think me the CAUSE neither of her family's malice and resentment. It is all in their hearts. I work but with their materials. . . . I only point the lightning and teach it where to dart, without the thunder: in other words, I only guide the effects; the cause is in their malignant hearts" (464). The reader is left to wonder whether the conflicts that Richardson has announced exist at all or whether Clarissa is merely unaware of them.[3]

Clarissa is not the only character to maintain that all is well in the obviously disturbed Harlowe household. If the early letters of the novel often lead us to believe that Clarissa's excellence defines itself in contradistinction to her less wonderful, undeserving family, they also assure us that Clarissa's family, like the general public, enjoys the comparison and takes pride in their kinswoman's obvious superiority. In a letter to Clarissa's nurse, Mrs. Harlowe gives what seems an unlikely account of Clarissa's early years, yet to deny its truth is to reject the perceptions of both mother and daughter:

> Have you not heard strangers, as she passed to and from church, stop to praise the angel of a creature, as they called her; when it was enough for those who knew who she was, to cry, WHY, IT IS MISS CLARISSA HARLOWE! . . .
>
> For my own part, I could not stifle a pleasure that had perhaps a faulty vanity for its foundation, whenever I was spoken of, or addressed to, as the mother of so sweet a child: Mr. Harlowe and I, all the time, loving each other the better for the share each had in such a daughter. . . .
>
> She was our glory when abroad, our delight when at home. Everybody was even covetous of her company; and we grudged her to our brothers Harlowe, and to our sister and brother Hervey—No other contention among us, then, but who should be favoured by her next—No chiding ever knew she from us, but the chiding of lovers, when she was for shutting herself up too long together from us, in pursuit of those charming amusements and useful employments which, however, the whole family was the better for.
>
> Our other children had reason, good children as they always were, to think themselves neglected. But they likewise were so sensible of their sister's superiority, and of the honour she reflected upon the whole family, that they confessed themselves eclipsed without envying the eclipser.
>
> . . . The dear creature, you know, Norton, gave an emi-

nence to us all. And now that she has left us, so disgracefully left us! we are stripped of our ornament, and are but a common family! (584)

This early declaration stands in marked contrast to Clarissa's repetition of a resentful complaint from the "eclipsed" elder sister: "that I next-to-bewitched people . . . that nobody could be valued or respected but must stand like cyphers wherever I came" (194), yet Mrs. Harlowe's letter reveals more about the family inconsistencies than she perhaps realizes. She has disclosed a system of evaluation in which the family's eminence rests on its contradistinction to, and possession of, Clarissa. Whether Clarissa's blazing brilliance may be courted or resented, her absence renders the Harlowe family not evil, says her mother, but only common, just as her presence renders her siblings insignificant in comparison, mere ciphers, common. Months later Lovelace will purposefully place himself in a similarly odd position in regard to this heroine, arguing that, if he abandons his "overmatched" contest with Clarissa, he will "be but a common man . . . another dull heavy creature" (907).

The emphasis on contest and possession in Mrs. Harlowe's epistle is quite emphatic. It seems that, in order for the Harlowe family to retain its notability, Clarissa must maintain her status as an "uncommon" young lady; in doing so, she is unwittingly forced to accept a predetermined position of honor, a position that implies a subtle comparison. Although she must continue to be different from those around her, Clarissa must belong to her family, must grace the Harlowe home as a precious "ornament," bestowing glory and eminence through her mere presence. Her employments and achievements are theirs; her parents love each other for their "share in her," yet her superiority can only be acknowledged at the expense of each individual member of the Harlowe family.

Clarissa does not have to do anything to retain her status as a legend; she merely has to be—and to be different from, yet part of, the family. Unfortunately, this formula for belonging leaves little room for becoming. Nor does it encourage healthy, developing relationships with parents and siblings and a normal sense of self-determination.[4]

Psychologists have long regarded this type of situation as potentially explosive. In one study of seemingly perfect children, Alice Miller points out the dangers of regarding even an exceptional child as a family treasure: "As soon as the child is regarded as a possession for which one has a particular goal, as soon as one exerts control over him, his vital growth will be violently interrupted." Miller explains, "The [acclaimed] child is never encouraged to become a distinct individual, with needs and impulses clearly differentiated from those of his parents. Ironically, this child, usually the youngest daughter, has always been considered the 'best' child, the perfect one, emphatically superior to her siblings." Quite often, she has been "looked upon as a precious possession, in need of the very best of care," but denied recognition of her own individuality.[5]

The Harlowes, as portrayed in Mrs. Harlowe's unguarded, seemingly loving letter, uncannily fit our understanding of the stereotypical dysfunctional family, the type of family in which we are most likely to find overly prized children, disordered eating behavior, gender and identity conflicts, oppression and confusion. It is easy to regard such a family in terms of the conflicting needs of its members by rationalizing their disputes as instances of competing interests, yet such an approach suggests that each member is merely a victim of the ill will of the others.[6] If, however, we posit that each character is an active participant in the system, whether or not he or she is capable of perceiving or admitting his or her complicity, the familial system can be understood not merely in terms of misunderstandings but, rather, in terms of the problematics of understanding oneself in relation to others.[7]

The insight that a child can be a regarded as a possession and that a family can be rigidly united against such a child deserves far more attention than it has received in previous discussions of *Clarissa*. Accounts of family dynamics and mother-daughter relationships from the period give no indication that Mrs. Harlowe's adoration of her daughter would have been considered normal. "Motherhood was no doubt a source of satisfaction . . . but it was not the central, only and defining role of women," writes historian Alan Macfarlane. "Women's satisfactions and securities came from many sources, of which children were only one."[8]

After 1750 the death rate of aristocratic children under the age of five dropped by 30 percent in England over a period of twenty-five years. This trend has been attributed to the disappearance of the plague, wider acceptance of childhood vaccination, and improvements in medical care and nutrition in general. Historians have also speculated that more humanistic trends in child rearing contributed to improved health.[9] It is a period widely associated with a sudden increase in maternal responsibility for child raising and interest in children as companions. Historian Lawrence Stone explains:

What was happening in the eighteenth century was a steady shift away from prime reliance on physical punishment in the upbringing of children to reliance on the reward of affection and the blackmail threat of its withdrawal. . . . The rise of individualism among the middling and upper ranks in society brought with it, as a logical corollary, the rejection of that determination to crush the child's will that had so obsessed educators and parents in the sixteenth and early seventeenth centuries.[10]

Mrs. Harlowe's letter does not suggest that the family promotes their child's sense of self-determination by urging her to earn their affection; rather, she suggests that she and her husband are best loved for their "share in [Clarissa]," that their child "reflects" honor on the family that she "eclipses." This attitude is virtually antithetical to that which, in the early eighteenth century, Lady Mary Wortley Montagu attributes to those mothers whose devoted interest in their children is overly possessive: "[They] generally look on their children as devoted to their pleasures, and bound by duty to have no sentiments but what they please to give them; playthings at first, and afterwards the objects on which they may exercise their spleen, tyranny, or ill humour."[11] Although Clarissa will eventually become the focus of her family's anger, the mother's early belief that Clarissa is superior to a "common" family on whom she bestows an "eminence" is decidedly out of character with all recorded writings concerning eighteenth-century attitudes toward daughters.[12]

That Clarissa's family considers itself eminent is revealing. The family of the "perfect child" may well be financially and socially successful and very concerned with upward mobility, writes Hilde Bruch. The parents are excessively preoccupied with appearances, proud of the child's considerable academic performance and popularity. Often, both the parents and daughter remember her childhood as having been particularly, unrealistically, happy. Rosy pictures of family members whose only contention has been how best to love one another suggest that the important process of discovering and respecting differences that marks the development of all normal, healthy families has been suppressed, denied, or somehow forgotten.[13] Members find themselves caught in an active family collaboration through which they define one another and themselves.

Like so many disturbed families, the Harlowes are conspicuously successful; many of their neighbors feel that they are too newly wealthy for their own good. "Never," writes her grandfather, in the preamble to his will, "was there a family more prosperous in all its branches" or a granddaughter like Clarissa, "from infancy a matchless young creature . . . admired by all who knew her as a very extraordinary child" (53).

At eighteen Clarissa is an independent heiress, divinely beautiful, the intellectual match of her own minister, an industrious housekeeper, record keeper, philanthropist, designer, writer, musician, composer, painter. She has a facility at learning languages, is fluent in French and Italian, is teaching herself Latin. She is capable of designing and running her grandfather's dairy as well as her parents' estate. She even has a natural facility for science and has achieved a comfortable knowledge in "those branches of science which she [has] aimed at acquiring" (1468), yet, as Anna explains, being matchless has its drawbacks: "Such a sun in a family where there are none but faint twinklers . . . they must look upon you as a prodigy among them: and prodigies, you know, though they obtain our admiration, never attract our love" (129).

Clarissa's brilliance, however natural it is thought to be, will always necessitate comparisons that can bring her little unconditional love. Even Anna's mother cannot help reflecting on her daughter's friend as a measure of Anna's own inadequacies. "My mother takes very kindly your compliments in your letter to her," Anna writes. "Her words upon reading it were: 'Miss Clarissa Harlowe is an admirable young lady. Wherever she goes, she confers a favour; whomever she leaves, she fills with regret.' And then a little comparative reflection: 'Oh my Nancy, that you had a little of her sweet obligingness!'" "No matter . . . I think myself as well as I am," Anna can respond with confidence (60). "I set not up for a perfect character" (274).

Clarissa, however, enjoys a widespread reputation for perfection and is unable to harbor the same confidence. She is not only Clarissa but "the divine" Clarissa, "a" Clarissa, "our" Clarissa. She is earnestly eager to accommodate the prescriptions of a very demanding set of admirers and does so under the guise of self-determination. "How soothing a thing is praise from those we love!" she relates.

> Whether conscious or not of deserving it, it cannot but give us great delight to see one's self stand high in the opinion of those whose favour we are ambitious to cultivate. An ingenuous mind will make this farther use of it, that if it be

sensible, that it does not ALREADY deserve the charming attributes, it will hasten, before its friend finds herself mistaken, to obtain the graces it is complimented for: and this it will do, as well in honour to itself, as to preserve its friend's opinion, and justify her judgement!—May this be always my aim!

Although Clarissa insists that she is "incapable of flattery" (240), she does not realize that the perfection she demands of herself is dictated by others. When Anna rightly suggests that her friend's desire to be thought superior and in "command of yourself" is nothing more than a "struggle between YOU and YOURSELF" (292), she cannot know just how dangerous this duality will be. In her desire to please, Clarissa has internalized a prescribed perfection, a perfection that will eventually render her incapable of perceiving herself as a self-governing character capable of transforming her situation.[14]

Prescribed perfection is now accepted as a common factor in adolescent disturbance. "When personhood or selfhood is not recognized as a value but rather possessions and appearances are esteemed," contends family counselor Avis Rumney, "the child learns caretaking is not a response to her demands or needs, but is a result of her doing something particularly pleasing . . . love is conditional and she must prove herself worthy of her parents' love . . . since rarely does she receive unconditional warmth and mothering, she believes she herself does not merit love and it is only her actions that might be rewarded."[15]

In Richardson's novel Clarissa is made well aware that her compliance to family demands is expected, even required, if she is not to be banished from meals, confined to her room, or forbidden to correspond with her friends or parents. "Remember," warns Clarissa's beloved Norton, as she urges the girl's acceptance of an unworthy suitor, "there would not be any merit in your compliance, if it were NOT to be against your own will. Remember also what is expected from a character so extraordinary as yours" (179).

Norton's words seem cruel until we realize that Clarissa's "character" has led her entire family, and Clarissa herself, to expect the compliance they suggest. They are honestly puzzled when their kinswoman rebels, apparently for the very first time. It is this tendency to confront Clarissa as an object, a body that can be manipulated in spite of the will, rather than as a self-directed identity, which blinds the family to their child's real distress and the child herself to her own potential for self-realization.[16]

Bruch's studies reveal that, of the many obstructions to communication in the dysfunctional home, this attitude toward perfection is precisely the most dangerous. She writes, "Parents' failure to see their child's distress and their persistent perception of her in unrealistic terms, according to the image they carry in their own mind, are the very factors that have interfered with the child's developing a realistic self-concept and reliable self-esteem."[17] Perfection has become exaggerated. These children are never just good but emphatically better than others; they take extraordinary pride and pleasure in doing something difficult. Similarly, they are devastated and disgraced when they cannot comply with their families' demands. This disgrace is inevitable, painful, and extremely dangerous. Bruch explains:

> Those in charge of the well-being, care and education of these youngsters need to become alerted to the fact that the "never-giving-any-trouble" child is already in trouble, that the overconscientious, overstudious, and compliant performance is a warning sign of something wrong. In many ways these children fulfill every parent's and teacher's idea of perfection, but they do it in an exaggerated way. It is the extra push, the being not good but "better," that makes the significant difference between these unhappy youngsters who starve themselves and other adolescents who are capable of enjoying life. True prevention requires that their pleasing superperfection is recognized early as a sign of inner misery.[18]

The emphasis placed on Clarissa's "innate" perfection effectively disrupts her ability to perceive herself other than in contradistinction to others, other than as an unworthy exemplar, and therefore taints all communication and interaction between Clarissa and her environment. She grows to perceive herself as powerless, constrained, and predetermined. After her rape, for example, she clings to this contradistinction as a rationalization of her predicament, blaming her own nature, rather than her situation, for her distress. Merging the myth of her natural superiority with the myth of her relative superiority, she informs Belford that "[he] must not blame her parents: ... what an enormity was there in her crime, which could set the best of parents (as they had been to her till she disobliged them) in a bad light for resenting the rashness of a child, for

16

whose education they had reason to expect better fruits! . . . no ONE body, throughout the whole fatal transaction, had acted out of character, but HERSELF" (1101).

The apparent contradiction between this belief that she has consciously acted out of character and her insistence that she has been "tricked out of herself" is perhaps less a contradiction than the duality of a person caught in the logical fallacy of naturalized polarities, inappropriately perceived.[19] Because Clarissa allows her perception of herself to be prescribed by her oppressive family, she perceives herself as both innocent and criminal simultaneously. "I know not how it comes about, but I am, in my own opinion, a poor lost creature: and yet cannot charge myself with one criminal or faulty inclination. Do you know, my dear, how this can be?" she pleads to Anna (565). The duality is equally apparent to her family; "You have showed yourself so silly and so wise, so young and so old, so gentle and so obstinate, so meek and so violent," chides Arabella, "that never was there so mixed a character" (230). "How willingly would I run away from myself, and what most concerns myself, if I could!" Clarissa responds miserably (237).[20]

Clarissa's thwarted attempts at establishing blame or responsibility for her actions create great confusion for her entire family. Within the system that dictates her perfection, the disturbed patterns and demands controlling her are subtle, often camouflaged by conventional behavior. Bruch notes that no one isolated act or attitude in the dysfunctional home is actually abnormal or abusive; rather, it is the aggregate of these influences which convinces the child that nothing she expresses or feels is important in itself but must be done for the family's sake, that she does not own her own body, is not self-directed, and cannot communicate with or sufficiently please her parents. In most cases the parents' conviction that they are correct obstructs all signals indicating the increasing doubt and frustration that their child is suffering.

Early attempts at interpreting such environments, explains Bruch, traditionally conceived of the daughter as a victim, a casualty of the contradictions and inconsistencies under which she had grown up.[21] Recent studies, however, present a more complex, challenging perspective in which the child is also an active participant; her actions, in turn, affect the family. Instead of focusing on isolated behavioral traits of any individual in the family, one must investigate the dynamic interaction between all members and the roles they play in regard to one another. This approach can provide the only clue to a system in which the distinction between victim and manipulator is blurred because the child has been, and wants to be, a "good" child who does what she is told.[22]

"None but parents know the trouble that children give: they are happiest, I have often thought, who have none. And these women-grown girls, bless my heart! How ungovernable!" laments Mrs. Howe to Mrs. Harlowe (1112).

If Anna and Clarissa share an inviolable friendship, their mothers share a considerable concern over how best to raise the perfect daughter. Anna Howe speaks her mind with great assurance, teases her mother and mocks her mother's choice of a suitor for herself, and threatens to rebel at the least provocation. Angry words, accusations, even an occasional slap pass between Anna and her mother, yet, unlike the "perfect" Clarissa, Anna remains at home, fairly happy. She boldly illustrates her relationship with her mother to Clarissa in terms of defiance: "Mind my mamma, when you are not with us—YOU SHALL, I TELL YOU, NANCY!—I WILL HAVE IT SO!—DON'T I KNOW BEST!—I WON'T BE DISOBEYED—How can a daughter of spirit bear such language! such looks too with the language; and not have a longing mind to disobey?" (432). In spite of her pride in recalcitrance, however, Anna maintains that she enjoys a real friendship with her mother. She writes, "If we are not well together at one time, we are not ill together at another. And while I am able to make my mamma smile in the midst of the most angry fit she ever fell into on the present occasion (though sometimes she would not, if she could help it), it is a very good sign—a sign that displeasure can never go deep or be lasting" (433). The dialogues between these two lively and headstrong women are considerably witty and entertaining, never really hostile.

Clarissa's relationship with her mother initially appears to be practically antithetical to Anna's with Mrs. Howe, yet beneath a facade of affection there rages a real contest. Her letters insist that they are unusually close, mutually dependent. "My mamma has been very ill and would have no other nurse but me," Clarissa writes to Anna in the fifth letter of the novel. "I have not stirred from her bedside, for she kept her bed, and two nights had the honour of sharing it with her" (54). This attachment does not go unnoticed by the rest of the family. Arabella resentfully declares that she "hates" her younger sister for "playing your little, whining tricks; curling, like a serpent, about your mamma; and making her cry to deny you anything your little obstinate heart was set upon!" (195). An early dialogue between Clarissa and her mother, however, allows one to wonder whether Clarissa's heart may not be less her own than her parent's:

> The heart, Clary, is what I want.
> Indeed, Madam, you have it. It is not so much mine, as my mamma's!
> Fine talking! As somebody says, if words were duty, Clarissa Harlowe would be the dutifullest child breathing.
> . . . Leave me, my dear!—I won't be angry with you—if I can help it—if you'll be good. (103)

The emphasis on conditional love in this interchange, the mother's insistence that Clarissa consider the mother's emotions before expressing her own, reflects the real distortion in role allocation between these two women. The relationship between Mrs. Harlowe and her daughter is so disturbingly intimate that they often seem to reverse roles. Clarissa, we find, is a nurturing figure at home, selflessly acting as nurse, advisor, even marriage counselor, to her parent. She is abnormally concerned with her mother's well-being, often confusing her mother's needs with her own. Confined to her room, abandoned even by her beloved mother, she relates: "I am extremely affected on my mamma's account—more, I must needs say, than on my own—And indeed, all things considered, and especially that the measure she is engaged in is (as I dare say it is) against her own judgement, she DESERVES more compassion than myself. Excellent woman!" (112).

Embracing the myth of her daughter's pliable perfection, Mrs. Harlowe maintains that Clarissa's humble superiority has rendered her naturally suited for this inappropriate role as child/counselor. After Clarissa's elopement she explains to "Mamma" Norton (for whom Clarissa also cares, both financially and emotionally):

> In her bosom, young as she was, could I repose all my griefs—sure of receiving from HER prudence, advice as well as comfort: and both insinuated in so humble, in so dutiful a manner, that it was impossible to take those exceptions which the distance of years and character between a mother and a daughter would, from any other daughter, have made one apprehensive of. (584)

One cannot help but wonder what Mrs. Harlowe means by "any other daughter." Any other daughter in the world? Or Arabella? Once again the myths of Clarissa's natural and relative superiority have merged.

Although Mrs. Harlowe obviously does not hesitate to privilege her adolescent daughter with discussions of family affairs and marital problems, this tender confidence is far from gratuitous. Not only does Mrs. Harlowe rely on Clarissa's ability to accommodate both her desires and behavior to another's needs, but she makes this conformance the condition of her love for her daughter. Her letters to Clarissa, usually written in the conditional and future tenses, are punctuated with *ifs* and highlighted by occasional imperatives and threats. A typical letter suggests that truly maternal love can only follow obedience and that this obedience is to be cheerful as well: "if you now at last comply.... But, you know the terms.... If you come directly, and, as I said, CHEERFULLY, as if your heart were in your duty ... I shall then, as I said, give you the most tender proofs, how much I am your truly affectionate mother" (188–89).

When Clarissa is unable to reconcile her desires and behavior to her mother's wishes, she eventually comes to believe that she does not deserve the parental love she ought to have received unconditionally. She internalizes her mother's prescriptions, applying them to her own behavior in her parent's absence.[23] Even on her deathbed, abandoned by her family, she suppresses and denies her feelings of resentment, addressing herself to her beloved mother in the language she has been taught: "with all the consciousness of a self-convicted criminal supplicating her offended judge for mercy and pardon" (1372).

According to psychologists, confusion and suppressed feelings are typical of the disequilibrium felt by emotionally abused children. Alice Miller voices a current psychological consensus when she points out that a child has "an amazing ability to perceive and respond intuitively" to his or her parents' demand that he assume an assigned role. This role guarantees him his parents' love, and what child can risk losing that? There are many children, writes Miller, "who have not been free to experience the very earliest feelings, such as discontent, anger, rage, pain, even hunger and, of course, enjoyment of their own bodies" lest they lose their mother's approbation and affection. Such children are compelled to assume a false, conforming disposition, even to perceive their own needs according to their parents' perceptions. As counselors James Hogg and Mary Lou Frank explain, such children "often do not know where they end and others begin. Consequently, they live for others, feel responsible for others, and attempt to regulate the world around them." Their covert message is: "Your needs are more important than mine so I'll be whatever you need."[24]

Often, Miller argues, these children appear to be naturally suited to their roles, almost "predestined to be used,"

> intelligent, alert, attentive, extremely sensitive, and (because they are completely attuned to her well-being) entirely at the mother's disposal and ready for her use. Above all, they are transparent, clear, reliable, and easy to manipulate—as long as their true self (their emotional world) remains in the cellar of the transparent house in which they have to live.

In such cases the child has an intensely strong compulsion to be loyal, a compulsion one family therapist calls "a radarlike sensitivity" to the parents' expectations and demands.[25] More important, "This feeling is stronger than intellectual insight that it is not a child's task or duty to satisfy his parent's narcissistic needs." Because this conditioning has its beginnings in life's earliest period, it is exceptionally intense and obdurate. In effect, the mother has communicated a "mirrored framework" to which the child must accommodate himself. Looking into the mother's eyes, he will see not himself but, instead, the mother's insecurity, anxiety, fear, and perhaps hostility. He will never learn to know himself in separation from his mother's needs and estimation.[26]

If we consider Clarissa and her mother as "mirrored" partners, the discrepancy between their perceptions of Clarissa's past and the relations of other family members becomes understandable, even predictable. It is perhaps no coincidence that Clarissa and her mother, reinforcing each other's needs, are the only two characters in the novel who cherish memories of uncontested joy, in each other.[27]

While the mirroring of the mother's needs provides Clarissa with a simple formula for obtaining love, it also creates a painful confusion, the confusion that results from never being able to identify one's own image with certainty that it is solely one's own. What is perhaps most confusing to a child who responds to the demands of the mirror, writes Bruch, "are the actions of a mother who is continuously preoccupied with herself; whatever a child does, it is interpreted as expressing something about the mother."[28] Similarly, within such an enmeshed framework, claim Minuchin and others, "the usefulness of children as sources of feedback and as extensions of and reflections of [parental] self overrides any parental ability to perceive them as potential persons."[29]

Mrs. Harlowe's earliest attempts at addressing Clarissa's proposed marriage to Mr. Solmes are characteristic of the mirrored framework that she shares with her daughter and of the contorted communications, merged needs, and "active" passivity in the Harlowe family. Her arguments center almost exclusively on her own marriage; little attention is paid to Clarissa's desires or needs. The family assumes exclusive importance as the mother invites her daughter to join her in self-abnegation for the sake of family unity, equating refusal of this role with a refusal of the mother herself. Clarissa describes one of these strange sessions with her mother in great detail; they are obviously extremely moving and confusing interviews for her:

> And drawing her chair still nearer to mine, she put her arms round my neck and my glowing cheek, wet with my tears, close to her own. . . .
>
> You know, my dear, what I every day forgo and undergo, for the sake of peace. Your papa is a very good man and means well; but he will not be controlled, nor yet persuaded. You have seemed to pity ME sometimes, that I am obliged to give up every point. Poor man! HIS reputation the less for it; MINE the greater; yet would I not have this credit, if I could help it, at so dear a rate to HIM and to MYSELF. You are a dutiful, a prudent and a WISE child, . . . you would not add, I am sure, to my trouble. You would not wilfully break that peace which costs your mamma so much to preserve. . . . I charge you, on my blessing, that all this my truly maternal tenderness be not thrown away upon you. . . .
>
> On this one quarter of an hour depends the peace of my future life, the satisfaction of all the family. (89)

Clarissa's confusion over such a communication can be readily understood. She is being asked to ensure the happiness of her mother's marriage by entering into an extremely undesirable marriage herself. In an ironic twist Clarissa is encouraged to seal the family happiness by leaving the family. In her own understanding she is "to be given up to a strange man; to be engrafted into a strange family . . . to be obliged to prefer this strange man to father, mother—to everybody" (148), entirely because she prefers her parents and her family.

That Clarissa's mother is submissive to her father would not have surprised Richardson's original readers, although her position might seem insupportable to contemporary women. Eighteenth-century writings concerning marriage reflect strict notions of submission, propriety, and duty in a wife.[30] As late as 1782, Henry Home Kanes, in *Loose Hints upon Education,* writes that to "make a good husband is but one branch of a man's duty; but it is the chief duty of a woman to make a good wife. Woman, destined to be obedient, ought to be disciplined early to bear wrongs, without murmuring. This is a hard lesson; and yet it is necessary even for their own sake; sullenness or peevishness may alienate the husband; but tend not to sooth his roughness."[31] Mary Astell complains that "a wife must never dispute with her Husband . . . and if she shews any Refractoriness, there are ways enough to humble her; so that by Right or Wrong the Husband gains his Will."[32]

It is perhaps for these very reasons that so many women in the eighteenth century chose to have very affectionate relationships with their children. The rise in maternal affection toward children in the eighteenth century, particularly among the bourgeoisie and squirarchy, has been amply documented,[33] and writings show that many mothers were far closer to their daughters (both in childhood and adulthood) than they were to their husbands; yet Mrs. Harlowe's willingness to sacrifice a child she professes to love is grossly out of character with what is known of devoted mothers of the period.[34] Few mothers would have counseled a daughter to accept a despised suitor on any terms, least of all a woman whose own marriage was unhappy. Lady Mary Wortley Montagu had been pressured to accept a suitor she found repulsive, and found a "near resemblance of my maiden days" in the novel, yet even she labeled Clarissa's situation "most miserable" and "unusual for its time."[35]

Clarissa's odd relationship with her mother has baffled generations of readers. In *Becoming a Heroine* Rachel Brownstein points out that the story takes on a nightmarish quality as, without warning, "the house is transformed, changed from a haven to an arena where her parents, turned monsters, force her to marry a man she loathes." She does not attempt to explain the sudden transformation, but she does imply that it has to do with marriage politics in a world in which "women dress themselves like so much meat for their devourers."[36] Critical discussions of the novel have, with few exceptions, unquestioningly accepted some variation of this stance, arguing that Clarissa's role in a symbolically patriarchal family is necessarily that of a possession.[37] For many readers patriarchal economics and politics seem the only possible explanation for the Harlowes' united cruelty, a cruelty that is as sudden as it is total, a cruelty that results in her starving herself to death.[38]

Although patriarchal expectations offer a convenient explanation for Clarissa's trials, historical writings demonstrate that the tradition of arranged, economic marriages was rapidly becoming archaic in Richardson's time. Because marriage was considered such a serious contract, such marriages were always discountenanced when they did occur.[39] Malthus described as "little better than legal prostitutions" those marriages between fair young women and unattractive older men,"[40] and the extremely popular book *The New Whole Duty of Man* maintained that if

> parents offer to their children what they cannot possibly like, and what all considerate people cannot but disapprove, there is no doubt to be made, but that, in such a case, children may refuse; and if their refusal be made with decency and humility, that it will not fall under the head of sinful disobedience.[41]

Although marriage laws privileged the prerogative of the husband, throughout the century writers comment on the freedom of children to choose their own spouses and the importance of marrying for love (if it can be done without great impropriety or financial ruin). When Lady Mary Wortley Montagu visited Turkey with her husband, she noted a huge contrast between the importance in England of the future couple's feelings compared with a total lack of regard for the couple's sentiments in a society in which all marriages were arranged.[42] Montesquieu noted that English daughters "frequently" married "according to their own fancy," whereas French women had, by law, to obtain the consent of their fathers.[43]

In the eighteenth century, throughout Europe, men under the age of twenty-five and women under twenty could not marry without parental consent; in England, however, marriages needed no consent or witnesses to be valid. From the twelfth to the twentieth century any man over the age of fourteen and woman over twelve could marry simply by giving their free consent to each other.[44] Macfarlane writes, "It is difficult to envisage a more subversively individualistic and contractual foundation for a marriage system."[45]

Between 1753 and 1823 Hardwick's Law made it illegal for those under twenty-one, not being widows or widowers, to marry without the consent of parents or guardians; however, Macfarlane points out that even during this period "a marriage, like any other contract, was not valid *without* the free consent of the partners to the contract themselves . . . such was the law in the eighteenth century, and it was widely recognized."[46] For Clarissa's mother to urge her into a marriage that she did not want would have been considered not only improper but also illegal and blasphemous to her contemporaries. According to the law, a valid marriage needed "full, free and mutual consent"; without "free" consent there was no marriage.[47]

While children could legally marry without their parents' consent, it was widely accepted that a dutiful child should attempt to obtain it. Clarissa's desire to oblige her parents, if at all possible, would have been considered not only commendable but also practical (even financially advisable) by her contemporaries. Buchan observed, "An advantageous match is the constant aim of parents; while their children often suffer a real martyrdom betwixt their inclinations and duty."[48] Because Clarissa's trials represent a literal martyrdom to her parents' wishes, the negotiations portrayed in *Clarissa Harlowe* have been of interest not only to literary critics but to historians as well. Macfarlane writes, "Negotiations are evident in many eighteenth-century sources, with no apparent softening on the parents' side, particularly in relation to daughters," yet admits that there are no documented cases that are not "a far cry from the more extreme form of parental pressure represented in Richardson's *Clarissa Harlowe*, where Clarissa is finally driven to elopement and shame as the only protection against family pressure to marry an unattractive suitor."[49]

Even by eighteenth-century standards, then, the role that Mrs. Harlowe has asked her daughter to assume is an unthinkable one, until we consider that it is a role that the mother herself has played for a long time. Clarissa, we find, is part of a pattern stretching back across at least one generation.

Although Mrs. Harlowe's pleas and manipulations make it easy to perceive her as an oppressor and her daughter as a victim, the two women are, in fact, cast in remarkably similar, mutually reinforcing positions. Like her daughter, Mrs. Harlowe is generally respected as a diplomat, holding the family together as contentious spirits threaten to rip it asunder, yet she has been able to accomplish this unification only by resigning her own will. She is portrayed as a passive presence, a silent voice, and is publicly acclaimed for her condescending passivity in relation to her unreasonable, oppressive husband.[50] Like her lovely daughter, Mrs. Harlowe is regarded as a unitive force in the family because she is better "natured," but this role has left her unable to commend herself for exerting her own will, for displaying the natural qualities for which she is respected. She is a woman who grounds her sense of personal worth on her ability to submit to others.

While her mother's oppression is obvious to Clarissa, she does not realize the extent to which it influences her behavior. "Have I any encouragement to follow too implicitly the example which my mamma sets of meekness and resignedness to the wills of others?—Is she not for ever obliged to be, as she was pleased to hint to me, of the FORBEARING side?" Clarissa wonders, but soon she realizes that this passivity is a type of action in itself. The oppressed Mrs. Harlowe causes the very oppression that she laments, Clarissa decides, simply by refusing to accept it as unnatural rather than as merely unfortunate. "In my mamma's case," she determines, it may well be that "those who will bear much shall have much to bear" (105).[51] Furthermore, in the present crisis Clarissa discovers that her mother must be labeled "naturally" stubborn in order for the family to manipulate her without differentiating her too thoroughly from the clan. She, too, must become separate but not different.

If Mrs. Harlowe presents her daughter with a mirrored framework in which to read herself, it can only be a darkened and cracked mirror, a distorted reflector. In order to maintain unity Mrs. Harlowe must embrace the conflicting myths of her own natural superiority and the willing weakness for which her superiority renders her suited; Clarissa must apply the same unwieldy equation to her mother. As the conflict in the Harlowe household escalates, their discourse becomes almost a code, a jumble of mixed signals through which they attempt to communicate with each other as individuals and, simultaneously, as polarized symbols. There is even a distressing sympathy between them, a common understanding between victims cast in uncomfortable roles. Clarissa and her mother struggle like two gladiators, compelled to fight each other to the death yet united in their disdain of the compulsion. "Never was there a countenance that expressed so significantly, as my mamma's, an anguish, which she struggled to hide under an anger she was compelled to assume," Clarissa relates (111).[52] Their conversations become heavily weighted with the burden of interpreting what is said as an individual, what as an ambassador.

In addition to addressing her mother's pleas, demands, and conditions, Clarissa must determine the extent to which her mother's role as emissary and politician is willingly assumed for the family's sake, misguided in its good intentions for Clarissa, or spiteful in its own right. We see all her interpretive powers at war in seemingly simple protestations:

> I thought it hard to be thus given up by my mamma, and that she should make a will so uncontrollable as my brother's, her will. . . . Did not this seem to border upon CRUELTY, my dear, in so indulgent a mamma?—It would be wicked (would it not?) to suppose my mamma capable of art—But she is put upon it; and obliged to take methods her heart is naturally above stooping to; and all intended for my good, because she sees that no arguing will be admitted anywhere else. (97)

"I advise as a friend, you see, rather than command as a mother," Mrs. Harlowe assures her frustrated daughter, yet, because all notions of authority have now become suspect, it is impossible for Clarissa to determine the distinction between either the verbs or the nouns.

Occasionally, Clarissa attempts to break through the verbal politics with a direct appeal, but she is never able to receive an answer that does not reflect her mother's concern for her own position and for the family's "status"; Clarissa's feelings are always secondary considerations. During one horrible interview Clarissa frantically clings to her mother's gown, pleading: "Do not renounce me totally!—If you must separate yourself from your child, let it not be with ABSOLUTE reprobation on YOUR OWN part!—My uncles may be hard-hearted—my papa may be immovable—I may suffer from my brother's ambition and from my sister's envy!—but let me not lose my mamma's love; at least, her pity." "You HAVE my love! You HAVE my pity! But, oh my dearest girl—I have not yours" is the mother's prepossessed response (111). "She therefore entreated me in the most earnest and condescending manner," relates Clarissa: "'To signify to my papa, on his return, my ready obedience; and this, she was pleased to say, as well for HER sake, as MINE.'" Clarissa later tells Anna that she finds herself highly affected by her mother's plea, particularly "by that part of her argument which related to her own peace" (110).

As an adult, a child who has interiorized the lesson that she is loved not so much for what she really is as for her beauty and achievements, will always be dependent on the affirmation of others, will always question her own desires. There is a strange paradox in her situation, Miller explains:

> According to prevailing attitudes, these people—the pride of their parents—should have had a strong and stable sense of self-assurance. But exactly the opposite is the case. In everything they undertake they do well and often excellently; they are admired and envied; they are successful whenever they care to be—but all to no avail. Behind all this lurks a sense that their life has no meaning. These dark feelings will come to the fore as soon as . . . they are not "on top," not definitely the "superstar," or whenever they suddenly get the feeling they failed to live up to some ideal image and measure they feel they must adhere to.[53]

There are, of course, several sorts of mechanisms against these feelings of emptiness, desertion, shame, and fear. The person who learns to accommodate parental needs tends to become an "as if personality," developing in "such a way that he reveals only what is expected of him, and fuses so completely with what he reveals that . . . one could scarcely have guessed how much more there is to him" (a situation with which Mrs. Norton and the Harlowes come to be familiar when Clarissa suddenly ceases to conform to their expectations).[54] But there is always a subdued "false self" behind the masked hero or heroine. This true self remains in a "state of noncommunication," according to therapists, until it is forced into the open by crisis or therapy. It will, however, make itself felt as a general sense of emptiness, futility, or homelessness because the child has actually allowed a living, spontaneous part of herself to be temporarily killed.[55] Such children often dream that they are dead or are being killed.[56]

As her family pressures her to accept a horrible suitor at the expense of her happiness, and Lovelace pressures her to escape with him at the risk of her reputation, Clarissa dreams that her oppressors have killed her between them; her dream is quite disturbing:

> Methought my brother, my uncle Anthony, and Mr. Solmes had formed a plot to destroy Mr. Lovelace; who discovering it turned all his rage against me, believing I had a hand in it. I thought he made them all fly into foreign parts upon it; and

afterwards seizing upon me, carried me into a churchyard; and there, notwithstanding all my prayers and tears, and pro-testations of innocence, stabbed me to the heart, and then tumbled me into a deep grave ready dug, among two or three half-dissolved carcases; throwing in the dirt and earth upon me with his hands, and trampling it down with his feet.

I awoke with the terror, all in a cold sweat, trembling, and in agonies; and still the frightful images raised by it remain upon my memory.

But why should I, who have such REAL evils to contend with, regard IMAGINARY ones? (342–43)

Although Clarissa dismisses the incidents in her dream as imaginary, the patterns of interaction they reveal are entirely recognizable as those existing in her life. If Clarissa were able to express her innocence and rage, to be listened to and believed, her "real" self could stay alive. In her dream, however, as in her life, prayers, tears, expostulations, and pleadings are equally ineffective. When Clarissa awakens, she finds that her desire to be self-determined, her self-esteem and confidence in her ability to govern herself, must still be buried in deference to duty, family loyalty, and obe-dience.[57]

Death and burial are obviously themes that preoccupy the heroine, even while awake. She often declares that she prefers to die, or even be buried alive, rather than marry Mr. Solmes. Immediately after her night-mare, Clarissa writes to Lovelace, resolving to run away with him, but expresses a desire to die rather than to join him as well. More important, however, she bases her preference for death on the anticipated effect her flight will have on others, "if not" on herself. She writes: "Could I, without an unpardonable sin, die when I WOULD, I would sooner make death my choice than take a step which all the world, if not my own heart, will con-demn me for taking" (350). Once again Clarissa has problems establish-ing the extent to which she can legitimately accommodate her own desires and decisions before considering the expectations of others. Throughout this letter Clarissa laments the compulsion and the irresolution that at-tend her decision to leave home.

Perhaps the most noticeable aspect of Clarissa's dream is the fact that in it, as in life, she plays the role of the innocent, passive victim, somehow caught in tensions between others. Clarissa's death at Lovelace's hands is sacrificial; she is merely the focal point of his rage against Solmes and her family. The heart he stabs is a heart that belongs to others, not to him and obviously not to Clarissa. Lovelace forces her into a grave to revenge her apparent collusion with her family, the very family and suitor she is attempting to escape, in real life, by eloping with him.

Although this dream can easily serve, in the course of the novel, as a foreshadowing of Lovelace's role in Clarissa's death, it is intriguing to examine it from a psychological perspective, in terms of what it might reveal at the time it occurs. As she dreams, Clarissa feels that she suffers through being associated with, identified with, and compared with others, although she does not understand her role in this process. In her sleep, as in Anna's first letter, Clarissa is being "blamed . . . for the faults of others." To remain a Harlowe, an acknowledged, accepted Harlowe, Clarissa finds that her own voice must remain as impotent as if she were indeed dead. Only in her dream, however, will she perceive the heavy implications of this system with real lucidity.[58]

TRIANGLES AND UNITY

"You know my dear, that there is a good deal of solemnity among us. But never was there a family more united in its different branches than ours. Our uncles consider us as their own children, and declare that it is for our sakes they live single. So that they are advised with upon every article relating to, or that may affect, us," writes Clarissa in an early letter (56). We become almost immediately aware, however, that this close-knit extended family is not the affectionate democracy it seems to be.

In order to function as a unit, the Harlowe family must negate the autonomy of its individual members; conflicts and competitions must be internalized until they become part of one interminable argument whose boundaries, origins, and issues can no longer be distinguished at all. The general atmosphere is always oppressive, and most discussions end in sterile generalities, accusations, stalemates. Although the only conflict in the Harlowe home appears to concern Clarissa's refusal of Solmes, an issue that should be resolved in a matter of days, the question has become so entangled in a web of jealousies and hostilities that Clarissa is unable to address one argument without becoming ensnared in another; her refusal of Solmes is immediately interpreted as a love for Lovelace, a disrespect for her brother, a pride in her financial independence from her father, a disregard for her mother's marital problems.

Throughout the rest of the novel, as in her dreams, Clarissa's conflicts are seldom linear, involving only herself and one antagonist. Her relationship with her mother invariably involves her mother's relationship with her father. Her struggles with Lovelace always contain her family; his dealings with her are constantly tempered by his hatred for the Harlowes, as her relationship with him can never be free of her sense that it has been paid for at the price of her family's goodwill. On a grand scale even Clarissa's elopement with Lovelace does not affect merely herself but must have implications for her entire sex. She can, without hesitation, accommodate her mother's accusation that "she [Clarissa] has deceived everybody's expectations. Her whole sex, as well as the family she sprung from, is disgraced by it" (585). This pattern of mediated, triangular relationships, relationships in which two parties perceive their alliance in terms of its effect on others rather than on themselves, is a pattern that typifies the dysfunctional family.

Although triangles would seem to be insidious affairs, thwarting any attempt at real communication between individuals, they are actually an attractive defense against the pain and anxiety that so often accompany intimacy. The triangular, mediated pattern of demands and conditional love between Clarissa and her mother, for example, is particularly seductive to both because it serves to reduce the tensions between other family members. In focusing attention on parental issues, blaming Clarissa for their contentions, Clarissa's parents avoid confronting the very real problems in their marriage, just as their love for the previously perfect child allowed them to "love each other the more" for their share in her. "Signify . . . your compliance with our wishes . . . and you will once more make us happy in you, and in one another" her mother pleads (189), allowing Clarissa to assume the burden of her parents' marital happiness. Similarly, the jealousies of siblings, the rivalry between Arabella and James, Mrs. Harlowe's distress at being unable to control her husband and children, at having a "will without a power" (586), are completely ignored, overcome by the family's concern for Clarissa's ungovernable behavior. In functioning as a family, uniting against Clarissa, the Harlowes achieve a stability that would be impossible were its members to insist on self-determination.

The unity in the Harlowe family is, of course, more a precarious stability than a real unity. It can be broken as soon as any member acknowledges a feeling that the other members do not wish to accommodate. Such a troublemaker will be immediately accused of "breaking up the family." In particular, Mrs. Harlowe's role as peacekeeper depends on her ability to weld the family together by remaining passive in the face of family contentions, a role similar to that demanded of her daughter (although somehow the public has decided that she is less an angel than a martyr for having assumed it). When she is coerced into accepting an active role, that of trying to convince Clarissa to succumb to family pressures to marry, she accuses Clarissa of destroying the family unity and finds the same charge levied against herself. Clarissa agonizes over her mother's complaint that "she had a very hard time of it between my father and me . . . she was charged, she said, with dividing the family into two parts; she and her youngest daughter standing against her husband, his two brothers, her son, her eldest daughter and her sister Hervey" (109).

In trying to express her feelings, to communicate with her family, Clarissa has discovered that she, too, can hold the family together only as an image of difference—either as an exemplar or as a disgrace. What is more important, however, is the fact that she must be recognized as such by *all* members simultaneously. "Remember," warns Norton, "there would not be any merit in your compliance, if it were NOT to be against your own will. Remember also what is expected from a character so extraordinary as yours: remember it is in your power to unite or disunite your whole family for ever" (179).

To collapse the polarity between Clarissa and the rest of her family is, ironically, to divide the family in half. For this reason she must never be allowed to present herself as an individual to individuals, but, rather, as a segment to the rest of the family en masse. Clarissa becomes painfully aware of the political nature of this system when she attempts to address her family as a family. Her mother explains, "Your papa has given his sanction to your brother's dislikes, and they are now your papa's dislikes, and my dislikes, your uncles [*sic*] and everybody's!—No matter to WHOM owing" (124). "It was hard," she continues, "if a father and mother, and uncles and aunt, all conjoined, could not be allowed to direct [Clarissa's] choice" (97). Clarissa sadly muses, "It was doubtless much more eligible to give up a daughter, than to disoblige a husband, and every other person of the family" (122). Later, Lovelace will accuse Clarissa of the same cruel preferences, protesting, "How my heart rises at her preference of them [the Harlowe family] to me, when she is convinced of their injustice to me! . . . But she cannot surely be so mean as to purchase her peace with them at so dear a rate. She cannot give a sanction to projects formed in malice and founded in a selfishness (and that at her own expense) which she has spirit enough to despise in others" (145).

The roles within the Harlowe family have become so deeply entrenched that the patterns of behavior between members have become predictable, naturalized; because the antagonisms between members are necessary to avoid even greater chaos, each character tends to accept his role as his perception of himself, allowing it to carry over into other relationships outside the family. Conditioned to believe that his personal worth lies in his possession of the family fortune, James's inappropriate role as a lawgiver and arrogant chieftain makes itself felt in the community, at college, in his address to Anna, in his duel with his sister's lover. Arabella, too, intensely competitive, vies for the favor of parents and lovers, admitting her feelings of inadequacy or mistrust only in terms of mediated hostility. If Mrs. Harlowe or Lovelace or Grandpa have loved Clarissa more than her sister, the fault, reasons Arabella, in typically triangular style, must surely be Clarissa's—not theirs and surely not her own. "Did you not bewitch my grandfather?" she cries in a painfully unguarded dialogue. "Could anything be pleasing to him, that YOU did not say or do? . . . Yet what did YOU say, that WE could not have said? What did YOU do, that WE did not endeavour to do?" (194). As in her dream, Clarissa becomes the focal point for everyone's rage.[59]

Such a family as the Harlowes, says psychiatrist John Sours, "superficially functions well and is a polite family. But unlike the well-functioning family that interacts within its system, confronts conflicts, allows interpersonal differentiation, and permits separation and autonomy as the child gets older, the [dysfunctional] family enmeshes its members, is overprotective, rigid, lacks the ability for conflict-resolution, and involves the child in parental conflicts."[60] Most noticeable about these families is their lack of flexibility and the barriers to communication they construct. Such a family is "dependent on the mental and behavioral deviations of their . . . offspring as a means of preventing disintegration."[61]

Clarissa's defiance does indeed unite the otherwise contentious members of her family. In its efforts to force Clarissa to marry, the divided Harlowe family soon becomes "an embattled phalanx," in Uncle John's words, and its members "have agreed ALL to be moved, or NONE; and not to comply without one another" (150). In spite of this conspiracy, Clarissa is never encouraged to develop an autonomous identity or to assess her feelings independently of their impact on the rest of the family.

If Clarissa is unable to distinguish the oppressive nature of the Harlowes' possessive interest in her affairs, this is, perhaps, because the family's animosity assumes the same contentious and acquisitive form that its members' love has always taken. Even as she is dying, Clarissa will remember her family members' love in terms of their struggles to possess her:

> I was the joy of their [my uncles'] hearts; and, with theirs and my father's, I had three houses to call my own; for they used to have me with them by turns, and almost kindly to quarrel for me; so that I was two months in the year at one's house; two months at the other's; six months at my father's; and two at the houses of others of my dear friends, who thought themselves happy in me: and whenever I was at any one's, I was crowded upon with letters by all the rest, who longed for my return to them. (1106)

As Clarissa becomes increasingly aware of herself as a separate individual whose choices express her opinions about herself, rather than her sense of gratitude, duty, or fear, she finds it necessary to define herself in terms of continuous interaction with individual members of her family, yet the family continues to insist on being approached as an aggregate—an "embattled phalanx." Clarissa finds it impossible to make sense of the perplexing shifts in communication and role allocation which characterize her home at this time. Hers is a situation distinguished by an ambiguous and circuitous system of information which will soon become a nightmare of guessing for Clarissa and a rather confusing muddle for the reader as well.[62]

TRIANGULAR COMMUNICATION AND CONDITIONAL CONSUMPTION

"My father and mother industriously avoid giving me opportunity of speaking to them alone," Clarissa worries to Anna (61). "What my brother and sister have said against me I cannot tell—But I am in heavy disgrace with my papa" (63). The hideous Solmes "courts them. . . . His courtship, indeed, is to THEM; and my brother pretends to court me as his proxy, truly! . . . I have no opportunity of saying No, to one who asks me not the question" (62).

This is the situation between Clarissa and her relations as she prepares to describe one of her last meals with the family. The emphasis on her ineffective voice, the impossibility of addressing any family member as an individual, her loss of identity in association with her family, have become familiar. Clarissa has just been informed by her brother, "upon my aunt's report," that she is not to correspond with anybody outside the house. Soon after, her sister announces, "I am to tell you that it will be taken well if you avoid visits or visitings for a week or two, till further order." The deliberate use of the passive, the cruel lack of agency in this message, unnerves Clarissa far more than the prohibition itself. "Can this be from those who have authority—," she pleads. "I have delivered my message," Arabella responds abruptly (63).[63]

James, explains Clarissa, has also enjoyed an inappropriate relationship with the parent of his own gender. She relates, "[He] gave himself airs very early: 'That his grandfather and uncles were his stewards; that no man ever had better'" (77). As the novel opens, Mr. Harlowe is withholding judgment on Clarissa's betrothal until James can be consulted and is thanked, on his son's return, "in such a manner," Clarissa claims, "as a superior would do when he commended an inferior for having well performed his duty in his absence" (48).

Although James has been "programmed" in a number of inappropriate and disruptive ways, this programming is attributed not only to his place as eldest male heir but also to his "natural" abilities. Repeating a pattern that has been applied to herself, Clarissa imputes her brother's defiance less to economics and to the conditioning influence of her parents' overpermissiveness than to James's natural disposition. "My brother!" she exclaims to Anna. "What excuse can be made for his haughty and morose temper? He is really, my dear, I am sorry to have occasion to say it, an ill-tempered young man, and treats my mamma sometimes—indeed he is not dutiful" (55).

If Clarissa has always been the unnaturally perfect child, James has always been a publicly acknowledged horror. "How happy might I have been with any other brother in the world but Mr. James Harlowe; and with any other sister but HIS sister!" (65–66), writes Clarissa. "His temper and arrogance are too well known," Anna replies, explaining that she once refused his offer of marriage because he rendered it, in a manner foreshadowing Austen's Mr. Darcy, "with the air of a person intending to confer, rather than hoping to receive a favour" (68).

As Clarissa's trials increase, we begin to detect an impatience toward her parents accompanying her comments on her brother's natural disposition, a desire to implicate others in her contention with her brother. She begins to perceive that, however natural her brother's faults may seem to be, they have been accommodated in a most unnatural way. "He had from early days by his violent temper made himself both feared and courted by the whole family," she tells her friend, adding, "My father himself, as I have lately mentioned, very often (long before [James's] acquisitions had made him still more assuming) gave way to him, as to an only son who was to build up the name and augment the honour of it. Little inducement therefore had he to correct a temper which gave him so much consideration with everybody" (80). Apparently, this child, too, has been given a role to play, a role in which his family's needs and ambitions are of far greater importance than his own, a role to which he has accommodated himself only too well.[64]

In attempting to assign blame, to determine the ultimate cause of her brother's actions, Clarissa blinds herself to a dangerous pattern of interrelationships, a pattern that psychotherapist Harriet Goldhor Lerner, in a study of triangular relationships, calls the "dance of anger."[65] "It is tempting," writes Lerner,

> to view human transactions in simple cause-and-effect terms. If we are angry, someone else CAUSED it. Or, if we are the target of someone else's anger, we must be to BLAME; or, alternately—if we are convinced of our innocence—we may conclude that the other person has no RIGHT to feel angry. The more our relationships in our first family are fused (meaning the togetherness force is so powerful that there is a loss of the separate "I's" within the "we"), the more we learn to take responsibility for other people's feelings and reactions and blame them for our own. . . . Likewise, family members assume responsibility for CAUSING other people's thoughts, feelings, and behavior.
>
> Human relationships, however, don't work that way—or at least not very well. . . . We ARE responsible for our own behavior. But we are NOT responsible for other people's reactions; nor are they responsible for ours. Women often learn to reverse this order of things: WE PUT OUR ENERGY INTO TAKING RESPONSIBILITY FOR OTHER PEOPLE'S FEELINGS, THOUGHTS, AND BEHAVIOR AND HAND OVER TO OTHERS RESPONSIBILITY FOR OUR OWN. When this happens, it becomes difficult, if not impossible, for the old rules of a relationship to change.

No relationship is really linear (A causes B or B causes A), Lerner insists, but, rather, all relationships are circular (A and B are mutually reinforcing): "Once a pattern is established in a relationship, it is perpetuated by both parties."[66] In many cases these patterns can be traced back for generations.

The real problem with circular relationships is that they seldom stay circular. Lerner explains, "Underground issues from one relationship or context invariably fuel fires in another." This process occurs when two parties attempt to reduce the anxiety of their relationship by focusing on a third party, pulling him or her into the situation to lower the emotional intensity of the original pair. Such a pattern is called a "triangle." Although triangles can operate harmlessly enough on a transient basis, Lerner maintains, they can also become "rigidly entrenched, blocking the growth of the individuals in them and keeping us from identifying the actual sources of conflict in our relationships."[67]

According to Lerner's theories, triangles can help to keep painful rivalries and hostilities underground. When they are disrupted, the participants are forced to confront each other on a person-to-person basis, without the interference or mediation of a third party. Because this is so emotionally difficult, dependencies on triangular relationships are extremely addictive, so much so that the original triangle can quickly become an interdependency on numerous interlocking triangles. Dysfunctional families typify the complexity of this situation. The dependencies and distortions of their relationships are so tangled and interconnected that it is impossible to approach problems in terms of cause and effect. No one person is to blame; the very process of assigning blame fuels the contentions in the family, aggravating and perpetuating its problems.[68]

Considered from this psychological perspective, Clarissa's struggle with her family becomes doubly tragic because it must be viewed as a double struggle. Clarissa cannot accept responsibility for herself without blaming herself for being herself. This very process of blaming, philosophizing, trying to understand, actually thwarts her efforts to know herself separately from her family. Considered in terms of family dynamics, Clarissa's confusion is not merely the result of her frustrated attempts to resist her family's demands but a consequence of her inability to perceive her complicity with deeply entrenched conflicts.

As Clarissa begins a regime of missed meals and sleepless nights, which is instantly naturalized, she enters a circular confrontation that Bruch has called the "Frankenstein Theme." As the child internalizes her parents' prescriptions and becomes convinced of her status as a possession and a creation, she cannot help but turn, monsterlike, against her creators in a desperate effort to change them so that they can undo their errors and recast her in a more tolerable mold.[69] In fact, we can easily question the extent to which Clarissa is even conscious of her own physical needs, since these functions, like her emotions, have become prescribed by her family. The delusion of not having an identity of her own renders her incapable of perceiving herself as a self-governing character capable of transforming her situation and herself. She perceives herself, instead, as "caught up" in an unalterable reality, capable only of recognizing and enduring its cruel ways. Although she can feel her needs, she cannot emerge from the system that oppresses her sufficiently to comprehend their cause. Nor does she realize that she perpetuates the very tensions that she laments when she attempts to focus her attention on the cause of her problems, assigning or accepting blame, rather than on her own options for change.

As Clarissa becomes increasingly dissatisfied with her mother, and with her whole family, she learns to take control over herself by manipulating a system that her family has already put into motion, a triangular pattern of accepting food in order to signal her acceptance of something else and of refusing food in an equally political, mediated way. This pattern of consumptive transference is common in dysfunctional families, families in which issues and identities commonly become transferred to, or engulfed in, others.[70] Researchers highlight the likelihood that "family communication and conflict [will] escalate in this setting, in which all family members come together to share a common task."[71] Family counselor Avis Rumney explains that, because of the perpetual distortions in communication in such households, "A disproportionate amount of attention is focussed on food in the family, and meals and behaviors around food are highly ritualized."[72] As a focal point of family unity, all meals become symbolic, political, part of a vicious interchange of prerogatives and conditions that strengthen a collaborative system of deceptively polarized enemies.

PATTERNS OF CONDITIONAL CONSUMPTION

"Dinner is near ready," blusters Mr. Harlowe, surprising Clarissa and her mother during one of their unsatisfactory contests. "Let us have you soon down—your daughter in your hand, if worthy of the name." Mr. Harlowe's emphasis on the conditional is typical, and Clarissa is concerned that her presence should imply her acceptance of his demands. "My mamma, seeing my concern, seemed to pity me," she relates, and offered, "Dinner will be upon table presently—Shall we go down?" Clarissa returns, "What, madam, go down, to let it be supposed we were talking of PREPARATIONS!—Oh my beloved mamma, command me not down upon such a supposition" (93).

Clarissa never makes it to this dinner or to most of the meals after dinner. Meals have become the ground for a battle of wills, a test of endurance. "I will go down," her mother urges, after this refused dinner, "and excuse your attendance at afternoon tea, as I did to dinner; for I know you will have some little reluctances to conquer. . . . And so you SHAN'T come down, if you choose NOT to come down—Only, my dear, don't disgrace my report when you come down to supper. And be sure [to] behave as you used to do to your brother and sister; for your behaviour to them will be one test of your cheerful obedience to us" (97).

Mrs. Harlowe's demand for cheerful compliance, encompassing Clarissa's behavior not only toward her mother but toward everyone else as well, is a part of a well-worn pattern. Unfortunately, she has embraced a procedure with which family therapists are becoming well acquainted; she has decreed the family repast the condition of compliance, the stage for the battle. "If I meant to show my duty and my obedience, I must show it in THEIR way, not MY OWN," Clarissa realizes, and the result, as she tells Anna, is that her mamma "went down to tea and kindly undertook to excuse my attendance at supper" (101).

Clarissa's letter the next morning reveals what will become a disturbingly predictable pattern of mediated self-denial. "I have not been in bed all night; nor am I in the least drowsy," she writes. "I stepped down at my usual time, that it might not be known I had not been in bed, . . . My mamma went down to breakfast. I was not fit to appear; but if I had been better, I suppose I should not have been sent for; my papa's hint, when in my chamber, being to bring me down, if worthy of the name of daughter. That, I doubt, I never shall be in HIS opinion, if he be not brought to change his mind as to this Mr. Solmes" (103).

If Clarissa's attendance at meals has become contingent on her compliant behavior, her parents seem oddly to favor delineating Clarissa's trials by the boundaries of their own repasts. "Your father both dines and sups at your uncle's, on purpose to give us this opportunity," confides the mother, and "I have made a short as well as early dinner, on purpose in order to confer with you" (107). Apparently, meals must be curtailed, even avoided, in order for Clarissa's mother to chat with her. This is trying, as Clarissa can discuss her affairs with her father only through her mother's mediation; her mother is too manipulated herself to perform the role of mediator with any real success.

This conference does not go well. Clarissa refuses to comply with her father's demands. She retreats to her room in disgrace and writes to Anna: "My father is come home, and my brother with him. Late as it is, they are all shut together. Not a door opens; not a soul stirs. . . . The angry assembly is broke up. My two uncles and my aunt Hervey are sent for, it seems, to be here in the morning to breakfast. I shall then, I suppose, know my doom. . . . (The next day) They are at breakfast together . . . What a cruel thing is suspense!" (116–18).

The Harlowes have always functioned as a unit, enmeshing family members in contentions that are so tangled and knotted that resolution is no more possible than independence from the struggle. Psychologists warn that, when this situation inevitably comes to revolve around mealtime, the traditional highlight of family interaction, the "perfect" child, is well on her way to developing an eating disorder.[73] "The preanorectic daughter," writes psychiatrist John Sours, "still as a leaf barely clinging, lives in a state of fear, expecting punishment and wishing that she could tell what her parents are thinking, which further blurs the family subsystem boundaries. The gentlest breeze makes their windows rattle, and the house grows shadows around the family. The anorectic must mediate parental conflict. Each family member says what the other means; no one speaks about his feelings, the windows are nailed and boarded."[74]

This rather Gothic scenario expresses perfectly the atmosphere we have come to expect of the Harlowe mansion; even before Clarissa ceases to enjoy meals with her family, family interaction at meals is characterized by unspoken passions, cruelly courteous intimidation, and a nightmarish quality of impending disaster. One early meal upsets Clarissa to such an extent that she relates it dramatically to Anna; this repast characterizes the pattern for conditional, mediated behavior and the barriers to communication which she can anticipate from her family:

> Such a solemnity in everybody's countenance!—My
> mamma's eyes were fixed upon the tea-cups; and when she

looked up it was heavily, as if her eyelids had weights upon them, and then not to me. My papa sat half-aside in his elbow-chair, that his head might be turned from me; his hands folded, and waving, as it were, up and down; his fingers, poor dear gentleman! in motion, as if angry to the very ends of them. My sister sat swelling. My brother looked at me with scorn, having measured me, as I may say, with his eyes, as I entered, from head to foot. My aunt was there and looked upon me as if with kindness restrained, bending coldly to my compliment to her as she sat; and then cast an eye first on my brother, then on my sister, as if to give the reason . . . of her unusual stiffness . . .

I took my seat. Shall I make tea; madam, to my mamma? . . .

No! a very short sentence in one very short word was the expressive answer.

This meal is over almost instantly. Clarissa relates nothing that is said, nothing that is eaten. Abandoned by the others, she is uncertain even of her own actions. "I did not know what to do with myself," she admits. And then:

Just after the second dish out stepped my mamma—A word with you, sister Hervey! taking her in her hand. Presently my sister dropped away. Then my brother. So I was left alone with my papa.

He looked so very sternly that my heart failed me, as twice or thrice I would have addressed myself to him; nothing but solemn silence on all hands having passed before.

At last, I asked, if it were his pleasure that I should pour him out another dish?

He answered me with the same angry monosyllable which I had received from my mamma before, and then arose and walked about the room. (63–64)

The foreboding aloofness of Clarissa's family is particularly disturbing here because it takes place over tea. It is somehow horribly indecorous, like a brawl in a nursery. Her ostracism is especially distressing because she has been invited to share in the meal, a signal that she should be able to expect courtesy and dialogue and to rely on the format of the meal itself as interactive. Interaction, however, is never a simple process at Harlowe Place. The family manages to pop out of the room, one by one, in a not very subtle way, but the maneuver that is so amusing in *Pride and Prejudice* is frightening in the Harlowe mansion; the empty dining room becomes a symbol of desertion, of betrayal, as unjust as Miss Havisham's ghastly empty wedding banquet in *Great Expectations*, yet the brooding presence with whom she is left is none other than her "papa."

Clarissa's only face-to-face confrontation with her father takes place as though she were not even present. As in her dream, both her body and her voice are ignored. The meal ends with no interchange between them. Her father merely repeats a formula to which she has become accustomed: "No words—I will not be prated to!—I will be obeyed!—I will have no child, but an obedient one," thunders her father when he finally manages to break the heavy silence. "I will be obeyed, I tell you!—and cheerfully too!—or you are no child of mine!—" (63–65).

Months later, as Clarissa lies a vanquished prisoner in a brothel, she will write a frantic note to her father, pleading, "You are my own dear papa, whether you will or not—And though I am an unworthy child—yet I am your child" (890). It is perhaps no coincidence, however, that her plea to her father corresponds with a defiant resolution that she will never eat or drink again.

2

The Hungry Lover
Clarissa and Lovelace

A CONDITIONAL KIND OF LIKING

Clarissa's first meals in London do not take place, as though missing them were a test of her ability to govern her own choice. She relates:

> While we were talking at the door, my new servant came up with an invitation to us both to tea. I said HE might accept of it, if he pleased; but I must pursue my writing; and not choosing either tea or supper, I desired him to make my excuses below, as to both; and inform them of my choice to be retired as much as possible; yet to promise for me my attendance on the widow and her nieces at breakfast in the morning.
>
> He objected particularity in the eye of strangers as to avoiding supper.
>
> You know, said I, and can tell them that I seldom eat suppers. My spirits are low. You must never urge me against a declared choice. (525)

Lovelace accepts the political implications of Clarissa's decision, and their correspondence henceforth centers around the dining room. Predictably, Clarissa's letter continues, "I am exceedingly out of humour with Mr. Lovelace . . . for he would not let me rest till I gave him my company in the dining-room" (526).

In keeping with the early patterns her family has taught her to respect, Clarissa finds that both her presence and behavior at meals are to be considered representative of her compliance with the terms and wishes of others. She is now free of the mother who urged, "Don't disgrace my report when you come down to supper. And be sure [to] behave as you used to do to your brother and sister" (97), but Lovelace instantly steps into this empty parental role. As her mother had once informed the household that Clarissa would marry Solmes, Lovelace claims that he has informed the household that he and Clarissa are actually man and wife. This initial breakfast will signify her compliance with his lie. "Let me beseech you, madam, if my behaviour shall not be to your dislike, that you will not tomorrow at break-fast-time discredit what I have told them," Lovelace pleads (527).

The plea is familiar—with one exception. Lovelace twists the pattern, implicating himself in her compliance by making Clarissa's behavior conditional on his adherence to conditions set by herself. "The moment I give you cause to think that I take any advantage of your concession, that moment revoke it and expose me as I shall deserve," he offers (527). Because Lovelace has designated meals as signifiers of acceptance, Clarissa's food-related behavior can serve as an excellent index of the extent to which she can accept Lovelace on his own terms, terms that he leaves open to Clarissa's subjective evaluation.

Lovelace's plea follows earlier assurances that Clarissa's will shall be always superior to his in their dealings together, an assurance reminiscent of Clarissa's oaths of loyalty to her mother. "May I perish eternally if your will shall not be a law to me in everything!" (376), he swears as he urges Clarissa to run away with him during the fateful interview before she does just that. Clarissa's first letters from St. Albans relate, "My pleasure should determine him, he said, be it what it would. . . . [he assured] me that my will should be a law to him in every particular" (390). This language of self-denial is so familiar to both Clarissa and to her suitor that they do not question the efficacy of beginning a relationship upon it.

Accepting Lovelace at his word, Clarissa heartily embraces her role as reformer, immediately instructing Lovelace that he is in his "novitiate" (458), that he has a great deal to correct before he might aspire to her hand, and that he should indeed prefer her satisfaction to his own. "He seems," she tells Anna, "to be one who has always had too much of his own will to study to accommodate himself to that of others" (410). "He imagines himself, I find, to be a very polite man, and cannot bear to be thought otherwise . . . I had a mind to mortify a pride that I am sure deserves to be mortified" (458).

Lovelace's terms are effectively baffled as Clarissa insists on judging her lover by what she has heard of him (Lovelace has developed as legendary a character as Clarissa's) rather than according to her own experience. In this respect she treats him as she herself has always been treated by those who have heard of her. Lovelace can only protest this strategy, pleading: "What cause have I given you to treat me with so much severity, and so little confidence? . . . My general character may have been against me: but what of your knowledge have you against me?" (489). Startled, Clarissa responds that general character is sufficient to merit dislike and finds herself miserable when her hasty answer forces her to reject a much wished-for proposal of marriage, a proposal strategically offered as a punishment for her prejudice.

In her attempts to "reform" Lovelace, Clarissa follows her family's strategy for her own reformation, demanding not only that he become what she would have him be in order to deserve her love but also insisting that he desire to do this. Her first attempts at correction thus sound very much like bullying:

> You talk of reformation, sometimes, Mr. Lovelace; and in so talking acknowledge errors. But I see you can very ill bear the reproof which perhaps you are not solicitous to avoid GIV-ING occasion for—Far be it from me to take delight in finding fault. I should be glad for both our sakes, since my situation is what it is, that I could do nothing but praise you. But failures which affect a mind that need not be very delicate to be affected by them are too grating to be passed over in silence by a person who wishes to be thought in earnest in her own duties. (458)

Lovelace apparently thinks so too. He interrupts her several times, referring to her desire to correct as a "pleasure in mortifying." In spite of his terms for acceptance, his promise to be governed by Clarissa's will, Lovelace responds with genuine irritability to the implication of conditional love, love that is to be transferred from her former "friends" to himself, love that is to be granted less to his self than to his actions and accomplishments. Baffled, Clarissa can only complain, "like a restive horse he pains one's hands, and half disjoints one's arms to rein him in" (128).

The pattern for conditional love, of course, is familiar to Clarissa, and we will find that it has been part of her suitor's background as well. This dangerous pattern is complicated by Clarissa's refusing, in characteristically triangular fashion, to accept the responsibility for her own decisions, decisions regarding both her feelings and her activities in relation to Lovelace. She displaces this responsibility, insisting that she cannot determine her future actions until she has received letters from Aunt Hervey, her sister, Anna Howe. "There is no taking any resolutions till I hear from my friends," she insists (461), provoking Lovelace to exclaim bitterly, "So father-sick! so family-fond! what a poor chance stands a husband with such a wife, unless, forsooth, they vouchsafe to be reconciled to her and CONTINUE to be reconciled?" "I hourly pray that a man may see whether she can love anybody but her father and mother!" (521).[1]

These triangular perceptions effectively distort all communication between Lovelace and his supposed bride, forcing them to perceive each other as adversaries and marriage as an alternative to family love and self-esteem. Lovelace's most resentful, painfully confused invectives against Clarissa invariably carry an awareness of the conditional nature of her love, a bitter perception of Clarissa's love as a triumph over him. Above all, Lovelace can never be sure that he is loved unconditionally, loved for himself rather than for his submission both to Clarissa and to her "allies." Although he has pledged to conduct himself according to her guidance, Clarissa's association with her family will not allow him to accept the submission that such a pledge involves. In a particularly complex epistle he laments to Belford:

> She will not trust me. She will not confide in my honour. Doubt, in this case, is defiance. She loves me not well enought [sic] to forgive me generously. She is so greatly above me! How can I forgive her for a merit so mortifying to my pride! She THINKS, she KNOWS, she has TOLD me, that she is above me. These words are still in my ears, "Begone, Lovelace!—my soul is above thee, man!—Thou hast a proud heart to contend with!—My soul is above thee, man!" Miss Howe thinks her of the same opinion. Thou, even thou, my friend, my INTIMATE friend and companion, art of the same opinion. I fear her as much as I love her—How shall my pride bear these reflections? . . . Myself to be considered but as the second person in my own family!—Canst thou teach me to bear such a reflec-

tion as this!—To tell me of my acquisition in her, and that
she, with all her excellencies, will be MINE in full property, is a
mistake—It cannot be so—For shall I not be HERS; and not
MY OWN?—Will not every act of her duty (as I cannot deserve
it) be a condescension, and a triumph over me? . . . a daughter
of the Harlowes thus to excel the last and, as I have heretofore
said, not the meanest of the Lovelaces—forbid it! (734)

The familiar language of acquisition, of the loved one and of oneself
as possessions, of self as reputation, cannot be ignored here; it is familiar
as the language of the treasured child, the competitive, insecure family
possession. Nor can we ignore Lovelace's triangular insistence on judging
his relationship with Clarissa according to everyone else's view of it.

As a treasured child, a family object, it has been Lovelace's experience, as well as Clarissa's, that someone must always be first in the family,
a single voice around which all others will rally. It is perhaps no wonder
that each resents and fears the other's apparent aspiration toward this
position. Each character believes that only one person's will can be dominant, thus their engagement cannot be otherwise than a battle for su-
premacy. This triangular battle, involving all who would interfere between
them, allows the two lovers to avoid the frighteningly strong feelings they
have for each other and the personal insecurities these feelings unleash.

Although Lovelace and Clarissa are commonly viewed as adversaries
and opposites by critics eager to interpret the novel according to a polarized moral scheme, it is important to recognize that Lovelace's situation
and character are, in many ways, remarkably similar to those of the heroine; it is this similarity in perspectives which compels them to view each
other as adversaries and to turn meals into trials, negotiations, and political competitions.[2]

Like Clarissa, Lovelace has interiorized a prescribed identity, a role
that he both accommodates and resents. He, too, is a highly competitive
person, obsessed with appearances, inordinately attractive, bright, wealthy,
popular; and he is equally used to distorted communications, secrets, and
conditional love. His prolonged siege of Clarissa is fueled and aggravated
by family members who are as insistent as the Harlowes that he marry
their choice—whatever his own might be. A typical letter from Lord M.
reads: "I have no manner of doubt now but that you will marry . . . I know
you have vowed revenge against this fine lady's family: but no more of

that, now. You must look upon them all as your relations; and forgive and forget. . . . Love your lady. . . . Be a good husband. . . . Do this; and I, and your aunts, will love you forever" (664–65).

If Clarissa's family members have insidiously held their love for her as a hostage in their battle for authority, Lovelace's relatives follow an economic strategy in addition to this emotional one, pooling their united resources into a hypothetical inheritance that Lovelace will forfeit by not complying with their wishes. This is easily accomplished because, like Clarissa, Lovelace has grown up in a highly mediated surrounding, a home without parents, a world in which his rights, his possessions, his identity, depend on the favor of a united clan of relatives.

A typical meeting at Lord M.'s to discuss Lovelace's inveteracy toward Clarissa is not significantly different from mealtime trials at Harlowe Place, although Lovelace's position as male heir allows him to withstand the trial with greater assurance. We recall Clarissa's narration of averted faces, glum silence, her father's fingers in angry motion on the tabletop, as the family meets to discuss her marriage to Solmes. Lovelace's description of a family gathering to discuss his intentions toward Clarissa (following his deliberate absence from both breakfast and dinner in order to "punish" his family) is painfully similar; he relates:

> NOW I ENTER UPON MY TRIAL[.]
> With horrible grave faces was I received. The two antiques only bowed their tabby heads; making longer faces than ordinary; and all the old lines appearing strong in their furrowed foreheads and fallen cheeks.
> . . . I took my seat. Lord M. looked horribly glum; his fingers clasped, and turning round and round, under and over, his but just disgouted thumbs; his sallow face, and goggling eyes, cast upon the floor, on the fireplace, on his two sisters, on his two kinswomen, by turns; but not once deigning to look upon me. (1026–27)

Although the silence and despondency of this meeting are surely justified by Lovelace's forgeries, perjuries, and sexual crimes, the family's tendency to close into an "embattled phalanx," insisting that its members will act as a unit rather than as individuals, immediately warns the reader that channels of communication at The Lawn are unlikely to produce obedience on the part of a young person who perceives himself as self-determined. We will see, declares Lady Sarah during this conversation,

> whether we [herself and Lady Betty], and my Lord M. (your nearest relations, sir) have, or have not, any influence over you. And, for my own part, as your determination shall be in this article, such shall be mine, with regard to the disposition of all that is within my power.
>
> LADY BETTY. And mine
>
> And mine, said my lord: and valiantly he swore to it. (1035)

Just as James is to be made the recipient of the Harlowe brothers' joint wealth, we find that Lovelace is the sole heir of his relatives' fortunes, and, like James, he has been strongly encouraged to assume a position of inappropriate confidence in his family. It is for this reason, as Carol Kay points out, that "his family cannot sustain a punitive disapproval."[3] The threat of disinheritance is obviously less effective than the polarity it entails, a distinct gap between the culprit and the family as a whole, a gap whose closure depends on Lovelace's abandoning his right to self-determination. Whatever he may think of the request, it is unlikely that Lovelace will accommodate it under these conditions. "Far be it from me to think slightly of favours you may, any of you, be glad I would deserve. But as far be it from me to enter into conditions against my own liking, with sordid views," he declares (1035), revealing the same sentiments with which Clarissa received her family's proposal of a suitor. To Belford he protests, "He [Lord M.] has sometimes threatened to disinherit ME: but if I should renounce HIM, it would be but justice, and would vex him ten times more than anything he can do will vex me" (648).

Clarissa's only hope for a happy marriage with Lovelace lies in her ability to bridge this gap, yet she has been cast in a neatly polarized position of allegiance with all the antagonists whom Lovelace resents. Lovelace's family has thoughtlessly portrayed her as an alternative to their own child, Lord M. announcing, "Let me tell you, if you do not make the best of husbands to so good a young lady, and one who has had so much courage for your sake, I will renounce you; and settle all I can upon her and hers by you, and leave you out of the question" (665). Ignoring the conditions attached to Lord M.'s threat, Lovelace naturalizes his guardian's preference, declaring, "THIS I know, that were I to marry this lady, he would rather settle upon her all he has a mind to settle, than upon me. . . . Another reason why a Lovelace should not wish to marry a CLARISSA" (669).

Convinced that Clarissa's love for him is conditional on his reformation and secondary to her love for a family he despises, distressed by constant reminders that Clarissa is actually his superior in all ways and preferred, for this reason, by his own family, it is perhaps inevitable that Lovelace should come to see the woman he loves as a dangerous competitor. While one can easily interpret his pride as mercenary, surely it can as easily be read as a sign of Lovelace's own insecurity, his distress at being compared to "a CLARISSA."

Lovelace's distress at this point exactly parallels Clarissa's former battles with her family. John Stevenson argues brilliantly that Clarissa is shocked at her family's proposal of Solmes because he represents "her substitute, the new sibling, who is privy to their plans." He writes, "[Clarissa] is especially horrified at the robbery of his relations that his settlements imply—a horror that probably derives, in part, from her fear that he has already acquired a new family and no longer needs his own."[4] Clarissa is not only shocked at being replaced but at being replaced for economic reasons. Lovelace is similarly shocked to discover that his aunts plan to "adopt" Clarissa as their own child, replacing the Harlowes as her parents. Lady Sarah exclaims tearfully, "She shall be my daughter!" (1039), yet Lovelace notes with annoyance that these professions of affection are immediately followed by an "inquisition into the lady's fortune; into the particulars of the grandfather's estate; and what her father, and her single-souled uncles, will probably do for her" (1040). Lovelace is embarrassed and frightened by his family's mercenary charity. Although he acknowledges to Belford that Lady Sarah is "very indolent and melancholy" and Lady Betty is "officious and managing" as well as generous, he cannot help adding, "She is *my aunt,* Jack" (1039).

To his consternation Lovelace finds that his family's horror at his abduction and seduction of Clarissa is less owing to his actions than to his choice of a victim. "For such a pretty little miss as this to come to so very great a misfortune must be a very sad thing: but tell me, would not the losing of any ordinary child, of any other less considerable family, of less shining or amiable qualities, have been as great and as heavy a loss to that family as the losing this pretty little miss to hers?" he demands of Belford (971). He finds himself strangely indignant that his family is less concerned for Clarissa as an individual than for her position as a member of her wealthy family. "Their family is of standing. All gentlemen of it, and

rich, and reputable," Lord M. insists; to which the young man replies, obviously with his lover in mind: "They are a narrow-souled and implacable
family. I hate them" (1036).

Always a legend at home, Clarissa has now become an incarnation of
wisdom and perfection to Lovelace's relatives. She is as unquestionable as
one of Lord M.'s proverbs. Nothing she says will be doubted. Her virtue
cannot err. Lovelace knows from experience that he cannot hope to influence his family in a declared preference of this kind. "His lordship takes
pleasure in writing to me in a corrective style," he complains:

> When a boy, I never asked anything of him, but out flew a
> PROVERB; and if the tendency of that was to deny me, I never
> could obtain the least favour. This gave me so great an aver-
> sion to the very word, that when a child I made it a condition
> with my tutor, who was an honest parson, that I would not
> read my Bible at all, if he would not excuse me one of the
> wisest books in it: to which, however, I had no other objec-
> tion than that it was called THE PROVERBS. And as for Solomon,
> he was then a hated character with me, not because of his
> polygamy, but because I had conceived him to be such an-
> other musty old fellow as my uncle. (610–11)

Unfortunately, Clarissa is also fond of proverbs (she amuses herself
before her death by copying long lists of them for meditation), and Lovelace
once again finds himself conditioning for ways of avoiding such formu-
laic wisdom. If his relatives will prefer the apparently perfect Clarissa to
their own child, even after his supposed reformation and marriage, how
can Lovelace ever hope to be loved—by them or by her? As Clarissa's father once cursed her for despising his wishes, Lovelace's uncle bellows
that he must marry Clarissa or "May the curse of God follow you in all
you undertake!" (1037). "I cannot bear this," Lovelace agonizes to Belford.
"What mortifies my pride is, that this exalted creature, if I were to marry
her, would not be governed in her behaviour to me by love, but by generosity merely, or by blind duty" (669). "Oh Belford, Belford! I cannot, cannot (at least at present I cannot) marry" (657).[5]

Lord M. is not the only well-intentioned person who unwittingly
forces Clarissa to face Lovelace from across an emotional gap. At precisely
the same time Lovelace is relating his family's threats and interventions to

Belford, Anna Howe is urging Clarissa to accept Lovelace's proposals of marriage by proxy. She exclaims: "He promises by them [Lady Betty Lawrence and Lady Sarah Sadleir] to make the best of husbands; and my lord and his two sisters are both to be guarantees that he will be so. . . . Nor doubt they of a thorough reformation in his morals from your example and influence over him." Apparently, Anna accepts without question the right and ability of Lovelace's family to mediate and to make intimate moral promises for him. She continues, in a manner similar to Lord M., to speak of the importance of family ties:

> But come, since what is past cannot be helped, let us look forward. You have now happy prospects opening to you: a family, ALREADY NOBLE, ready to receive and embrace you with open arms and joyful hearts; and who, by their love to you, will teach another family (who know not what an excellence they have confederated to persecute) how to value you. Your prudence, your piety, will crown all: it will reclaim a wretch that for an hundred sakes more than for his own one would wish to be reclaimed. (1042–43)

Like Lovelace's relatives, the only consideration Anna does not mention in her argument for Clarissa's marriage to Lovelace is the quality of Clarissa's feelings for her future husband and of his for her. The possibility of their coming to love each other does not appear of much importance. Only settlements, reputations, and reconciliations are mentioned, matters that embroil both families in the economic affairs of the two people most concerned in the marriage.[6] In fact, the marriage partners are actually urged to marry in terms that designate them as enemies: Clarissa in order to "reclaim a wretch," Lovelace in order to "do justice" to a lady far his superior. Both characters are advised to bury their own desires in order to accommodate more "important" principles and expectations;[7] both are strangely encouraged to view this sacrifice of self as a noble gesture to oneself. "If you would not have him for YOUR OWN sake," Anna entreats her friend, "Have him you must, for MINE, for your FAMILY's, for your HONOUR's sake!" (1045).[8]

Tragically, both Clarissa and Lovelace often accept this mediated situation without hesitation. They seem actually unable to consider marriage other than as a secondary affair that will affect their relationships with their families. Should she marry, Clarissa tells Anna,

> I, who have now but one only friend, shall most probably,
> and if it be not my own fault, have as many new ones as there
> are persons in Mr. Lovelace's family; and this whether Mr.
> Lovelace treat me kindly, or not. And who knows, but that by
> degrees, those new friends, by their rank and merit, may have
> weight enough to get me restored to the favour of my rela-
> tions? Till which can be effected, I shall not be tolerably easy.
> Happy I never expect to be. Mr. Lovelace's mind and mind
> [sic] are vastly different; different in essentials." (671)

"All the ground I have hitherto gained with her is entirely owing to
her concern for the safety of people whom I have reason to hate," Lovelace
rightly laments (142). "I would have her [my wife] look after me when I
go out, as far as she can see me, as my Rosebud after her Johnny; and meet
me at my return with rapture," he muses (669), idealizing the only couple
he knows that seem to love each other unconditionally, yet Lovelace ad-
heres to this triangular pattern too. "What my motive, dost thou ask?" he
queries. "[I] will secure her mine, in spite of them all, in spite of her own
inflexible heart; mine, without condition. . . . Then shall I have all the
rascals and rascalesses of the family come creeping to me: I prescribing to
them; and bringing that sordidly-imperious brother to kneel at the foot-
stool of my throne" (145).

It is no wonder, given this mediated battle combined with the genuine attraction between these two characters, that each is confused, miserable, angry with the other and with him- or herself. "How little confidence!
as if we apprehended each other to be a plotter rather than a lover," muses
Lovelace (650). Letters to friends confess their bewilderment, despair, frustrated love, yet their conversations with each other are heavy with the
weight of interlocking triangles, conditions, myths of submission, and
estranged duties.[9]

It is important to remember that, while Clarissa and Lovelace are victims of families that indirectly urge them to oppress each other, they are
not merely passive victims. Each of these perplexed characters accommodates the system. The triangular pattern of mediated relationships allows
a collaborative hostility through which Clarissa and Lovelace avoid confronting the sources of conflict in their relationship. It enables Clarissa to

avoid thinking about just how conditional her "conditional kind of liking" for Lovelace might be (135), and Lovelace need not address his fear
of marriage and his feelings of inadequacy. Their attempts to discuss their
feelings for each other are inevitably undermined as problems from other
relationships are substituted for more personal and direct concerns. Each
attempt to blame, criticize, or analyze thwarts these individuals' ability to
regard themselves as self-governing, as belonging to themselves, as having
the right to their own feelings.

Clarissa and Lovelace continue to torment each other, assigning and
accepting blame, but never really explore their options for change. One
message from Clarissa to Anna relates a typically frustrating conversation
that takes place between herself and her lover at five o'clock in the morning—in the dining room. The letter reads:

> [Clarissa] DUTY and NATURE, sir, call upon me to make the
> submissions you speak of: there is a father, there is a mother,
> there are uncles, in the one case, to justify and demand those
> submissions—What, pray, sir, can be pleaded for the CONDE-
> SCENSION [toward himself], as you call it?—Will you say your
> merits, either with regard to THEM, or to MYSELF, may?
>
> [Lovelace] This to be said, after the persecutions of those
> relations! After what you have suffered! After what you have
> made me hope! Let me ask you, madam (we talked of PRIDE
> just now), what sort of pride must HIS be, which could dis-
> pense with inclination and preference in his lady's part of it?—
> What must be that love—
>
> [Clarissa] LOVE, sir! who talks of LOVE?—Was not MERIT the
> thing we were talking of?—have I ever professed, have I ever
> required of YOU professions of a passion of that nature? (592)

After this admission that her alliance with Lovelace can be founded
only on admiration of his reformed character, not on love of himself,
Clarissa suggests that they conclude their relationship. Her proposal is
met with a violent outburst that so terrifies her that she flees to her chamber, there to indulge in a flow of tears. "In half an hour," she relates, "He
sent a little billet expressing his concern for the vehemence of his behaviour,
and praying to see me." She confesses, in genuine perplexity, "I went—
Because I could not help myself, I went" (593).[10]

Only once does Clarissa confess unqualified love for Lovelace. Significantly enough, the incident that elicits this demonstration is a violent stomach disorder brought on by Lovelace's having purposefully swallowed ipecacuanha. Lovelace is quite sure that news of his having vomited blood will force his beloved to disclose what all his expostulations and promises have not revealed. Little does he realize that this forced confession is conditional as well. "One cannot, my dear, hate people in danger of death, or who are in distress or affliction," Clarissa writes to Anna in a letter that surely would not satisfy the least demanding lover (679), yet even this guarded admission that the incident has "taught me more than I knew of myself" strikes Clarissa as dangerous. She writes:

> You will not wonder that I am grave on this detection—
> DETECTION, must I call it? What can I call it?—I have not had
> heart's ease enough to inspect that heart as I ought.
> Dissatisfied with myself, I am afraid to look back upon what
> I have written. And yet know not how to have done writing. I
> never was in such an odd frame of mind—I know not how to
> describe it—was YOU ever so? (679)

Lovelace's letters to Belford are equally expressive of mixed passions. "Let me perish, if I know what to make either of myself, or of this surprising creature," he writes (932). "Do not despise me, Jack, for my inconsistency—in no two letters perhaps agreeing with myself. . . . But I am mad with love—fired by revenge . . . drawn five or six ways at once—Can SHE possibly be so unhappy as I?" (694).

Less than two weeks later Clarissa has been drugged, raped, and imprisoned in a brothel. It is impossible to excuse Lovelace's actions; however, considered in terms of his tangled emotions, his desperate need to be loved unconditionally, Lovelace's plot to seduce Clarissa can become, if not less offensive, at least more understandable. Viewed within the context of competing, interlocking triangles, Lovelace's rape of Clarissa becomes a desperate and impossible attempt to separate his self from his actions, to somehow confirm that he is loved for his self rather than for his compliance to a prescribed behavior, a conditional role.[11]

Because he has interiorized the oppressive system of conditional love, Lovelace decides to test Clarissa by conditioning with her, by forcing her to forgive the very behavior she has most emphatically forbidden as a condition of her love: he determines to violate her sexually. In what must surely be one of the most psychologically complex and poignant passages of the novel, Lovelace asserts that only Clarissa's unconditional forgiveness and uncontested loyalty can become the basis of his own unqualified love for her:

> Let me see that she loves me well enough to forgive me for my OWN sake. Has she not heretofore lamented that she stayed not in her father's house, though the consequence must have been, if she HAD, that she would have been the wife of the odious Solmes? If now she be brought to consent to be mine, seest thou not that the RECONCILIATION with her DETESTED RELATIONS is the INDUCEMENT, as it ALWAYS was, and not LOVE of ME?—Neither her virtue nor her love can be established but upon full trial; the last trial—But if her resistance and resentment be such as hitherto I have reason to expect they will be, and if I find in that resentment less of hatred of me, than of the fact, then shall she be mine in her own way. Then . . . will I MARRY HER. (838)

"Less of hatred of ME, than of the fact." The fallacy in Lovelace's plan is, of course, that he can somehow sever himself from his actions; it is a fallacy of which he is painfully aware, and yet he has become, like Clarissa, a dual character and cannot correct the duality that torments him. As Jocelyn Harris points out, "Lovelace's two desires, to deflower her and to make her love him, are mutually contradictory."[12]

If Lovelace is a cruel character in his dealings with Clarissa, he is also a tortured one, and this is surely part of the tragedy of their relationship. "I hate compulsion in all forms; and cannot bear, even to be COMPELLED to be the wretch my choice has made me!" he agonizes to Belford. "I am a machine . . . and no free agent. Upon my soul, Jack, it is a very foolish thing for a man of spirit to have brought himself to such a height of iniquity, that he must proceed, and cannot help himself; and yet to be next to certain that his very victory will undo him." This pathetic letter continues:

> What a happiness must that man know, who moves regularly to some laudable end, and has nothing to reproach himself with in his progress to it! When by honest means he attains

this end, how great and unmixed must be his enjoyments! What a happy man, in this particular case had I been, had it been given me to BE only what I wished to APPEAR to be! (848)[13]

Lovelace's earnest battle with himself is further exacerbated by his friends' attempts to help him to determine his interests and actions. Because other characters' opinions are mediations, no character can give Lovelace advice without frustrating his own purpose. Belford's anxious pleadings on Clarissa's behalf may well contribute to her rape. "I charge thee, write not a word to me in her favour, if thou meanest her well; for if I spare her, it must be all *ex mero motu*," warns Lovelace, a warning Belford does not heed (668). Even McDonald's appeal for mercy undermines its own purpose when Lovelace perceives his intervention as yet another alternative to self-determination. "Jack, this pitiful dog was such another unfortunate one as thyself—his arguments serving to confirm me in the very purpose he brought them to prevail upon me to give up," Lovelace argues, with scorn and misguided defiance.

> Had he left me to myself, to the tenderness of my own nature, moved as I was when the lady withdrew, and had sat down and made odious faces, and said nothing; it is very possible that I should have taken the chair over-against him, which she had quitted; and have cried and blubbered with him for half an hour together. But the varlet to ARGUE with me! To pretend to CONVINCE a man, who knows in his heart that he is doing a wrong thing!—He must needs think that this would put me upon trying what I could say for myself. (837)

As friendless as she is, Clarissa is not friendless enough to escape the violence of a man who has been taught to perceive all interference on her behalf as an attempt to undermine his right of self-determination and to exalt her at his expense. As much as he may desire to comply with his relatives' wishes, Lovelace cannot be true to his own desires without feeling that he is betraying his right of refusal, his right of choice. "I have often more than half ruined myself by my complaisance and, being afraid of control, have brought control upon myself," he ruminates, unable to unravel the tangle of notions that inform his fears and dictate his actions (961).

Lovelace's perplexity is not appreciably different from that of his prisoner. "I am very uneasy to think how I have been DRAWN on one hand, and DRIVEN on the other, into a clandestine, . . . lover-like correspondence, which my heart condemns," Clarissa worries (117). She, too, determines that "those who will bear much shall have much to bear," resolving that "we poor mortals, by our OVER-solicitude to preserve undisturbed the qualities we are constitutionally fond of, frequently lose the benefits we propose to ourselves from them; since the designing and encroaching, finding out what we most fear to forfeit, direct their batteries against these our weaker places and, making an artillery, if I may so phrase it, of our hopes and fears, play it upon us at their pleasure" (105).[14] Unfortunately, this conviction will not allow either Clarissa or Lovelace to exercise the precious control of self without sacrificing that control to suspicion.

GRANDIOSITY, NARCISSISM, AND THE COMPULSION TO REPEAT

Lovelace's duality, his agonized struggles with himself, have been often ignored in critical treatments of Richardson's novel. These poignant and disturbing passages are easily overwhelmed by his audacious boasts, his outrageous threats, his cocky taunts and caricatures, and, most of all, his impudent treatment of all things feminine. Bold, rash, reckless, wild—capable of extraordinary energy and ingenuity—Lovelace is easily one of the most brazen libertines in the annals of literary history. He is not, however, consistently brazen, nor does he find his own behavior fulfilling.

Critical attempts to blame Lovelace for the events of the novel (according to his arrogant boast that he manipulates all the characters in the book like puppets), to posit Lovelace as the only problem in the text, ignore the possibility that the novel, like the world it aspires to reflect and teach, contains countless reinforcing interactions, multiple causes, unlimited conflicting perceptions. Critics such as Jocelyn Harris have neatly labeled Lovelace "a tyrannical Filmer," the incarnation of "all that is tyrannous in the sex,"[15] yet Lovelace's months of deliberating, scheming, doubting, and fearing himself do not support the argument that the rape is an unmixed act of tyrannical lust.[16] Such an argument must rest on an elemental antagonism between two characters who spend much of the novel admitting their perplexed love for each other.

Unless Lovelace and Clarissa are considered in terms of the complexities of interrelationships that influence their perceptions and actions, unless they are viewed as characters in a situation that is itself problematic, each will necessarily appear inconsistent and hypocritical. Readers will find themselves caught in the narrow reasoning Clarissa employs when she labels her brother, sister, and lover naturally manipulative, all the while discovering that the same charge is being applied, quite successfully, to herself. An examination of the conflicting impulses within these unhappy characters may allow Richardson to be given even further credit for having written a profoundly rich and psychologically sophisticated text.

It is not difficult to understand how Lovelace might be labeled a villain and a tyrant; his chauvinistic comments concerning women and his frivolous treatment of Clarissa are stereotypically villainous and tyrannical. Considered separately from the influence of other characters, however, Lovelace's personality and behavior are no more excessive than those of any character in the novel. James, Arabella, the Harlowe parents and servants, Clarissa, Lovelace's friends and servants, Madam Sinclair and her whores—all appear emphatically demanding or exemplary in one way or another. Neither the angelic nature of the divine Clarissa nor the evil tendencies of her aggressive lover nor the unwavering resentments of her siblings and parents are immediately believable. They seem to be mythic tendencies, fantastic and seductive qualities intended to lure the reader into a symbolic world for a moral purpose.[17]

Critics such as Carol Flynn have explored the possibility that the actions of characters such as Clarissa and Lovelace are too extreme to exist except on a mythic level. Flynn writes, "While Clarissa and Lovelace push each other into polarities, playing angel to devil, victim to rapist, light to darkness, tragedy to comedy, heaven to hell," Richardson examines the process of creating the self but "loses interest in his characters once they perfect themselves."[18] Such an approach ignores the expectations imposed on two very perplexed and complicated perfectionists and the difficulties they encounter in attempting to "create the self" on their own terms. If Richardson is to be given credit for the astounding psychological complexity of his characters, a realistic intricacy that continues to impress psychologists two hundred years after the novel's publication, it is necessary to consider the complications that arise in the nonfictional world whenever a child is pronounced perfect and expected to excel, particularly when excellence is defined as compliance.[19]

That Clarissa and Lovelace do excel in so many ways may indicate that they have been born gifted, but it may also suggest that they have accommodated themselves to the expectation of their own perfection. If we entertain this latter possibility and examine its implications within the narrative, the transgressions of the characters become less the inconsistencies of mythic characters "driven out of their paths" than the natural resentments of individuals compelled to assume prescribed roles. Many of Lovelace's disturbing remarks can be reconciled with what we know of him as a troubled character.[20] His seemingly lascivious exclamation "To carry off such a girl as this in spite of all her watchful and implacable friends . . . What a triumph!—What a triumph over the whole sex!" (147) falls neatly into what we have come to expect as a tendency to plan his actions concerning Clarissa around their potential effects on other relationships—in this case, his hostilities toward the Harlowes.

Psychotherapist Arthur Robbins notes that such displacements onto groups or abstractions ("What a triumph over the whole sex!") are common in grandiose adults whose parents often posited the demands of abstractions (God, the family, proper social conduct) as a way of forcing the child to comply with the parents' wishes. Because these concepts are inviolate in the child's mind, there is no one against whom the child can safely vent anger over his or her lack of freedom. "In adulthood," Robbins explains, "this anger is displaced onto institutions, onto society at large, and periodically onto specific individuals, resulting in the paranoia which is characteristic of the grandiose when they are confronted with social demands which they can no longer escape"[21]

In fact, Lovelace's vow of revenge may be even more circular than it initially seems. He proposes to revenge himself on all women through Clarissa, precisely because he has been wounded by the infidelity of his first love, a woman who taught him the pain of being loved for one's accomplishments and position rather than for oneself. "I thought she loved me at least as well as I believed I loved her," he remembers. "My friends were pleased with my choice. . . . I could not bear that a woman should prefer a coronet to me" (143–44).

Lovelace moves quickly from his narration of the conditional love of this first lady to his love for Clarissa: "an angel," he exclaims, "eyes so sparkling; limbs so divinely turned; health so florid; youth so blooming; air so animated . . . but here's her mistake. . . . How my heart rises at her preference of them [her family] to me, when she is convinced of their injustice to me!" (145). Once again, what seems to be a direct antagonism reveals itself as a circular, mediated resentment. Such deflections, explain psychologists Nancy McWilliams and Stanley Lependorf, are typical of the narcissistic personality, an individual incapable of admitting error, apologizing, or accepting the responsibility for his or her actions; rather, this person will defensively rationalize them, blaming the victim of his or her aggression, appealing on the grounds of having had good intentions. Lovelace's claim that, if he is forgiven, he will marry Clarissa "on her own terms" is also familiar as a narcissistic tendency to "substitute some other kind of interpersonal transaction for an apology." "What a narcissistically defended person seems to do instead of apologizing is to attempt a repair of the grandiose self in the guise of making reparation with the object," the authors write. "What is repaired is not the damage to the relationship, but the subject's illusion of perfection."[22]

Lovelace's tendency to refer to Clarissa as exemplary is complicated. His belief that Clarissa might serve as a substitute for his first "fair jilt" and as a symbol for women in general, a sentiment that sounds intensely chauvinistic within the context of his letter, is commonly pronounced by most of the women of Clarissa's acquaintance, including her mother and her best friend. "Oh miss, miss, what have you to answer for," chastises Mrs. Howe. "The whole sex is indeed wounded by you: for who but Miss Clarissa Harlowe was proposed by every father and mother for a pattern for their daughters?" (975). It is impossible to determine, finally, the extent to which Lovelace imposes the distinction of paragon on Clarissa or merely accommodates the perceptions of others once again.[23]

Lovelace's troubled inability to differentiate his true feelings and perceptions from those he is compelled to assume, his uncertainty about his very right to feel, is not a situation he can "cure" simply by distinguishing the origins of his perceptions. Psychologists admit that people who perceive themselves as devalued cannot gain control over their uncertainties merely by recognizing them. David Lindgren explains: "Grandiose men seek external answers to internal dilemmas. This type of man runs as fast as he can to avoid feeling the depth of despair that is required for him to . . . become a whole man."[24] Thus, neither the perfection-driven Clarissa nor the proud Lovelace can be expected to resolve easily the mixture of rage, resentment, and frustrated love they feel toward families and lovers who have rejected them, tacitly confirming their feelings of inadequacy and uncertainty. As psychoanalyst Johanna Tabin explains, grandiosity is "a state of mind independent of actual status or achievement."[25]

Because they have been forced to regard their natural feelings as wrong and to repress them, because they have come to believe that only perfection, brilliance, and compliance can earn love and that their true, repressed selves therefore do not deserve to be admired, Clarissa and Lovelace are often as adversarial toward themselves as they are toward the persons who ignite these resentments. "You were always so ready to accuse yourself for other people's faults, and to suspect your own conduct, rather than the judgement of your relations," Anna chastises Clarissa (1151), who replies, "I am more grieved . . . for OTHERS, than for MYSELF. And so I OUGHT" (1161).

In a similarly self-distrusting vein Lovelace admits: "Oh Belford, Belford, how have I puzzled myself as well as her! . . . Had I NOT been a villain in her sense of the word, she had not been so much an ANGEL . . . [yet] I had rather all the world should condemn ME, than that HER character should suffer the least impeachment. The dear creature herself once told me that there was a strange mixture in my mind" (735).

Such suppressed emotions can only be controlled if they can be acknowledged, psychologists claim. There are several ways in which this can be accomplished. Object relations theorists suggest that, in order to be felt, suppressed emotions must be brought to the surface and experienced in an act of transference, an externalizing of what theorists call the original narcissistic wound. The original narcissistic wound occurs when, like Clarissa, a child is denied her earliest need, the need to have her mother at her disposal, the need to find, mirrored in the mother's eyes, herself rather than the mother's own predicaments and demands. If a child is lucky and has a mother confident enough in her own maternal role that she can allow herself to be made use of ("narcissistically cathected") by the child, then, as Miller explains, the child will be able to concentrate on the mother's activities only as they regard herself, almost as if the mother were an extension of the child.

This egocentrism is the "only attitude possible" during the earliest stage, Miller notes. It allows the child to develop the "unquestioned certainty that the feelings and wishes [he] experiences are a part of himself," as normal as his pulse:

> This automatic, natural contact with his own emotions and wishes gives an individual strength and SELF-ESTEEM. He may live out his feelings, be sad, despairing, or in need of help, without fear of making the introjected mother insecure. He can allow himself to be afraid when he is threatened, or angry when his wishes are not fulfilled. He knows not only what he does not want but also what he wants and is able to express this, irrespective of whether he will be loved or hated for it.[26]

Eventually, this "healthy narcissism" will result in a healthy self-feeling that will encourage separation and autonomy, the autonomy of a child who is free to feel his own feelings without questioning their effects on others.[27]

Although such an adult may well choose not to act on his passions, he will not find it necessary to deny feeling them in the first place. He will not need to ridicule his emotions, to suppress or belittle them, to look for distraction when he is moved or angry, transferring his antagonisms, in typically triangular style, to avoid confronting his interiorized guilt at feeling emotions that a "good" child should not feel. Unhealthy narcissism is typically the result of a "mirrored framework" that did not reflect the child's individual needs. Mahler writes:

> If [the mother's] primary occupation with her child, i.e., her mirroring function during the period of early childhood, is *unpredictable, insecure, anxiety-ridden* or *hostile,* or if her confidence in herself as a mother is shaken, then the child has to face the period of individuation without a reliable framework for *emotional* checking back to his symbiotic partner. The result is a disturbance in his primitive "self-feeling."[28]

Such an adult "can only be fully aware of his feelings if he has internalized an affectionate and empathic self-object," Miller explains. "People with narcissistic disturbances are missing out on this. Therefore they . . . will only admit those feelings that are accepted and approved by their inner censor, which is their parents' heir. Depression and a sense of inner emptiness is the price they must pay for this control." In such instances the true self will be unable to communicate itself; it will remain unarticulated, masked by depression or frightening grandiose fantasies.[29]

If Lovelace's defiance is combined with his constant grandiose fantasies concerning women and considered from this psychological perspective, these fantasies instantly become part of a familiar pattern of self-mistrust and perplexity rather than symptoms of what Jocelyn Harris calls a "maggoty brain."[30] In his fantasies Lovelace is no longer the submissive vassal, the nephew whose inheritance teeters on a will, the lover whose acceptance depends not only upon his reformation but also upon a reconciliation with his worst enemies. In his imagination Lovelace effectively changes places with his perceived conditioners, positing himself as the ultimate lord of wealth and of love:

> Had I been a prince!—To be sure I should have made a
> most NOBLE prince! I should have added kingdom to king-
> dom, and robbed all my neighbour sovereigns in order to have
> obtained the name of ROBERT THE GREAT. And I would have
> gone to war with the Great Turk, and the Persian, and the
> Mogul, for their seraglios; for not one of those Eastern mon-
> archs should have had a pretty woman to bless himself with,
> till I had done with her. (762)

He imagines that he is a conqueror but, more important, that he is
beloved for his ability to conquer. "Women, as Miss Howe says, and as
every rake knows, love ardours!" (636), he proclaims to Belford, insisting
that he has only "to single out some ONE of the sex to make HALF A SCORE
jealous." "I can tell thee," he brags, "many an eye have I made to sparkle
with rival indignation: many a cheek glow; and even many a fan have I
caused to be snapped at a sister-beauty, accompanied with a reflection,
perhaps, at being seen alone with a wild young fellow who could not be in
private with both at once" (143). In his fantasies, however, Lovelace does
not find himself spurned for a coronet or a family reunion. It is he who
drifts away, returning to a mistress who pines during his loss, loving him
the more for his having briefly bestowed his regal regard on a "sister-
beauty."

Lovelace's fantasies are typical, we are told, of the man who fears that
he has always been loved conditionally. A person who comes to believe
that the admiration he has earned has not been meant for him as he really
is but, rather, for his beauty, obedience, and achievements may discover
that he has indeed been a dual character for much of his life. He will come
to mourn the child who was never allowed to be a child and resent being
loved only for his accomplishments or accommodating reputation.[31]

As Lovelace's relationship with Clarissa develops, he comes to realize
that it is somehow different from his previous trysts, yet he cannot help but
treat her in the same maddening manner as his former mistresses. He comes
to realize that the admiration of other women is due not "so much to particular liking of me, as to their own self-admiration. They looked upon me as
a connoisseur in beauty. They would have been proud of engaging my attention, as such: but so affected, so flimsy-witted, mere skin-deep beauties!"
(1026). While the disdainful Clarissa and her defiant friend Anna disrupt
this pattern of superficial admiration, they provoke an equally strong resent-

ment of conditional admiration, an equally strong fear of rejection.

Lovelace's fear of rejection has typically been characterized by critics as an inability to feel.[32] From the viewpoint of the object relations theorist, however, his dilemma is characteristic of love object relationships. Fairbairn notes that the conflicting desires and fears in such relationships "are an intense and devastating drama of need, fear, anger and hopelessness. To attempt to account for this by a hedonistic theory of motivation, namely that the person is seeking the satisfactions of oral, anal and genital pleasure, is so impersonal and inadequate that it takes on the aspect of being itself a product of schizoid thinking."[33]

As Lovelace becomes increasingly angry at Clarissa and Anna, we find that the language of his fantasies changes. Like the anxious child whose compulsion to repeat leads him to provoke situations in which his fear of rejection has a basis in reality, Lovelace finds that he is compelled to transfer his attentions to women who, like his dead mother and "musty" relatives, are not available to him. His relationships with these women are decidedly marked by characteristics of narcissistic cathexis and a compulsion first to conquer and then to desert them.

In characteristic style Lovelace repeats the very pattern he resents in order to allow himself a sense of control over it. This compulsion to repeat is evident both in his pursuit of the indignant Clarissa and in the fantasies that accompany this chase. In an explanatory letter Lovelace relates to Belford that he has been able to retain his senses after his humiliating first love only through "a vehement aspiration after a novelty." "Those confounded poets," he claims, "fired my imagination and set me upon a desire to become a goddess-maker . . . I must create beauty and place it where nobody else could find it: and many a time have I been at a loss for a subject when my new-created goddess has been kinder than it was proper for my plaintive sonnet she should be" (143).

Lovelace evidently equates a worthy subject with the difficulty of attaining it. Lounging at his uncle's estate after Clarissa's escape, he writes: "What heart, thinkest thou, can I have to write, when I have lost the only subject worth writing upon? . . . having HER, I shall never want a subject. Having lost her, my whole soul is a blank" (1023). "Do thou find her for me, as a subject worthy of my pen," he implores Belford (1026). The irony in this statement is, of course, that Lovelace has never truly possessed Clarissa in the first place; the hunt has been his subject. When he discovers the runaway Clarissa in her hiding place at Hampstead, he elatedly writes, "the subject is now become worthy of me" (762), a sentiment he is to repeat when Clarissa's outraged letters stir the resentment of the entire Lovelace family against him, compelling him to the chase again. "Now, Jack, have I a subject with a vengeance" he declares (1026). With elaborate transference Lovelace collapses his fantasy with his narcissistic needs. He has lost both Clarissa and himself, thus his subject must be the simultaneous pursuit of both.[34]

Because Lovelace equates power with pursuit, his sense of powerlessness cannot be resolved by acquiring what he pursues. Therapist Olga Cheselka argues that there are four strategies that people use to pursue interpersonal power, some more narcissistic than others: one can dominate another by controlling his or her actions; one can engage in fantasies of omnipotence either through a feeling of one's own grandiosity or through an imagined unity with another person who is perceived as having power; one can work to achieve recognition from others; and one can engage in reciprocal influence—the ability to affect and be effected by another person. As Cheselka points out, the narcissist whose feelings of power are limited to fantasies or domination of another is substantially limited. Such a person must have constant access to that individual and must rely on him or her to want to continue to act a submissive role. She explains, "The more we have to exert control to experience power the less powerful we feel."[35] Often, relates Sydney Smith,

> committing oneself to a relationship or to accepting what is offered or available represents [to the narcissist] an admission that the fantasy cannot be realized. . . . thus, what [he] has in hand he is willing to let go in the interests of looking endlessly for new possibilities, searching for the one person who will at last fulfill him so completely that he will experience the longed-for bliss the fantasy promises.[36]

"The transition from dominance to reciprocal influence is possible when both people are able to take a risk and to allow the other's needs to predominate for awhile," Cheselka writes.[37] This reciprocity is impossible for someone whose own needs are confused with others' or whose sense of autonomy is compromised by an admission of reliance on others. As Clarissa's proclamations of indifference increasingly anger and stimulate this lover, who is compelled to pursue her virtually because she resists him, Lovelace relies increasingly on complex fantasies of dominance and grandiosity to support his narcissistically defended self-image. Certain that Clarissa's indifference is fueled by Anna's resentments, he casts both girls into the roles of concubines, fantasizing, "How sweetly pretty to see the two lovely friends, when humbled and tame, both sitting in the darkest corner of a rooom [*sic*], arm in arm, weeping and sobbing for each other!— And I their emperor, their then ACKNOWLEDGED emperor, reclined on a sophee, in the same room, Grand Signor-like, uncertain to which I should first throw out my handkerchief?" (637).

Lovelace's bizarre fantasy is actually quite common according to psychoanalysts who maintain that once an individual can recognize his repressed need for unconditional respect, understanding, and acceptance, he may find himself plagued by fantasies of grandeur, fantasies that mirror his desire for the unconditional acceptance he never had. For the adult male this need may take the form of the stereotypical "masculine dream," the experience of "being coddled by women like a baby and at the same time commanding them like a pascha."

This seemingly chauvinistic desire, claims Miller, effectively replicates "the infant's most genuine and legitimate need," the ability to demand from the mother without having to worry oneself with the mother's needs too early, to rule over the mother like a small lord without having to consider her feelings. Quoting a report in the German magazine *Stern* (8 June 1978) about regular visitors to St. Pauli, Hamburg's red-light district, Miller offers that the attraction of the masculine dream is "that the girls are available and completely at the customer's disposal, THEY DO NOT REQUIRE PROTESTATIONS OF LOVE LIKE GIRLFRIENDS. There are NO OBLIGATIONS, PSYCHOLOGICAL DRAMAS, nor PANGS OF CONSCIENCE when desire has passed: 'YOU PAY AND ARE FREE!'"[38] Therapist Sydney Smith relates that such a "golden fantasy" expresses "the wish to be totally gratified in a manner that underscores the [individual's] passivity and by someone who remains nameless and faceless but is somehow always present to assume responsibility and meet every need."[39]

Lovelace's constant fantasy of an unmarried life of honor seems to correspond to this need for affection without obligation, a need that directly conflicts with the highly conditional demands and promises of his loved ones. His thoroughly reasoned proposal of a Valentine's Day change for all married couples, an opportunity for each partner either to renew the annual marriage vow or to move on to another relationship, is a fascinating version of this masculine dream, rationalized to its limits (872–74).

Although Lovelace's tendency to treat such proposals with levity forces his female acquaintances to regard him with as much real concern as many current feminist literary critics do, this levity itself can be formulated as part of the narcissistic disturbance. Belford condemns this levity, arguing that "such an air of levity runs through thy most serious letters; such a false bravery, endeavouring to carry off ludicrously the subjects that most affect thee; that those letters are generally the least fit to be seen which ought to be most to thy credit" (1077). Lovelace admits: "This is my way. I mean no harm. I cannot let sorrow touch my heart. I cannot be grave six minutes together, for the blood of me" (1098).

This odd behavior puzzles his acquaintance; Anna remarks, "My mother, as well as Mr. Hickman, believes . . . that he is touched in conscience for the wrongs he has done . . . but, by his whole behaviour, I must own it seems to me that nothing can touch him for half an hour together" (1138), yet Lovelace cannot hide from himself what he hides from others. To Belford's accusations he finally responds in frank despair, "Thou severely reflectest upon me for my LEVITY . . . thou seest not my heart. . . . It is to DEEP CONCERN that my very levity is owing: "For I struggle and struggle, and try to buffet down these reflections as they rise; and when I cannot do it, I am forced as I have often said to try to make myself laugh that I may not cry; for one or other I must do" (1310).

Much of Lovelace's illusion of grandeur may stem from his perception of his obviously exceptional intellectual capacity. Like Clarissa, Lovelace is intelligent, well-educated, and eager to learn. What he cannot perceive is the extent to which these intellectual attributes may displace underdeveloped or suppressed emotional attributes, forcing him to rationalize his schemes even while he ridicules or ignores the disturbing emotions they unleash. The adult perfectionist is often an individual whose intelligence and sensitivity have rendered him well suited for parental manipulation in the first place. Such a narcissistically cathected person, claims Miller, "has the chance to develop his intellectual capacities undisturbed, but not the world of his emotions, and this will have far-reaching consequences for his well-being . . . his intellect will assume a supportive function of enormous value in strengthening his defense mechanism, but hidden behind that, his narcissistic disturbance may grow deeper."[40]

Lovelace's emotions are certainly present in his clever epistles, but they are often ridiculed or resented. When he finds his real concern for Clarissa crowding into his grandiose schemes for her seduction, he tends to personify this concern and then to dismiss it, in the language of an emperor, as a worthless servant or unloyal vassal. "Oh thou lurking varletess CONSCIENCE!" he exclaims in a typically agitated letter (658). "See what a recreant she had made me!—I seized her by the throat—HERE!—THERE, said I" (848). The language of this "in-voiced" battle with himself is not substantially different from the "tyrannous" language he uses to describe his battle with Clarissa; he continues:

> Puling, and IN-VOICED, rearing up thy detested head, in vain implorest thou my mercy, who, in THY day, hast showed me so little!—Take THAT, for a rising blow!—And now will THY pain, and MY pain from THEE, soon be over!—Lie there!— Welter on!—Had I not given thee thy death's wound, thou wouldst have robbed me of all my joys. Thou couldst not have mended me, 'tis plain. Thou couldst only have thrown me into despair. Didst thou not see that I had gone too far to recede?—Welter on, once more I bid thee!—Gasp on!—THAT thy last gasp, surely!—How hard diest thou!—ADIEU!—'Tis kind in thee, however, to bid me ADIEU!—Adieu, Adieu, Adieu, to thee, Oh thou inflexible and, till now, unconquerable bosom-intruder—Adieu to thee for ever! (848)

The only difference between this self-directed drama and the resentments he directs at Clarissa, Anna, or Belford is the tone of apology and justification. "Thou couldst not have mended me" is not a statement of tyranny; rather, it is a complicated, dualistic admission to himself that he is somehow acting in self-defense. "I must not trust myself with myself," Lovelace resolves (733).

The danger of Lovelace's dualistic approach to Clarissa's rape (that she can somehow be brought to condemn the act while forgiving the actor) is that this dualism fits so neatly into his grandiose formula.[41] Not only does Lovelace allow himself to assume heroic traits in his dealings with Clarissa, but he casts Clarissa in the role of the untouchable queen, the "Glorianna" (418), whose distance stimulates and enrages simultaneously. Harris claims that this desire to "confine" the soul of a queen in a mere woman's body allows "every man—whether father, brother, husband, or lover—[to] become her Domestic King,"[42] yet there is substantial evidence that just the opposite may be true.

Lovelace's fantasies may be attractive simply because the truly "worthy" subject is impregnable. Not only does her indifference stimulate desire by suggesting a renewed opportunity to obtain earlier unattainable affection, but it may seem to present a safe situation in which to work through these transferred feelings. Psychoanalyst Sydney Smith notes that all fantasies are characterized by "the wish to have all of one's needs met in a relationship hallowed by perfection." Two invariable features of fantasies are the subject's total passivity (he is cared for so completely that no demand is made on him), and the fact that the fantasy "touches on the deepest issues of one's life and that indeed one's very survival may depend upon its preservation. . . . It is as though the fantasy provided a self-definition."[43]

Lovelace's Glorianna is reassuringly self-sufficient, a woman who claims to have a "great and invincible spirit" (593). Her imperturbable regal bearing will allow Lovelace the comfort of believing that, in psychologist D. W. Winnicott's words, "I can destroy the object and it will still survive."[44] He can project her rape as an experience that her "invincible spirit" will survive, positing that the queen will magnanimously forgive his need of the experiment, if not the experience itself. "Let me tell thee that I have known a bird actually starve itself, and die with grief, at its being caught and caged—But never did I meet with a lady who was so silly," Lovelace offers, reminding Belford that Clarissa is "the noblest" of quarries, "the most noble of all chases" (577–59). Clarissa, however, does starve to death, and Lovelace's compulsion to pursue her does not result in a healthy sense of self-determination.

The repression of many of his feelings may have been a matter of early survival for Lovelace as well as for the "perfect" Clarissa, a prerequisite of family peace and acceptance.[45] Psychologists claim that if these legitimate feelings and needs can be experienced through the process of transference, an experience of adult repetition, the split can be overcome and integration can follow, but in Clarissa and Lovelace's case this transference has become so entangled in triangular battles, so connected to secondary considerations, that it cannot proceed smoothly. Neither character can break out of the pathological reciprocal role that narcissistic behavior typically induces. "I am so totally hers, that I cannot say how much I am thine, or any other person's," Lovelace confesses (575), unable to sever his sense of self-esteem from Clarissa's admiration yet equally unable to support his sense of self-esteem without narcissistically weakening it.

This type of anguish, writes Miller, is impressively portrayed in Fellini's film *Casanova*.[46] Robert the Great is surely such another anguished character, creating for himself as much misery as he inflicts on the objects of his desire. Because Clarissa herself is a disturbed character, equally overwhelmed by prescriptions of perfection, the demands of a self-centered mother, a mediated struggle for autonomy, the relationship between these two unhappy characters becomes the tragic story of their quests for independence from each other—through each other. "There is no end of these debatings," Clarissa recognizes sadly, "each so faultless, each so full of self—" (592).

CONSUMPTIVE TRANSFERENCE

"Now is my charmer shut up from me: refusing to see me; refusing her meals. Resolves NOT to see me, that's more—Never again, if she can help it. . . . No admission to breakfast, any more than to supper. . . . It won't do!" protests Lovelace (572). Mealtime in London, we find, is not substantially different from mealtime at Harlowe Place. Lovelace and Clarissa have been living together for roughly one month when Lovelace writes this frustrated epistle to his friend Belford. It seems that he has infuriated the lady by attempting to sneak off with a letter that she has dropped on the floor. Clarissa has detected his intended theft; she flies from the room to her own chamber, double-locks and double-bolts the door behind her, and refuses to eat. In short she recreates her confinement at Harlowe Place, and this confinement is no less rigid for being self-imposed.

Once again, Clarissa's seclusion provides her with an opportunity to be active by being passive; her refusal to participate actually becomes a means of interacting, of influencing her situation by detaching herself from it. Little does she suspect that this detachment constitutes, from Lovelace's point of view, the very activity that she most wishes to avoid. "All her forms thus kept up," he muses, "how must all this distance stimulate!" (619). "I never before encountered a resistance so much in earnest: a resistance, in short, so irresistible" (727).

Clarissa's misguided attempt to punish Lovelace by refusing her presence at meals—in fact, by refusing meals altogether—corresponds with her recognition that her body is the only resource in her power. As though to prove the truth of Henry Tilney's formula,[47] Clarissa discovers that, once she has left home, the power of refusing meals is the only power that she can call her own. She has arrived in London completely devoid of possessions, unsure even of the extent to which she might still call herself the person she once was. A letter written to her parents, requesting that her clothes, books, and money be sent, is answered by Arabella, addressed to "Sister that was." "You will have no answer from anybody, write to WHOM you will, and as OFTEN as you will, and WHAT you WILL," Arabella exclaims. "I know not what name you are PERMITTED or CHOOSE to go by . . . Clarissa, **what?**" (509).

Threatened with total dependence on a man she does not trust, informed by her sister that "it is wished [by your entire family] you may be seen a beggar along London streets!" (510), Clarissa's sojourn with Lovelace is almost immediately characterized by a claiming of territory, a fervid attempt to assure herself of how much time, space, or authority she might still possess. On their arrival at London lodgings Clarissa immediately claims certain areas of the house for her own use; she informs her beau that her apartment shall be her retirement, a place into which he must never intrude. The dining room is designated the only common ground, the only room in which they may meet to discuss their adventures, their relationship. It is not surprising, then, that the dining room becomes the scene of most of this couple's contentions and that absence from meals should immediately assume symbolic importance.

"How passion drives a man on!" exclaims Lovelace. "Now my resentments are warm, I will see, and perhaps will punish, this proud, this DOUBLE-armed beauty. I have sent to tell her that I must be admitted to sup with her. We have neither of us dined: she refused to drink tea in the afternoon—and I believe neither of us will have much stomach to our supper" (639). Clarissa and Lovelace follow a well-worn pattern when they determine to conduct their affairs only in the dining room, effectively ensuring that the vicissitudes of their relationship will direct their acceptance or refusal of meals. In fact, food may well serve as an analogue to self, as each character expresses mixed feelings through food-related behavior.

Clarissa enters the relationship with assurances that she seldom eats at all, thus appropriating to herself the power to refuse meals without having to account for her refusal in terms that involve Lovelace. "We had some talk about meals," she informs Anna. "The widow very civilly offered to conform to any rules I would set her. I told her how easily I was pleased, and how much I chose to dine by myself, and that from a plate sent me from any single dish" (532). Almost immediately, however, Lovelace becomes implicated in Clarissa's choices. "They thought me very singular [for choosing to dine alone]," she continues, "but as I liked them not so very well as to forego my own choice in compliment to them, I was the less concerned for what they thought. And still the less as Mr. Lovelace had put me very much out of humour with him" (532).

As Clarissa reinforces her claim that she seldom eats by declaring a preference of long standing for solitary meals, she sets up a pattern of absence from Lovelace which initially serves the needs of both quite well. "I told him [that] . . . he must second me, particularly in my desire of breakfasting and supping (when I DID sup) by myself," Clarissa relates (533), leading Lovelace to remark, "SOLA-generally at her meals . . . all is civility on both sides. Even married people, I believe, Jack, prevent abundance of quarrels by seeing one another but seldom" (617). At this point, however, Lovelace is content in his belief that Clarissa "can fly to no other protection," and Clarissa believes that her fiancé is actually negotiating to buy a private residence and will soon marry her.

Clarissa's insistence on private meals cannot remain free of political implications. As Lovelace begins to test her, to infringe on the conditions with which he has so ardently promised compliance, her absences increasingly come to be regarded as denials. "No admission to breakfast, any more than to supper," grumbles Lovelace, after the episode of the purloined letter. "I wish this lady is not a simpleton, after all" (573).

Clarissa's behavior is far from simple. As she continues to share a house with a man who is notorious for his lax morals, her uncles renounce her as a fallen woman. "Your uncle will have it that you are ruined," relates Anna, explaining, "He can believe everything bad of a creature who could run away with a man—with such a one especially as Lovelace" (587). "Wicked as the man is, I am afraid he must be your lord and master," Anna counsels (586).

Clarissa's next meeting with Lovelace strongly reveals her preoccupation with this admonition; her narration of the meeting shows the extent to which her mealtime denials can be occasioned by mediated resentments and fears. It is a lengthy letter but deserves to be quoted at length. "You are of the opinion that I must be his; and that I cannot leave him with reputation to myself, whether with or without his consent. I must, if so, make the best of the bad matter," Clarissa responds to Anna's advice, acknowledging the extent to which she perceives herself as powerless, unable to govern her own choices and actions. Her letter continues:

He went out in the morning; intending not to return to dinner, unless (as he sent me word) I would admit him to dine with me.

I excused myself. The man whose anger is now to be of such high importance to me was, it seems, displeased . . .

The contents of your letter, and my own heavy reflections, rendered me incapable of seeing this expecting man!—The first word he asked Dorcas was, If I had received a letter since he had been out!—She told me this; and her answer, That I had; and was fasting, and had been in tears ever since.

He sent to desire an interview with me.

I answered by her, That I was not very well. In the morning, if better, I would see him as soon as he pleased.

Very humble! was it not, my dear?—Yet he was too royal to take it for humility . . . said a rash word, and was out of humour; stalking about the room. (590–91)

After this rejection Lovelace and Clarissa continue their altercation, and the shared meal becomes the object of strategy on both sides: Lovelace characteristically conditions for an audience by agreeing to comply with Clarissa's prohibitions concerning conversation topics; Clarissa interprets this conditioning as behavior that she has been taught to regard as preparatory to her own compliance with distasteful conditions. The resulting dialogue, a seemingly innocent contention over a meal, is riddled with the terminology of freedom and compulsion:

Half an hour after, he sent again; desiring very earnestly that I would admit him to supper with me. He would enter upon no subjects of conversation but what I should lead to.

So I should have been at LIBERTY, you see, to COURT HIM! I again desired to be excused. . . .

He sent up to tell me, that as he heard I was fasting, if I would promise to eat some chicken which Mrs. Sinclair had ordered for supper, he would acquiesce—Very kind in his anger!—Is he not?

I promised him. Can I be more preparatively condescending—How happy, I'll warrant you, if I can meet him in a kind and forgiving humour!

I hate myself!—But I won't be insulted. Indeed I won't! for all this. (591)

Clarissa's angry affirmation recalls her defiance of her parents' strategies, "arts" that she felt degraded both her and them. She has, however, become so accustomed to delineating her feelings according to meals that she is unable to approach mealtime in a nonpolitical manner. Even when she and her lover are at ease together, meals are weighted with significance, tests of the extent to which Clarissa might govern herself. Clarissa approaches all meals with suspicion, insisting on treating them as obligations, favors, hostages in a battle of wills.

By 21 May Lovelace and Clarissa are enjoying their relationship. "I was at the play last night with Mr. Lovelace," Clarissa happily writes to Anna, adding, "His behaviour, . . . on this occasion, and on our return, was unexceptionable, only that he would oblige me to stay to supper with the women below when we came back." Because she is content with his behavior, Clarissa attends this meal, sitting up until almost one o'clock in the morning, yet, in a forced effort to ensure her future right of refusal, adds that she has refused to see or dine with him at all during the next day. "I was resolved to be even with him," she explains, "for I love to pass the Sundays by myself" (640).

Clarissa's love of solitude on Sunday is easily accepted; her refusal to dine with Lovelace, however, is difficult to reconcile with her profession that she has now submitted to compliance and has resolved to marry him. "He must study for occasions of procrastination, and to disoblige me, if now anything happens to set us at variance again," she avers, but this claim is immediately undermined by her insistence on viewing Lovelace's desire to dine with her as a danger. "He is very importunate to see me," she relates on Sunday morning. "He is angry that I have declined to breakfast with him. I was sure that I should not be at my own liberty if I had. . . . He is, it seems, excessively out of humour. . . . This is put on, perhaps, to make me dine with him. But I won't, if I can help it. I shan't get rid of him for the rest of the day if I do. . . . He was very earnest to dine with me" (640).

Determined not to undermine her power of refusing her company at meals, yet equally concerned lest that refusal be interpreted as resistance, Clarissa is forced to naturalize her refusal to eat in an attempt to prove that her abstinence is not political. "I was resolved to carry this one small point; and so denied to dine myself," she admits, relating that Lovelace has apparently accepted this strategy as well. In response to Clarissa's insistence that she be allowed to write rather than to eat, Lovelace retreats to his own room. "He was very busy in writing," Clarissa explains, "and pursued it without dining, because I denied him my company" (641).

This exchange rapidly becomes hostile once again. From self-denial each character quickly moves to demands, conditions, promises, threats, and, of course, anger and suspicion. Because Lovelace has been led to believe that shared meals will follow his compliance with Clarissa's will, that he will be rewarded for his good behavior, he interprets Clarissa's desire to be left to herself, in spite of his apparent reformation, as a mere act of tyranny. Although he has missed dinner, "he afterwards demanded, as I may say, to be admitted to afternoon tea with me," Clarissa relates, "and appealed by Dorcas to his behaviour to me last night; as if, as I sent him word by her, he thought he had a merit in being unexceptionable. However, I repeated my promise to meet him as early as he pleased in the morning, or to breakfast with him. Dorcas says he raved."

Clarissa's letter continues in terms that demonstrate the extent to which this single day, characterized by three highly controversial meals, has eroded their earlier satisfaction with each other. "He has just sent me word that he insists upon supping with me," she announces. "As we had been in a good train for several days past, I thought it not prudent to break with him for little matters. Yet, to be in a manner threatened into his will, I know not how to bear that." In spite of her reference to supper as a "little matter," however, Clarissa responds to this request angrily, forcing Lovelace to wait for her company, declaring: "'Tis hard . . . that I am to be so little my own mistress. I will meet you in the dining-room half an hour hence" (641).

While Clarissa views meals as instances of her forced compliance with the will of her demanding lover, Lovelace interprets these same meals in equally political ways. His relation of the long-awaited breakfast following this contentious Sunday is also riddled with the terminology of tyranny and oppression, humility and supplication; not surprisingly, however, Lovelace views Clarissa as the tyrant, himself as oppressed. "No generosity in this lady. None at all," he begins in a letter to Belford. "I was in the dining-room before six, expecting her. She opened not her door. . . . Thus till half an hour after eight, fooled I away my time; and then, breakfast ready, I sent Dorcas to request her company" (644).

When Clarissa does appear for this meal, a meal she has emphatically agreed to share with Lovelace, it is evident that she has no intention of partaking in the repast. She enters the dining room fully dressed for an outing, carrying her gloves and fan, bidding the servant to go immediately for a chair to take her to church. "Cruel creature," writes Lovelace. "I looked cursed silly, I am sure—you will breakfast first, I hope, madam, in a very humble strain: yet with an hundred tenter-hooks in my heart. . . . Yes, she would drink one dish; and then laid her gloves and fan in the window." "I was perfectly disconcerted," Lovelace admits (644).

The remainder of this epistle recalls strained meals at Harlowe Place and at The Lawn, meals during which participants did not meet one another's eyes, did not speak, certainly did not enjoy themselves. These were meals intended to express displeasure, to intimidate, to triumph. Lovelace's perception of this single cup of tea shared with his betrothed is painfully humiliating and deserves to be quoted in its entirety:

> I hemmed and hawed, and was going to speak several times; but knew not in what key. Who's modest now, thought I! Who's insolent now!—How a tyrant of a woman confounds a bashful man!—She was my Miss Howe, I thought; and I the spiritless Hickman.
>
> At last, I WILL begin, thought I.
>
> She a dish—I a dish.
>
> Sip, her eyes her own, she; like an haughty and impervious sovereign, conscious of dignity, every look a favour.
>
> Sip, like her vassal, I; lips and hands trembling, and not knowing that I sipped or tasted.
>
> I was—I was—I sipped—drawing in my breath and the liquor together, though I scalded my mouth with it—I was in hopes, madam—Dorcas came in just then—Dorcas, said she, is a chair gone for?
>
> Damned impertinence, thought I, putting me out of my speech! And I was forced to wait for the servant's answer to the insolent mistress's question. . . .
>
> What weather is it, Dorcas? said she, as regardless of me, as if I had not been present. . .
>
> I had no patience—Up I rose. Down went the tea-cup, saucer and all—Confound the weather, the sunshine, and the wench!—Begone for a devil, when I am speaking to your lady, and have so little opportunity given me.

Up rose the lady, half frighted; and snatched from the window her gloves and fan.

You must not go, madam!—by my soul, you must not—taking her hand.

MUST NOT, SIR!—But I must—You can curse your maid in my absence, as well as if I were present—Except—except—you intend for ME, what you direct to HER. (645)

This disrupted breakfast casts both characters in the role of tyrant. Each lover perceives the other's silence as an accusation; each considers the other's behavior a challenge. Most important, each attributes this antagonism to his or her own complaisance. Clarissa charges: "I like you not, nor your ways—You sought to quarrel with me yesterday for no reason in the world that I can think of, but because I was too obliging." Lovelace counters with a similar charge: "It is too plain to whom my difficulties are owing. . . . [Anna] would have YOU treat ME, as SHE treats Mr. Hickman, I suppose: but neither does that treatment become your admirable temper to offer, nor me to receive" (645).

Anna Howe's avowedly haughty treatment of her suitor, her insistence that he behave respectfully to her "in her day" lest she refuse to grant him a lifelong authority over her, is familiar ground to both protagonists. It is a relationship that is no less mediated and triangular than theirs. Mr. Hickman has long been caught in the middle of a battle of wills between Anna and her mother. "In the Harlowe style, she WILL be obeyed," Anna relates of her mother's insistence that her daughter no longer correspond with a runaway. "Mr. Hickman came in presently after. I would not see him. . . . Poor man! He stands a whimsical chance between us." This letter ends with Anna's admission: "I shut myself up all that day; and what little I did eat, eat alone. . . . an unreasonable command . . . [is] a degree of tyranny: and I could not have expected that at these years I should be allowed no will, no choice of my own" (476–77).

Anna's obviously triangular relationship with Mr. Hickman, a relationship that affects her own ability to appear at meals, has long been an indirect source of contention between Clarissa and Lovelace. Because Clarissa refuses to act without consulting her only friend, Lovelace attributes whatever indifference he may detect in her behavior to the counsel of Miss Howe. A contemptuous letter from Anna, intercepted and read in secret, inflames Lovelace against Clarissa for weeks. He cannot help but

assume that Anna's disdain must stem from Clarissa's own related sentiments yet believes, paradoxically, that Anna's insolence is ultimately responsible for those sentiments. Lovelace has, however, become so
accustomed to these triangles that he tries to manipulate them on his own
behalf. Resolved to marry the secluded Clarissa, he corners Mrs. Howe at
a ball and urges her to urge Anna to urge Clarissa to accept him (1134).[48]

Although Lovelace may acknowledge Anna's power to influence
Clarissa, Anna's active interference on Clarissa's behalf, like Belford's pleadings with Lovelace, not only undermines the confidence between the two
would-be lovers but also contributes to the conflict between Clarissa and
her family. Anna's attempts to warn Arabella of Clarissa's poor health result in a series of increasingly angry letters, letters in which each girl be-
littles the other for her desire to run away with a rake. Eventually, Mrs.
Harlowe begs Mrs. Howe to restrain her daughter's pen, arguing that the
family's resentment and distress have been augmented, not pacified, by
the exchange of these vicious epistles (1109–11). Anna's good intentions
send yet another reverberated shock through the series of triangles that
entangle her friend. The "freedoms you have taken with my friends . . .
give me great concern, and that as well for MY OWN sake, as for THEIRS;
since it must necessarily incense them against me," Clarissa admits. "I wish,
my dear, that I had been left to my own course on an occasion so VERY
interesting to myself" (1139).

As Lovelace and Clarissa continue to transfer their mediated resentments toward each other onto their own bodies, all pretense of a natural
eating behavior is dropped. Clarissa no longer avers that she seldom eats;
she openly admits that her refusal to join in meals indicates a contempt
for the man with whom she is compelled to share them, even a loss of
appetite stemming from disdain for him. "I am now almost in despair
of succeeding with this charming frost-piece by love or gentleness,"
Lovelace writes in early June. "Love is an encroacher" (704). In keeping with this theory, he disgusts Clarissa by insisting on a reluctantly
granted kiss on the lips, followed by a bold attempt to kiss the breast
of his shocked mistress. Convinced that she is once again being punished for her complaisance, Clarissa retreats to her self-imposed confinement. "In vain have I urged by Dorcas for the promised favour of
dining with her," Lovelace concludes. "She would not dine AT ALL.
SHE COULD NOT" (705).

Clarissa's refusal of meals has long been political in the sense that she has used it to indicate her approval or disapproval of Lovelace's behavior. As she comes to view her relationship with Lovelace with increasing despair and fear, she discovers that she can use the abstinence that her jailor has come to expect in a desperate attempt to win her freedom. The tables are turned as Clarissa's self-denial is transformed into an activism that confounds Lovelace.

Perhaps Lovelace's most intrepid plot to ravish this maiden is his purposeful firing of the house at two o'clock in the morning. Terrified by the screams of the servants, certain that she is in danger of being consumed in a blaze, Clarissa flies, half-dressed, from her chamber—right into the arms of the eagerly waiting Lovelace. Only her terrified pleading and threats of suicide thwart his resolution to seduce her. The next morning he writes confidently: "I must not expect she will breakfast with me: nor dine with me, I doubt. A silly soul, what troubles does she make to herself by her over-niceness!" (728).

The troubles Clarissa makes are, however, quite contrived. Lovelace does not question her ensuing declaration that she will be confined for the next week, that he must not intrude on her or compel her in any way. Thoroughly used to this demand, Lovelace leaves for a week, confident that his servants will guard the fretting prisoner easily. The servants find their mistress's behavior customary as well, and Clarissa discovers that she can use this routine abstinence to her advantage.

As soon as Lovelace has left the house, the servants acquaint Clarissa with his absence. As expected, she receives their intelligence in tears. "She refused either to eat or drink; sighed as if her heart would break," they later tell Lovelace. Then she proceeds with her plan; Lovelace explains, "Being resolved not to see me for a week at least, she ordered [Dorcas] to bring her up three or four French rolls, with a little butter, and a decanter of water, telling her she would dispense with her attendance; and that should be all she would live upon in the interim" (738). Because Clarissa's fasts are so customary, no one questions the oddity of her resolution to isolate herself for a week, living only on a few rolls. Her request is granted as quickly as her parents once granted a similarly routine request to dine alone in the Ivy summer house and with much the same result (532). Clarissa finds it relatively simple to slip out of the house in servant's garb, fleeing the brothel before her absence is even suspected.

Lovelace finds her with little difficulty. When the relationship is forcibly continued, Clarissa's eating behavior becomes erratic once again, and

80

the circle of debatably intentional self-denial and confinement resumes. Lovelace confides to Belford: "I went down with the women to dinner. Mrs. Moore sent her fair boarder up a plate; but she only ate a little bit of bread, and drank a glass of water . . . she seems to be inuring herself to hardships" (799). "It is your own house, Mrs. Moore—It is your own table—You may admit whom you please to it—Only leave me at my liberty to choose my company," Clarissa urges, immediately naturalizing her abstinence. "A bit of bread, if you please, and a glass of water; that's all I can swallow at present. I am really very much discomposed. Saw you not how bad I was?" (799).

By the third time Clarissa escapes, her appetite has become a problematic indicator of her needs. Her doctor warns the wasting girl that she will do very well if she will only resolve to eat something. He implores that she will eat some mild foods, "lest you should starve yourself." Clarissa responds meekly, "I have no appetite" (1129).

Clarissa is not the only one whose political manipulation of meals ultimately results in an inability to eat at all. Miss Montague informs Anna, in real concern, that Lovelace has been self-confined ever since Clarissa's unintended arrest. "He would not see us all that night; neither breakfast nor dine with us the next day," she worries. "He was out each day; and said he wanted to run away from himself" (1148–49). When he is informed that Clarissa's familiar confinement is, at last, necessary and that she is slowly dying, Lovelace responds miserably: "I can neither eat, drink, nor sleep. I am sick of all the world" (1340).

3

Saintly Hunger
Saint Clarissa's Story

"*Clarissa* is one of the rare novels which take Christianity at its face value," write Richardson's biographers T.C. Duncan Eaves and Ben Kimpel.[1] There is little doubt that Richardson meant this to be so. His postscript to the novel declares it to be a work "designed to inculcate upon the human mind, under the guise of an amusement, the great lessons of Christianity" (1495). While the overwhelming preoccupation with themes of reformation, redemption, and death in the last sections suggests that a religious approach is certainly in order, perhaps we ought not to accept unquestioned either Mark Kinkead-Weekes's common critical stance that "we are bound to see that Richardson's novel has finally shifted from the psychological to the directly religious"[2] or A. O. J. Cockshut's equally accepted claim that "Richardson is a psychologist first and a moralist second."[3] In *Clarissa* psychology and religion are not quite so easily separated.[4]

Clarissa's religious asceticism demonstrates a marked continuity of her psychological commitment to perfection. An interactive, multifaceted approach to Clarissa's beatification suggests that eating and food-related behavior are as central to her piety as they have been to her earlier attempts at self-determination, perhaps for many of the same reasons. Because Clarissa's body and the power to refuse food have long been the only resources available to her, her spirituality can easily be expressed in terms of food practices. Ideals of renunciation allow her suffering both to symbolize the collective values of her Christian society and to reinstate her as the perfect child she has always desired to be. Her suffering, whether saintly or secular, is distinctly serviceable and decidedly efficacious.

Critics have long considered Clarissa's perfection under duress to be a product of the irreconcilable differences between her inflexible virtue and the less rigid conventional morality against which she is counterpoised. She is treated as a character whose virtue renders her, finally, "independent of the world."[5] While such arguments recognize that Clarissa cannot be independent and perfect simultaneously, they rely on a natural polarity between Clarissa and her environment; little consideration is given to the elaborate interactive means through which Clarissa comes to accommodate an oppressive perfection. That her final, transcendent perfection is oppressive is made only too apparent through her prolonged suffering, however piously it may be accepted. As Cockshut notes, "She may be a saint, but she is not what parents want their daughters to be, a respectable and happy young woman."[6]

Both Clarissa and Lovelace discover that their individual means of rejecting society result not only in a continued superiority to it but also in a continued subjection to a demand that they be superior, even at the expense of their wills. As Eagleton notes, "What Clarissa will discover in particular is the most demoralizing double bind of all: the truth that it is not so easy to distinguish resistance to power from collusion with it."[7] Although their sufferings and deaths are generally accepted as moral contraries, they are intricately interactive, paradoxically collaborative. Considered in this way, Richardson's novel becomes richly psychological and moral, no longer an example of "contradictory signals" and "moral ambivalence" in the author and in his age.[8]

Clarissa has long been used to thinking herself superior to Lovelace, both in mind and in soul, yet readily admits that she can like him in spite of his defects. "Allowing, as he does, the excellency of moral precepts, and believing the doctrine of future rewards and punishments, he can live as if he despised the one, and defied the other," she writes to Anna, long before she has left her father's house, yet concludes, "I think that, with all his preponderating faults, I like him better than I ever thought I should like him; and, those faults considered, better perhaps than I OUGHT to like him. . . . were he NOW but a moral man, I would prefer him to all the men I ever saw" (183, 185).

Lovelace is not a moral man, but Clarissa's emphasis on the present suggests that the future might hold changes. Not only are his faults intriguing, but her assurance of her own superiority presents itself as an incentive to correct them, a prospect to which Clarissa can look forward with pride. Little can she know that her lover has been taught to mistrust morality as a tyrannical condition of his inheritance, a threat to his grandiose dreams. "These confounded girls. But for THEM, I could go to church with a good conscience: but when I do, there they are . . . here and there a covetous little rogue comes cross me, who, under the pretence of loving virtue for its own sake, wants to have me all to herself," he reasons (419–20).

Accustomed to being considered a possession, Lovelace mistrusts spiritual, no less than sensual, attractions; this very mistrust leads him to propose his own reformation as bait to catch Clarissa. "A proselyte, I can tell thee, has great influence upon your good people," he explains to Belford. "Such a one is a saint of their own creation; and they will water, and cultivate, and cherish him as a plant of their own raising; and this from a pride truly spiritual!" (1108).

In spite of Lovelace's elaborate plans, however, it is precisely when Clarissa determines never to accept him but, rather, to embrace virtue for its own sake that she ensures both his reformation and his total, unconditional devotion to her. "What a whirlwind does she raise in my soul by her proud contempts of me! . . . How does she sink me, even in my own eyes," laments Lovelace in a marked repetition of Clarissa's pathetic cry that she has been "ruined in her own eyes" (909). "To find her power over me, and my love for her, and to hate, to despise, and to refuse me! . . . to go away conqueress and triumphant in every light!—Well may she despise me for suffering her to do so," he protests, yet, narcissistically bound to what he cannot possess, Lovelace finds that he must "love her the more for her despising me" (1182–83).[9]

Lovelace agonizes over the duality that allows him to believe that Clarissa hates him for allowing her triumph yet forces him to love her for her triumphant disdain. Long before she is out of his power, he struggles with this same dilemma. After the penknife incident he writes, "And now it is time to set out: all I have gained, detection, disgrace, fresh guilt by repeated perjuries, and to be despised by her I DOAT UPON; and, what is still worse to a proud heart, by MYSELF. . . . She despises me, Jack!—What man . . . can bear to be despised—especially by his wife?" (952).[10]

Clarissa's absence from the brothel and the tale of her pious suffering only exacerbate Lovelace's agony, twisting it into strangely religious strains. "Soul all over, Belford! . . . How great, how sublimely great, this creature! . . .

There is no bearing the consciousness of the infinite inferiority she charged me with—But why will she break from me, when good resolutions are taking place?—The red-hot iron she refuses to strike—Oh why will she suffer the yielding wax to harden?" he asks miserably (853). He laments, "I have sinned! I repent! I would repair!—She forgives my sin! She accepts my repentance! But she won't let me repair!" (1208). "Dost think I will lose such an angel, such a FORGIVING angel, as this—By my soul, I will not!" (1204). "I must love her . . . if SHE abandon me, GOD will; and it is no matter THEN what becomes of her Lovelace!" (1182–84).

Casting Clarissa as God and himself as her possession, Lovelace ensures that she is, finally, completely invulnerable and unobtainable then sets himself to pursuing her single-mindedly. In doing so, he retraces his steps, enforcing the moral gap between them and following his familiar pattern of conditioning; this time, however, the stakes are much higher. Sequestered in London under the watchful eye of the reformed Belford, Clarissa receives Lovelace's plaintive pleas:

> Your angelic purity, and my awakened conscience, are standing records of your exalted merit and of my detestable baseness: but your forgiveness will lay me under an eternal obligation to you . . . consent to meet me upon your own conditions . . . I will submit to your pleasure; and there shall be no penance which you can impose that I will not cheerfully undergo . . . [encourage] me in this CONDITIONAL hope . . . for in YOU, madam, in YOUR FORGIVENESS, are centred my hopes as to BOTH WORLDS. . . . Your cause, madam, in a word, I look upon to be the CAUSE OF VIRTUE, and, as such, the CAUSE OF GOD. And may I not expect that He will assert it in the perdition of a man who has acted by a person of the most spotless purity, as I have done, if YOU, by rejecting me, show that I have offended beyond the possibility of forgiveness? . . . You appear to me even in a divine light; and in an infinitely more amiable one at the same time than you could have appeared in had you not suffered the barbarous wrongs that now fill my mind with anguish and horror at my own recollected villainy to the most excellent of women. (1185–86)

Lovelace's epistle accomplishes several crucial changes in their relationship. First, it redefines his relationship with Clarissa in terms of yet another triangle, in terms of the effect their correspondence will have on his relationship with God. As she once insisted that she could not forgive until he had reformed, he now claims that he cannot reform until she forgives.[11] Second, it posits that the reformation he has undergone is directly related to her suffering, rather than to her forgiveness. "I once indeed hoped . . . that I might have the happiness to reclaim him: I vainly believed that he loved me well enough to suffer my advice for his good . . . the rather, as he had no mean opinion of my morals and understanding: but now, what hope is there left for this my PRIME hope?" Clarissa writes to Anna before receiving Lovelace's letter (1116). After his note, however, she has found her answer and can declare with confidence, "I am not without hope that he will be properly affected by the evils he has made me suffer; and that when I am laid low and forgotten . . . [his family] will be enabled to rejoice in his reformation" (1186).

Finally, Lovelace's letter leads Clarissa to realize the extent to which her suffering is a form of power, an active means of serving herself while serving others. She is able, at last, to govern her own choices without appearing stubborn or willful; to dictate her desires while accommodating those of others. Her reply to Lovelace's plea for forgiveness indicates both her compliance with his request and her defiance, a defiance he finds tantalizing:

> Religion enjoins me not only to forgive injuries, but to return good for evil. It is all my consolation, and I bless God for giving me that, that I am now in such a state of mind with regard to you, that I can cheerfully obey its dictates. And accordingly I tell you that wherever you go, I wish you happy. And in this I mean to include every good wish. And now having, with great reluctance I own, complied with one of your compulsatory alternatives, I expect the fruits of it. (1191)

Lovelace's response to Clarissa's suffering is similar to those of all her former friends and antagonists. "Poor dear Miss Harlowe! her sufferings have endeared her to us, almost as much as her excellencies can have done to you," Charlotte Montague informs Anna (1047). Alexander Wyerly renews his proposal of marriage, declaring, "I will love you, if possible, still more than I ever loved you—and that for your sufferings . . . now that your sufferings, so NOBLY BORNE, have with all GOOD JUDGES exalted your character" (1267).

On 7 August, the day on which Clarissa receives Lovelace's plea for forgiveness, she receives a message from her implacable family as well. "Were we sure you had seen your folly, and were TRULY penitent, and at the same time that you were so very ill as you intimate, I know not what might be done for you," writes Uncle John. "Unhappy girl! How miserable have you made us all! We, who used to visit with so much pleasure, now cannot endure to look upon one another" (1192). Like Lovelace, Wyerly, and the gentry at The Lawn, it seems that the Harlowes are made miserable through Clarissa's misfortunes yet will love her the better for her suffering.[12]

Clarissa's response to them, as to Lovelace, allows her to assert independence while insisting on solidarity. Once again, Clarissa's difference will secure the family unity. "There was a kind of fatality, by which our whole family was impelled, as I may say; and which none of us were permitted to avoid," she explains to Wyerly (1268). Remembering Clarissa's dangerous childhood fevers, Norton reminisces, "All our lives were bound up in your life" (1154). Clarissa has little reason to doubt that all their lives will be bound up in her suffering as well. She is well on her way to sainthood, driven to it as she has been driven to perfection all her life, but she will at least have the consolation of knowing that those for whom she suffers share her suffering. Her family members are moved by the pathetic letters she sends "Mama" Norton and Anna. When Cousin Morden reads the affecting passages in which she takes her final farewell of Anna, saying, "You shall be happy," her brother reflects, "It is more than she will let anybody else be" (1322).

Clarissa's pathetic sufferings, however much her family may resent them, are in direct proportion to their demand for her sufferings. Her friends will hardly think that she can suffer too much, she tells Belford (1103–4), and later: "Alas! I have made them as miserable as I am myself. And yet sometimes I think that, were they cheerfully to pronounce me forgiven, I know not whether my concern for having offended them would not be augmented: since I imagine that nothing can be more wounding to a spirit not ungenerous, than a generous forgiveness" (1119).

Clarissa's generous forgiveness of her family and of Lovelace, however, is unhesitatingly offered with a clear understanding of the distress it will cause. "I suffer a thousand times more than ever I made thee suffer," Lovelace protests (1335). To Belford he pleads: "Tell the dear creature she must not be wicked in her piety. There is a TOO MUCH, as well as a too LITTLE, even in righteousness. Perhaps she does not think of that" (1308).

Apparently, Clarissa does think of this. Her forgiveness of Lovelace is as triangular as his request for it, involving not only her eternal father but also her temporal one. Tell your friend, she requests Belford,

> that I am trying to bring my mind into such a frame as to be able to PITY him (poor perjured wretch! what has he not to answer for!); and that I shall not think myself qualified for the state I am aspiring to, if, after a few struggles more, I cannot FORGIVE him too: and I hope . . . my dear EARTHLY father will set me the example my HEAVENLY one has already set us all; and by forgiving his fallen daughter teach her to forgive the man who then, I hope, will not have destroyed my eternal prospects, as he has my temporal! (1102)

Her letter, notes Lovelace, is "so written as to make herself more admired, ME more detested" (1169). Triumphant in her forgiveness, Clarissa admits: "The man whom once I could have loved, I have been enabled to despise: and shall not CHARITY complete my triumph? And shall I not ENJOY it?" (1254).

If Clarissa's suffering is serviceable, its lesson is not lost on her lover. Having once tricked her into demonstrating her love by feigning illness, Lovelace now takes his cue from her, resolving, "I will make her mine!— And be sick again" (1204). But he does not realize that it is not Clarissa's suffering that commends her to others; rather, it is the story of her suffering, a new version of her former tale.

Clarissa's story has not changed appreciably from the first letter of the novel, in which Anna urges her to "write the whole of [her] story" in order to justify herself when blamed for the faults of others (40). Once again, Clarissa's identity as a legend is founded on her ability to tread calmly among villains. The villains are no longer James and the Harlowe clan; Lovelace now provides an adequate hindrance to her virtue. Clarissa's story must be his story; her triumph must be his defeat; her virtue must be asserted at his expense. Moreover, this is a story that cannot be contested. "As you are so earnest to have all the particulars of my sad story before you, I will, if life and spirits be lent me, give you an ample account of all that has befallen me from the time you mention," she promises Anna. "But this, it is very probable, you will not see till after the close of my last scene: and as I shall write with a view to that, I hope no other voucher will be wanted for the veracity of the writer" (1018).

"Pity me, Jack, for pity's sake; since, if thou dost not, nobody else will," pleads Lovelace after the ineffective rape. "We are apt to attribute to the devil everything that happens to us which we would not HAVE happen: but here, being (as perhaps thou'lt say) the devil myself, my plagues arise from an angel. I suppose all mankind is to be plagued by its CONTRARY" (908). Lovelace's levity in respect to this topic is soon dispelled. What seemed merely annoying during his courtship of Clarissa ("Everything I do that is good is but as I OUGHT!—Everything of a contrary nature is brought into the most glaring light against me!—Is this fair?" [42]) becomes truly terrifying when Clarissa becomes saintly. He is universally blamed for her downfall and cannot defend himself except by condemning Clarissa, thus hurting himself further. "In truth, Jack, I have been a most execrable villain," he admits (1385), protesting, "And thus am I blamed for everyone's faults!—When her brutal father curses her, it is I. I upbraid her with her severe mother. Her stupid uncles' implacableness is all mine. Her brother's virulence, and her sister's spite and envy, are entirely owing to me. This rascal Brand's letter is of my writing—Oh Jack, what a wretch is thy Lovelace!" (1291).

Clarissa's story weaves Lovelace into her fate, inverting their original positions. If she has lost the esteem of her own family, she has certainly secured that of his. "He has not one friend left among us," declares Miss Montague, "for we shun each other; and one part of the house holds US, another HIM, the remotest from each other" (1182). Furious and miserable, denied access to his family unless he marries Clarissa and assured that Clarissa would rather die than marry him, Lovelace can only protest: "Surely, Belford, the devil's in this lady! . . . But she has heard that the devil is black; and having a mind to make one of me, brays together in the mortar of her wild fancy twenty chimney-sweepers, in order to make one sootier than ordinary rise out of the dirty mass" (1183). "Can PATHOS . . . alter facts?" (1107).

Convinced that he has not deserved his fate yet equally inclined to condemn himself, Lovelace vacillates between self-pity and self-condemnation—unable, for once, to shift his anxieties onto a third relationship.

"Have I nobody, whose throat, either for carelessness or treachery, I ought to cut in order to pacify my vengeance!" he pleads (971). "It is certainly as much my misfortune to have fallen in with Miss Clarissa Harlowe . . . as it is that of Miss Harlowe to have been acquainted with me" (970).

As the members of his family join in a general condemnation, reinforcing their original preference of Clarissa to their kinsman, Lovelace's desperation peaks. "Such lamentations for the loss of so charming a relation! Such applaudings of her virtue, of her exaltedness of soul and sentiment! Such menaces of disinherisons [sic]," he complains to Belford. "I, not needing THEIR reproaches to be stung to the heart with my own reflections, and with the rage of disappointment; and as sincerely as any of them admiring her—What the devil, cried I, is all this for? . . . Can I help her implacable spirit? . . . Were her death to follow in a week after the knot is tied, by the Lord of Heaven, it SHALL be tied, and she shall die a Lovelace" (1169).

While Lovelace's insistence on marriage may now seem a renewed attempt to conquer her, there is reason to believe that the insufferably competing triangles Clarissa has set in motion have brought him to a realization of the necessity of a linear relationship. "Methinks, I would be glad that this affair, which is bad enough in itself, should go off without worse personal consequences to anybody else; and yet, it runs in my mind, I know not why, that sooner or later it will draw a few drops of blood after it; except she and I can make it up between ourselves," he admits in an unusually candid letter to Belford (972).

His grandiose schemes come to an abrupt halt as Clarissa approaches death, and Lovelace confronts his anxieties more honestly than he has ever been able to do: "To give her a lowering sensibility; to bring her down from among the stars which her beamy head was surrounded by, that my wife, so greatly above me, might not too much despise me—this was part of my reptile envy, owing to my MORE reptile apprehension of inferiority." Having confronted his own attempts to lower her, he resents the saintly forgiveness that Clarissa uses to distance him, asking: "Why does she not execrate me? . . . Ever above me." Unfortunately, Lovelace cannot conceive of a relationship that does not depend on some form of submission. "If she recover," he promises, "the world never SAW such an husband as I will make. I will have no will but hers: she shall conduct me in all my steps: she shall open and direct my prospects, and turn every motion of my heart, as she pleases" (1344).

As Lovelace becomes increasingly entangled in his fears, compulsions, and self-doubts, increasingly certain that he and Clarissa may not be allowed to make it up between themselves, he experiences one of the frightening dreams of death so typical of disturbed children. "Methought, I had an interview with my beloved," he relates to Belford in a frenzied letter:

> I found her all goodness, condescension, and forgiveness. She suffered herself to be overcome in my favour by the joint intercessions of Lord M., Lady Sarah, Lady Betty, and my two cousins Montague, who waited upon her in deep mourning; the ladies in long trains sweeping after them; Lord M. in a long black mantle trailing after HIM. They told her they came in these robes to express their sorrow for my sins against her, and to implore her to forgive me.
>
> I myself, I thought, was upon my knees and with a sword in my hand, offering either to put it up in the scabbard, or to thrust it into my heart, as she should command the one or the other.
>
> At that moment her cousin Morden, I thought, all of a sudden flashed in through a window, with his drawn sword—Die, Lovelace, said he! this instant die, and be damned, if in earnest thou repairest not by marriage my cousin's wrongs!
>
> I was rising to resent this insult, I thought, when Lord M. run between us with his great black mantle, and threw it over my face: and instantly, my charmer, with that sweet voice which has so often played upon my ravished ears, wrapped her arms round me, muffled as I was in my Lord M.'s mantle: Oh spare, spare my Lovelace! And spare, Oh Lovelace, my beloved cousin Morden! Let me not have my distresses augmented by the fall of either or both of those who are so dear to me.
>
> At this, charmed with her sweet mediation, I thought I would have clasped her in my arms: when immediately the most angelic form I had ever beheld, vested all in transparent white, descended from a ceiling, which opening, discovered a ceiling above that, stuck round with golden cherubs and glittering seraphs, all exulting: Welcome, welcome, welcome! and, encircling my charmer, ascended with her to the region of seraphim; and instantly, the opening ceiling closing, I lost sight of HER, and of the BRIGHT FORM together, and found wrapped

in my arms her azure robe (all stuck thick with stars of em-
bossed silver), which I had caught hold of in hopes of detain-
ing her; but was all that was left me of my beloved Miss
Harlowe. And then (horrid to relate!) the floor sinking under
ME, as the ceiling had opened for HER, I dropped into a hole
more frightful than that of Elden and tumbling over and over
down it, without view of a bottom, I awaked in a panic; and
was as effectually disordered for half an hour, as if my dream
had been a reality. (1218)

Lovelace's dream closely resembles Clarissa's terrifying nightmare in
which she is stabbed by an angry Lovelace, toppled into a grave, and cov-
ered with dirt. Critical discussions that contrast these two remarkably similar dreams generally concentrate on the irony of the inverted assault; few
critics have examined the similarities or questioned why each character
should experience such nightmares. Because these dreams lend themselves
so well to commentaries on foreshadowing and didacticism, because they
so neatly support a plot that seems to depend on one character's villainy
and on the other's innocence, little regard has been paid to their significance in terms of the dreamer's sense of self at the time of the dream.[13]

Considered from a psychological perspective, Lovelace's nightmare
suggests that he now shares many of the uncertainties that haunted Clarissa
at the beginning of the novel.[14] As the dreaming Clarissa once found herself the focal point of Lovelace's fury toward her family, Lovelace now
finds himself the object of everyone's "sorrow for my sins against her." As
she once found herself compelled to marry a man drastically inferior to
herself, Lovelace now finds himself compelled to marry a lady too much
his superior. Equally unable to assert his power of refusal or to ascertain
that his desire to accept will be accommodated, Lovelace is on his knees,
offering the sacrifice of himself.

Lovelace's dream is a frenzied tangle of interruptions, intercessions,
and fragmented triangles. Clarissa has been brought to forgive him through
the joint intercessions of his entire family; her forgiveness, however, is
interrupted by Colonel Morden's violent demand. Lovelace's attempt to
interact with Morden is interrupted by Lord M.'s interference, and Lord
M.'s interference is immediately mediated by Clarissa's. Clarissa not only
comes between Lord M. and Lovelace but also between Lovelace and
Morden, entreating each to spare the other. Lovelace's final attempt to

grasp Clarissa, a desire that has been frustrated all along, is effectively disrupted by an entire heavenly host. His own self, now forever ineffective, falls away into a bottomless pit, defeated by his family, Clarissa's family, and the hosts of heaven. Nothing he has said has been heard; nothing he has attempted has been realized. Throughout the dream he is voiceless, impotent, and faceless; smothered in mantles and enfolded in arms.[15] He, too, is excluded from speech—suppressed, interrupted, or ignored. Clarissa is merely a glorified absence, an empty piece of cloth in his hands.

"Sleeping or waking, my Clarissa is always present with me," Lovelace muses (1218), unable to realize that the absence in his dream is the absence that torments his waking hours as well. He and Clarissa will never make it up between themselves because neither one belongs to him- or herself. Lovelace is merely part of a story—Clarissa's story.

Clarissa's Story: Saintly Suffering

If Clarissa's story is exemplary, it is also highly ambiguous, perhaps because so many others are implicated in its telling. Once Clarissa's absence from home and the story of her suffering combine to create a saint, it becomes impossible to determine the extent to which her sufferings are public or private—ultimately, all are affected. As Maud Ellmann argues, "Since food and words are circulating currencies . . . it is *circulation* . . . that underlies the art of hunger, and it is necessary to investigate this ruinous economy."[16] It is important to note, then, the ways in which Clarissa the woman and the story of Saint Clarissa interact to weave one person's sufferings into a complicated public and private affair.

Clarissa the woman is simply a girl of nineteen who does not eat. That she has lost her appetite is the only clue Richardson will give to the cause of her death, and even this is a questionable clue.[17] On first being examined by a doctor, Clarissa is found to be tired and depressed, generally malnourished, probably not consumptive. "A love case," declares her kindly and reputable physician. "We can do nothing here . . . but by cordials and nourishment." To the pallid lady he declares, "you can do more for yourself than all the faculty can do for you" (1081).

If the doctor is of the opinion that Clarissa's disorder is "in her mind," the apothecary is even more convinced that her grief has led to stubbornness. In response to Mr. Hickman's inquiries he declares: "The lady . . . will do very well if she will resolve upon it herself. Indeed you WILL, madam. The doctor is entirely of this opinion; and has ordered nothing for you but weak jellies, and innocent cordials, lest you should starve yourself. And, let me tell you, madam, that so much watching, so little nourishment, and so much grief as you seem to indulge, is enough to impair the most vigorous health, and to wear out the strongest constitution." He recommends nine hours of sleep, a dinner of "anything you like, so you will BUT eat," and "country air" (1129).

Clarissa's response to this advice completely problematizes the opinions of her physicians. Her sufferings, she insists, are not mental but physical. "What, sir, said she, can I do? I have no appetite. Nothing you call nourishing will stay on my stomach. I do what I can" (1129). Her words are immediately appropriated by Belford, on whom the burden of relating Clarissa's story has fallen, and accounted for in distinctly religious terms: "This lady had OTHER views in living, than the common ones of eating, sleeping, dressing, visiting, and those other fashionable amusements which fill up the time of most of her sex." Belford uses her lack of appetite to predict her death at a time when there can be little medical reason to expect it, explaining, "Her grief, in short, seems to me to be of such a nature that TIME, which alleviates most other persons' afflictions, will . . . GIVE INCREASE TO HERS" (1128). Clarissa's refusal, or inability, to eat has become both psychological and religious, self-imposed and unquestioned.

Clarissa's fasting is an important part of her story and may well reflect not her austerity but, rather, her biographer's admiration of it. Her abstinence, whether it is considered as starving or fasting, illness or obstinacy, inspires awe and admiration in those who hear of her sufferings.

While Clarissa's eating, or noneating, may be explained in terms of family dynamics, such an approach cannot account for the tremendous effect the story of her abstinence has on all who know of her. "In order to read *Clarissa* correctly, it is necessary to understand what Christianity meant to the heroine and her author," writes Margaret Doody.[18] Christianity may be too broad a topic to consider for the purpose of this study, but it is not difficult to ascertain what the story of the fasting female saint might have meant for Clarissa's contemporaries or how such stories might easily have influenced a young lady already prone to expressing herself through food-related behavior.[19]

Fasting girls have long been of interest to theologians, particularly because the model of the female saint is, in many respects, the mirror image of the stereotypical witch. As Caroline Walker Bynum points out in her excellent *Holy Feast, Holy Fast,* women who do not need to eat, who receive visions and private "assurances," who withdraw from the world and surround themselves with reminders of death, are deeply threatening.

By the beginning of the eighteenth-century, Bynum explains, theologians were heatedly debating whether the ability to live without eating signified sanctity. "Pope Benedict XIV (d. 1758) commissioned an appendix for his great work on canonization to consider whether the extended fasts claimed for certain Catholic women, several of them stigmatics, could be natural."[20] This question still haunts theologians and doctors. In 1912, long before the current interest in anorexia nervosa and its sister disorder, anorexia mirabilis, had become of popular interest, the Carnegie Institute conducted a study to determine how long human beings could survive without sustenance. This study, of course, could not completely address the issue of pious women's seemingly miraculous ability to survive almost solely on the Eucharist.[21]

Clarissa's suffering is decidedly ambiguous, yet any attempt to pinpoint its origin, either in Clarissa's self-induced starvation, depression, or consumption, would be both fruitless and irrelevant. If Belford's letters give little insight into the origins of her ailments, it is because he, like the rest of her admirers, is less concerned with the cause of her sufferings than with the way she bears them.[22]

Clarissa's fasts have always allowed her to manipulate herself and to manipulate others. Now, however, the mere story of her suffering changes her world. Bynum explains:

> The course of an individual [saint's] life can never explain why the depression or guilt in that life expresses itself in symbols such as "blood" and "hunger" or why a particular theological notion, such as the idea of service through suffering, emerges as a solution. We cannot understand the voluntary starvation of any particular woman unless we understand fully what food means to those among whom she lives . . . women manipulated more than their own bodies through fasting. They manipulated their families, their religious superiors, and God himself. Fasting was not merely a substitution of pathological and self-defeating control of self for unattainable control of circumstance. It was part of suffering; and suffering

was considered an effective activity, which redeemed both individual and cosmos.[23]

In the vitae of saintly women suffering is very important; its significance lies in its experience, not in its source, notes Bynum. In the Middle Ages, she explains, people "did not divide body and mind so sharply as we do or the senses from one another." Accounts of suffering are less attentive to its cause than to its meaning.[24]

If Clarissa's saintly behavior concerning marriage, money, family, and friendship are treated as isolated themes, she will indeed appear an inconsistent, even a hypocritical, character; however, once her food-related behavior is posited as a central theme in her renunciation of the world and considered from both a psychological and a religious perspective, her behavior in other areas falls into consistent patterns. Clarissa's apparent rejection of physicality, wealth, and sensual pleasures becomes an acceptance of the new possibilities of physicality, an intensely sensual spirituality that allows her to influence the physical world in a number of ways.

Clarissa's fast, to be properly understood, must be considered as a fast from food, vice, family, sex, and every thought that might trouble her serenity. There can be no doubt that Clarissa regards her suffering as penance, a purging and weaning experience that will leave her purified and ready to meet her maker. An early letter to Norton from the Smiths reads, "There is in the same house a widow-lodger of low fortunes, but of great merit . . . who has, as she says, given over all other thoughts of the world but such as shall assist her to leave it happily—How suitable to my own views—There seems to be a comfortable providence in THIS at least!" (987–88). "This widow," she explains in a later letter, "is the better for having been a proficient in the school of affliction. An excellent school! my dear Mrs. Norton, in which we are taught to know ourselves, to be able to be compassionate and bear with one another, and to look up to a better hope" (1122).

These lessons in renunciation do not come as easily to Clarissa as she might wish. Her declarations of forgiveness and other-worldly resignation are constantly undermined by an inability to accept her hardships with patience. Anna's cruel taunts, the result of a misunderstanding that arises when Lovelace alters a letter, lead her to lament, "I find, by the rising bitterness which will mingle with the gall in my ink, that I am not yet subdued enough to my condition" (996).

The cruelties of her family are similarly acknowledged: "My sister's taunting letter, and the inflexibleness of my dearer friends," she protests (1261). "Indeed I cannot call them my RELATIONS, I think!—But I am ill; and therefore perhaps more peevish than I should be . . . I am very much tired and fatigued—with—I don't know what—with writing, I think— but most with myself, and with a situation I cannot help aspiring to get out of, and above!" (1194). "What an inefficacious preparation must I have been making, if it has not by this time carried me above—But above what?—Poor mistaken creature!—Unhappy self-deluder!—that finds herself above nothing! Nor able to subdue her own faulty impatience!" (1261).

If Clarissa's suffering is a purgation, there is no reason to believe that her emotional distress is not as important to this process as her physical ordeal. She can convince herself, at times, that her "divine course" is a natural passion, that she truly is above temporal concerns, but this belief must always be problematized if Clarissa is to continue on course by suffering. "I hope that I cannot now be easily put out of my present course. My declining health will more and more confirm me in it," she assures Belford. "I presume to hope that I have a mind that cannot be debased, in ESSENTIAL INSTANCES, by TEMPORARY CALAMITIES: little do those poor wretches know of the force of innate principles, forgive my own IMPLIED vanity . . . who imagine that a prison, or penury, or want, can bring a right turned mind to be guilty of a wilful baseness, in order to avoid such SHORT-LIVED EVILS" (1103).

Prison and rejection, however, are not the worst of what Clarissa has to endure. Clarissa has brought herself to bear poverty admirably; she soon finds that she cannot bear being relieved of it. Belford's clumsy attempt to give her money causes her real pain. "I cannot bear it," she explains, refusing his generosity with genuine anguish (1103). Even love and forgiveness cause Clarissa distress. Of her family she says, "If they were any of them to come or to send to me: and perhaps if I found they still loved me, [I should] wish to live; and so should quit unwillingly that life which I am now really fond of quitting, and hope to quit, as becomes a person who has had such a weaning-time as I have been favoured with" (1277).

Clarissa's desire to die ("I must say I dwell on, I indulge [and, strictly speaking, I enjoy] the thoughts of death" [1306]); her evident enthusiasm in ordering, designing, and viewing her coffin; her thoroughly planned will and many posthumous letters seem to suggest either that she has rejected the world in disdain or that she has rejected the physicality of her body, yet the process of death itself is, for her, intensely physical, intensely pleasurable.

Clarissa's fasting—from food, from vice, from love and from generosity—also constitutes a feast, no less physical than the sensual pleasures she has denied herself. "Most happy has been to me my punishment here!—happy indeed!" she declares on the eve of her death. "You know not what FORETASTES—what ASSURANCES . . . ," and here she pauses, in "thankful rapture" (1362).

Clarissa's tendency to discuss her pain in terms of pleasure, her long fast as divine food, is not unusual saintly behavior. Bynum explains that modern notions of pain and pleasure as opposites can be extremely misleading for scholars of saintly suffering. In the terminology of piety, a terminology with which Clarissa's contemporaries would have been familiar, "sensations and senses that we differentiate from one another tend to be fused. . . . satiation is described as 'hungry' and discomfort is called 'delicious.'"[25]

"I have eaten ashes like bread," writes Clarissa in a meditation that suggests misery and suffering, yet, as Bynum explains, Clarissa's misery is not incompatible with her assurances that her punishment has been enjoyable. For the fasting female saint, "Food was a multifaceted symbol. . . . Fasting, feeding, and feasting were thus not so much opposites as synonyms. Fasting was flight not FROM but INTO physicality. Communion was consuming, i.e., becoming a God who saves through physical, human agony. . . . God is food, which is flesh, which is suffering, which is salvation."[26]

Clarissa is the only character, of the many who die in the novel, to take the Eucharist, to join in communion with her God by consuming him. Bynum's superb research shows that, although the Eucharist took on many meanings over the course of the Church's history, the basic equation of food as God remained, along with "the need to take account of (rather than merely to deny) matter, body, and sensual response." "To eat was to consume, to take in, to become God," she writes. "To lift one's own physicality into suffering and into glory."[27]

References to food abstention and eucharistic piety are customary in accounts of female saints and are commonly referred to in metaphors of both hunger and eating. Clarissa's raptures, her enjoyment of a punishment tempered by divine "foretastes," repeats a pattern that has been followed by saints for hundreds of years. Food has long been used as an image of the soul's desire for God, the mystical union of saint with savior. "To medieval exegetes and spiritual writers, such themes were not mere metaphors," writes Bynum.

> Intellect, soul, and sensory faculties were not divided, with a separate vocabulary to refer to each. Rather, God was known with senses that were a fusion of all the human being's capacities to experience. When medieval writers spoke of eating or tasting or savoring God, they meant not merely to draw an analogy to a particular bodily pleasure but, rather, to denote directly an experiencing, a feeling/knowing of God into which the entire person was caught up.[28]

Moreover, the physical joining of human and spirit might be expressed in metaphors of both pleasure and pain because to taste God is also to hunger for him, to experience a craving for oneness beyond satiety.[29] "GOD WILL HAVE NO RIVALS IN THE HEARTS OF THOSE HE SANCTIFIES," Clarissa tells Norton. "By various methods he deadens all other sensations, or rather absorbs them all in the love of Him" (1338). She has been so thrilled by these raptures, she claims, that she sometimes "could hardly contain herself and was ready to think herself above this earth while she was in it" (1272).

Similarly, once Clarissa's cause has become the cause of virtue, of God, those who know of her story can express their cravings for her in terms of hunger and sensual enjoyment. "I never more longed to see you in my life," John Harlowe writes to his saintly niece, "and even hunger and thirst, as I may say, to see you" (1366). Even Clarissa's memory elicits a sensual/spiritual response. "I am bewitched to her memory," Lovelace declares. "Her very name, with mine joined to it, ravishes my soul, and is more delightful to me than the sweetest music" (1483).

If union with God finds its expression in metaphors of eating and assimilation, wickedness is expressed in imagery of feeding without assimilation, as an endless process of being chewed, bitten, devoured. "Tremble and reform, when you read what is the PORTION OF THE WICKED MAN FROM GOD," warns Clarissa in her posthumous letter to Lovelace. "His strength shall be hunger-bitten, and destruction shall be ready at his side. The first-born of death shall devour his strength. . . . His meat is the gall of asps within him. . . . A fire not blown shall consume him. . . . The worm shall feed sweetly on him. . . . This is the fate of him that knoweth not God" (1427).

After the rape Clarissa writes and tears fragments of letters in a frenzied attempt to regain her sense of self. Paper VII (to Lovelace) is one of the most lucid and consistent fragments. Employing the same imagery of painful and destructive consumption to describe Lovelace's cruelty, Clarissa casts herself as the victim of a blight that destroys the early promises of spring, of a "pernicious caterpillar, that preyest upon the fair leaf of virgin fame, and poisonest those leaves which thou [Lovelace] canst not devour," of an "eating canker-worm that preyest upon the opening bud" (892).

Although Clarissa's self-denial functions as a private image of union with her God, it is important to recognize that it also constitutes a crucial image of union with her neighbors, a demonstration of her ability to transfer her wisdom and goods, to provide charitable service to others. The wealth she shares is both a physical and a spiritual wealth, effectively allowing her to bypass the traditional hierarchies of family and clergy without seeming to do so. Clarissa's individual and direct union with God allows her to usurp a clerical authority that she has long desired but never has been able to attain. She is able to assume an unquestioned role as teacher, comforter, chastiser, and reformer, a role that would certainly have been prohibited to an ordinary nineteen-year-old girl, however sweet and pious she might have been.

As she takes leave of her physicians for the last time, having insisted on selling her clothes rather than accepting their services for free, Clarissa prays: "[I] beg of God . . . that it may be in the power of you and of yours to the end of time, to confer benefits, rather than to be obliged to receive them. This is a god-like power, gentlemen: I once rejoiced in it, in some little degree; and much more in the prospect I had of its being enlarged to me" (1248). In a letter to Belford, received after her death, she writes, "The great Duke of Luxemburgh, as I have heard, on his death-bed declared that he would then much rather have had it to reflect upon that he had administered a cup of cold water to a worthy poor creature in distress, than that he had won so many battles as he had triumphed for" (1367).

Clarissa has no need to compare herself to the duke; her Godlike charity is well documented. "You have heard, sir, how universally my dear cousin was beloved. By the poor and middling sort especially, no young lady was ever so much beloved. And with reason: she was the common patroness of all the honest poor in her neighbourhood," Morden explains to Belford (1397). Anna completes the story by explaining Clarissa's daily regimen, in which one hour of each day was set aside "to visits to the neighbouring poor; to a select number of whom, and to their children, she used to give brief instructions and good books" (1471).

Clarissa did not content herself with the mere feeding of bodies; she delighted in feeding the spirit as well. "One of my delights was to enter the cots of my poor neighbours, to leave lessons to the boys, and cautions to the elder girls," she tells Anna after her abduction, wondering sadly: "How should I be able, unconscious and without pain, to say to the latter, Fly the delusions of men, who had been supposed to have run away with one? . . . What then . . . can I wish for but death?" (1117).

Clarissa's death, accompanied by the story of her glorious suffering, renews her reputation, validating her spiritual guidance and ennobling her memory.[30] Her excellencies are revived and enhanced, relates Morden, her perfections "called up to remembrance and enumerated: incidents and graces, unheeded before or passed over in the group of her numberless perfections, now brought into notice and dwelt upon!" "The very servants [are] allowed to expatiate upon these praiseful topics to their principles!" he explains in astonishment:

> To see them [the family] . . . encouraging the servants to repeat how they used to be stopped by strangers to ask after her, and by those who know her to be told of some new instances to her honour—how aggravating all this!
>
> In DREAMS they see her, and DESIRE to see her: always an angel, and accompanied by angels: always clad in robes of light: always endeavouring to comfort THEM, who declare that they shall never more know comfort!
>
> . . . Her conversation how instructive! how sought after! The delight of persons of all ages, of both sexes, of all ranks! Yet how humble, how condescending! Never were dignity and humility so illustriously mingled!
>
> At other times, how generous, how noble, how charitable, how judicious in her charities! In every action laudable! In every attitude attractive! . . . LIKE or RESEMBLING Miss Clarissa Harlowe they now remember to be a praise denoting the highest degree of approveable excellence, with everyone, whatever person, action, or rank, spoken of.
>
> . . . Not one fault remembered! (1448)

After Clarissa's death her wealth is transferred to a fund, to be dispensed first by Norton then by Anna, "as she shall think will best answer my intention (to relieve the temporary wants of the industrious and sober poor)" (1419). The Poor's Fund is contributed to by all those who bless Clarissa's memory and serves to perpetuate her memory. In dispensing the much-needed relief, Anna "teaches everyone whom she benefits TO BLESS THE MEMORY OF HER DEPARTED FRIEND; to whom she attributes the merit of all HER OWN charities, as well as that of those which she dispenses in pursuance of her will" (1492).

The generosity of saintly women "captured the popular imagination by its courage," notes Bynum. "To empty family cupboards in defiance of husbands and fathers, to renounce family support, to work or beg in order to feed the poor—these were heroic and sometimes dangerous acts."[31]

The estate that was once so fiercely contested by Clarissa's relatives has now become part of Clarissa's story of charity and service, the more so because her insistence on poverty, her refusal to litigate with her father in order to relieve her distress, has enabled her to aid the community in a way that is both dramatic and charismatic.

It would be a mistake to assume that Clarissa's death alone allows this transformation from forgotten sufferer to counselor and financial patron. Long before she has actually expired, Clarissa ministers to the spiritual and physical needs of those who would comfort her. Although she seldom eats herself, she treats her friends to frequent repasts (1129, 1188, 1273). "I never saw so much soul in a lady's eyes, as in hers," writes Belford (1072); "Methinks I have a kind of holy love for this woman" (1080). Her apothecary tells her, on his first visit, "Your aspect commands love, as well as reverence" (1082).

Clarissa's meditations are copied and circulated, her prayers offered for others. Her example almost immediately reforms Belford. With her dying breath she urges him to see the error of his rakish ways, vouchsafes that Norton will most probably be, one day, a saint in heaven, and reassures her admirers that she has had divine "assurances" of a heavenly crown (1362). Friends crowd around her deathbed to receive her last blessing ("Bless—bless—bless—you all" [1362]).

Clarissa's sanctity impresses the clergymen who deal with her even more than it impresses the laymen. The parson who gives her the last sacrament stays less than a half-hour in the presence of this "lovely skeleton" (1231); as he leaves, he announces, in "a faltering accent, . . . You have an angel in your house" (1245). When Dr. Lewen attempts to impose his authority as her minister, writing, "Your religion, your duty to your family, the duty you owe to your honour, and even charity to your sex, oblige you to give public evidence against this very wicked man" (1251), his letter is answered with a courteous insistence that she be allowed to follow her own principles, judgments, and insights. Clarissa even presumes to remind him of his own precepts: "I believe your arguments would have been unanswerable in almost every OTHER case of this nature but in that of the unhappy CLARISSA HARLOWE," she responds, adding:

> In full conviction of the purity of my heart, and of the firm-
> ness of my principles (why may I not, thus called upon, say what
> I am conscious of, and yet without faulty pride; since all is but a
> DUTY, and I should be utterly inexcusable, could I not justly say
> what I do?—In this full conviction) he has offered me marriage.
> He has avowed his penitence: a SINCERE penitence I have reason
> to think it, though perhaps not a CHRISTIAN one.... Have not
> you, sir, from the BEST rules, and from the DIVINEST EXAMPLE,
> taught me to forgive injuries? (1253–54)

Clarissa's purity will effectively end the family's favor to the officious and low-minded pedant Mr. Brand. She will choose the scriptural passages for her own funeral and, in her final letters, will chasten her loved ones, directing their repentance and warning them of God's wrath.

Saintly visions and assurances of salvation often allowed women to exercise, if not bypass, ecclesiastical control, writes Bynum. Many medieval saintly women actually founded orders and quarreled with popes. By claiming for themselves the minister's or priest's proximity to God, they became mediators between human and divine. Such religiosity was not necessarily an aping of clerical power but, rather, "an alternative to, and therefore a critique of and a substitute for, the characteristic male form of religious authority: the authority of office."[32]

If Clarissa's empowering purity is considered in this way, her posthumous letters cannot be spiteful acts of revenge from beyond the grave; rather, they become the words of a saint, appropriating to herself the clerical rights that her suffering has enabled her to exercise.[33] James is urged to control his temper and to avoid recriminations. "You would not arrogate to yourself God's province, who has said, VENGEANCE IS MINE, AND I WILL REPAY IT. If you would, I tremble for the consequence," she warns (1373). To Arabella, whom she reminds of the "severity" of her unrestrained virtue, she writes while "in imagination, purified and exalted . . . made perfect . . . through sufferings" (1375). She beseeches Anna to marry Mr. Hickman, "a sincere, an honest, a virtuous, and what is more than all, a PIOUS man" (1377).

Belford and Lovelace receive the most righteous letters. "Tremble and reform," she entreats Lovelace. "Set about your repentance instantly—be no longer the instrument of Satan. . . . Seek not to multiply your offenses till they become beyond the POWER, as I may say, of the Divine mercy to forgive; since JUSTICE, no less than MERCY, is an attribute of the Almighty" (1427). "Let me hope that I may be an humble instrument in the hands of Providence to reform a man of your parts and abilities," she implores Belford (1368).

Belford immediately complies with her hope. He remembers Clarissa's fast and death as he describes Mrs. Sinclair's agonies in graphic detail, noting particularly her "huge quaggy carcass: her mill-post arms held up, her broad hands . . . fat ears and brawny neck . . . wide mouth . . . huge tongue hideously rolling in it . . . [and] her naturally big voice" (1389).

"What woman . . . did she know what miry wallowers the generality of men of our class are in themselves and constantly trough and sty with, but would detest the thoughts of associating with such filthy sensualists, whose favourite taste carries them to mingle with the dregs of stews, brothels, and common-sewers?" Belford asks, stretching the imagery of eating to its limits. Reminding Lovelace of the "lovely skeleton's" admonitions and excellences, he concludes, "I came home reflecting upon all these things, more edifying to me than any sermon I could have heard preached" (1393–94).

BELFORD AND CLARISSA'S STORY

Clarissa's story is not an autobiography. Her choice of a biographer emphasizes the meaning she wishes her story to have; it is emphatically the story of her triumph over Lovelace. "It will be an honour to my memory, with all those who shall know that I was so well satisfied of my innocence, that having not time to write my own story I could entrust it to the relation which the destroyer of my fame and fortunes has given of it," she announces to Belford (1176), but this validation, she insists, will not be for her sake alone; Clarissa's story will continue the saintly work of redemption and reformation which she so enjoys. She continues,

> And who knows but that the man who already, from a principle of humanity is touched at my misfortunes, when he

comes to revolve the whole story placed before him in one strong light, and when he shall have the catastrophe likewise before him; and shall become in a manner interested in it: who knows but that from a still higher principle, he may so regulate his future actions as to find his own reward in the everlasting welfare. (1176–77)

Clarissa's story is typical of any saint's story and also typical of Clarissa's unique triangular tendencies.[34] It is not a twisted version of the truth nor a spiteful attempt at revenge, but, rather, a nonlinear attempt to influence those around her. The vitae of female saints tend to follow predictable patterns, explains Caroline Bynum. "They place a strong emphasis on charitable activity in the world. . . . They are also strongly male-oriented: these women saints often simultaneously dominate and are dominated by the confessors who eventually write their biographies." "Hagiography—no matter how elegant its structure—is notoriously stereotypical and exaggerated. The stories of saints sometimes express more clearly the expectations of authors and readers than the hopes and fears in the hearts of their retiring and earnest subjects."[35]

Clarissa's story does not seem appreciably different from other saintly women's stories in this respect. Belford is extremely proud of his position as Clarissa's confidant and of his own reformation, particularly as he has been Lovelace's dear friend and fellow rake. From the beginning he is telling her story for others, using it, with Clarissa's blessing, in triangular fashion to accomplish a number of ends. First, he presents her story to those who will not accept it from her own lips. "Is she not answerable to God, to us, to you, and to all the world who knew her, for the abuse of such talents as SHE has abused? . . . [yet] nothing she writes herself will be regarded," declares Mrs. Harlowe in a letter to Norton (1156–57). "God grant that you may be able to clear your CONDUCT AFTER you had escaped Hampstead; as all BEFORE that time was noble, generous, and prudent: the man a devil, and you a saint," cautions Anna (995). Belford will see that this justification is rendered.

Second, Belford's story supplies a sound meaning for what might otherwise seem a meaningless and unnecessary suffering. His record of Clarissa's sufferings, in many ways a standardized vita, emphasizes what is expected of the saintly woman: fasting, meditation, and eucharistic devotion. Because Clarissa is isolated from a public that has already chosen her for an exemplar and a martyr, it is easy for him to present her sufferings in such a way that they will appeal to the expectations of an audience ready for wonder, ready for pathos, ready for admiration.

Belford's role as biographer is by no means altruistic. He relates what will be of most value to Clarissa's reputation and to his own as he chronicles her story. On a personal level Clarissa becomes a hostage in his friendship with Lovelace as Belford uses his correspondence with Clarissa to torture, tease, and reform his friend. In so doing, he both cements his fellowship with Lovelace and defines himself in contradistinction to him (much as Clarissa once unified her otherwise "common" family by contradistinguishing herself from them). Belford becomes a reformed rake, both of the libertines' fraternity and above it.

Like Lovelace, Belford finds that he is part of Clarissa's story, part of her purpose. His evil past is proof of Clarissa's power to reform. "I have ever thought myself when blessed with her conversation, in the company of a real angel: and I am sure it would be impossible for me, were she to be as beautiful and as crimsoned over with health as I have seen her, to have the least thought of sex when I heard her talk," he tells Lovelace (1299), although he finds that his rakish reputation does not help Clarissa when Brand speculates on what his constant attendance in her private chamber might signify. Like Clarissa, he finds that he can chastise his fellow rakes and give orders concerning Lovelace in an almost paternalistic manner (1386). As William Warner points out, "Although Belford writes on Clarissa's behalf, one can't escape the sense that he is indulging HIMSELF."[36]

Clarissa has always served by suffering and suffered by serving. Her long addiction to imposed perfection allows her to embrace the role of saint with evident enthusiasm, and the physical aspects of her fasts provide the ideal focus for Belford's chronicle of her saintly suffering and of Lovelace's carnal crime.

Saintly vitae commonly stress denuding activities—the nakedness of Saint Francis of Assisi or the austerity of Clare of Assisi, for instance.[37] Clarissa's vita is no exception. As Clarissa slowly turns into a pallid, skeletal saint, she sells her clothes, insisting that they not be purchased by her friends. Belford describes these transactions in detail, accentuating Clarissa's purity and attributing each instance of her behavior to Lovelace's perfidy. "In vain dost thou impute to pride or wilfulness the necessity to which thou hast reduced this lady of parting with her clothes: for can she do otherwise, and be the noble-minded creature she is?" Belford asks Lovelace. He continues, with a cool lack of concern, "Miss Harlowe is firmly of opinion that she shall never want nor wear the things she disposes of" (1123).

On one occasion Belford attempts to purchase some of Clarissa's clothes himself. "I was forced to take back my twenty guineas . . . she mistrusted that I was the advancer of the money; and would not let the clothes go," Belford writes. "But Mrs. Lovick has actually sold, for fifteen guineas some rich lace, worth three times the sum: out of which she repaid her the money she borrowed for fees to the doctor, in an illness occasioned by the barbarity of the most savage of men. THOU KNOWEST HIS NAME!" (1090).

Lovelace refuses to accept his role in Belford's story of Saint Clarissa, insisting that Clarissa's story be treated as the factual account of a common girl.[38] He is sorry for her ill health and the savage arrest (of which, he says, everyone knows he was not guilty). The rest, he declares, is "a common case; only a little uncommonly circumstanced; that's all: why then, all these severe things from her and thee?" Confronted with the story of Clarissa's denuding, Lovelace responds pragmatically:

> As to selling her clothes, and her laces, and so forth, it has, I own, a shocking sound with it. What an implacable, as well as unjust set of wretches are those of her unkindredly kin; who have money of hers in their hands, as well as large arrears of her own estate; yet withhold both, AVOWEDLY to distress her! But may she not have money of that proud and saucy friend of hers, Miss Howe, more than she wants?—And should I not be overjoyed, thinkest thou, to serve her?—What then is there in the parting with her apparel but female perverseness?—And I am not sure, whether I ought not to be glad if she does this out of SPITE TO ME—Some disappointed fair ones would have hanged, some drowned, themselves. My beloved only revenges herself upon her clothes. (1099)

Belford's accounts of Clarissa's starvation are similar to his treatment of her sale of clothing; he writes to Lovelace with evident admiration of her abstinence, never questioning her motives or objecting to her severity, blaming every pang of grief or missed meal on Lovelace: "The lady shut herself up at six o'clock yesterday afternoon; and intends not to see company till seven or eight this; not even her nurse; imposing upon herself a severe fast. And why? It is her birthday!—Blooming, yet declining in her blossom!—Every birthday till this, no doubt, happy!—What must be her reflections!—What ought to be thine!" (1124). Again, he seems less concerned with the lady's hardships than with the effect his relation of them will have on Lovelace.

Belford's long narration of Clarissa's imprisonment is fascinating in its simultaneous detachment and subjectivity. Taking particular care to point out each occasion on which Clarissa refuses food, Belford relates the tale of a three-day fast yet never remarks on Clarissa's refusals other than to credit her actions to someone else's depravity. "[Sally] ordered the people to press her to eat and drink. She must be fasting: nothing but her prayers and tears, poor thing! were the merciless devil's words . . . dost think I did not curse [Sally]?" he writes (1054). The story continues:

> Sally inquired, in her presence, whether she had eat or drank anything; and being told by the woman that she could not prevail upon her to taste a morsel, or drink a drop, she said, This is wrong, MISS HARLOW! Very wrong—Your religion, I think, should teach you that starving yourself is murder.
>
> . . . *What thinkest thou, Lovelace, of this!—This wretch's triumph was over a Clarissa!*
>
> About six in the evening, Rowland's wife pressed her to drink tea. She said she had rather have a glass of water. . . . The woman brought her a glass, and some bread and butter. She tried to taste the latter; but could not swallow it: but eagerly drank the water; lifting up her eyes in thankfulness for that!!!
>
> *The divine Clarissa, Lovelace—reduced to rejoice for a cup of cold water!—By WHOM reduced!*
>
> . . . Sally then ordered a dinner, and said they would soon be back again, and see that she eat and drink as a good Christian should, comporting herself to her condition, and making the best of it. (1053–58)

Belford never comments on the validity of Sally's argument that self-starvation is unholy. He seems to admire Clarissa's ability to endure her fast; its cause is obviously less important than her stamina. "Who would think such a delicately-framed person could have sustained what she has sustained? We sometimes talk of bravery, of courage, of fortitude!—Here they are in perfection!" he applauds (1058).

Belford continues his story, noting, "'Tis twelve of the clock, Sunday night—I can think of nothing but of this excellent creature. Her distresses fill my head and heart" (1058). Clarissa has, at this point, eaten nothing for two days. Her food-related behavior expresses itself as a concern only for others, as charity rather than as a pleasure in which she willingly partakes. Once again, Clarissa's refusal of meals reflects her constant concern with her family's response to her suffering:

> Refusing anything for breakfast, Mrs. Rowland came up to her, and told her (as these wretches owned they had ordered her, for fear she should starve herself), that she MUST and SHOULD have tea, and bread and butter; and that, as she had friends who could support her if she wrote to them, it was a wrong thing both for herself and THEM to starve herself thus.
>
> If it be for YOUR OWN SAKES, said she, that is another thing: let coffee, or tea, or chocolate, or what you will, be got: and put down a chicken to my account every day, if you please, and eat it yourselves. I will taste it, if I can. I would do nothing to hinder you: I have friends who will pay you liberally, when they know I am gone.
>
> . . . Mrs. Rowland prevailed on her to drink a dish of tea, and taste some bread and butter, about eleven on Saturday morning: which she probably did to have an excuse not to dine with the women when they returned. . . . Sally came again at dinner-time, TO SEE HOW THEY FARED, as she told her; and that she did not starve herself: and as she wanted to have some talk with her, if she gave her leave she would dine with her.
>
> I cannot eat.
>
> You must try, MISS HARLOWE.
>
> And, dinner being ready just then, she offered her hand, and desired her to walk down.
>
> No; she would not stir out of her PRISON-ROOM.
>
> . . . Well, miss, you would not eat anything, it seems!— Very pretty sullen airs these! (1058–60)

Belford goes to Rowland's at six the next morning. Clarissa has not eaten for three days. She has offered to sell her clothes to pay her debt and is extremely ill. Shocked, Belford describes the filthy room in which he finds her, by her own choice, in majestic white, "illuminating that horrid corner," casually noting the blooming sprigs of flowers in a broken vase. "I thought my concern would have choked me," he confesses, yet his concern is directed against everyone but Clarissa: "Con-Con-Confound you both, said I to the man and woman, is this an apartment for such a lady? Could the cursed devils of her own sex, who visited this suffering angel, see her, and leave her, in so damned a nook?" "Sir, we would have had the lady to accept of our own bedchamber; but she refused it," reply the sympathetic couple, gatherers of the blooming sprigs (1065).

Belford never can bring himself to accuse Clarissa of harming herself, any more than he can bring himself to admit his passive complicity in her rape. In yet another triangle Clarissa's story becomes a means of burying Belford's guilt, foisting it onto other relationships. Although he has ample evidence that she deliberately refuses meals, money, better furnishings, his concern for her behavior always expresses itself as an accusation of his former associates and of Lovelace in particular.

As Clarissa's absence from home renders her story peculiarly moving for those who love her, Lovelace's absence from Clarissa's prison and death chamber makes him a suitably devilish scapegoat against which Belford can measure his own comparatively passive part in Clarissa's destruction. "Why, Lovelace, wast thou not present thyself?—Why dost thou commit such villainies as even thou thyself art afraid to appear in; and yet puttest a weaker heart and head upon encountering with?" Belford demands (1067). Comparing his love for Clarissa with his love for Lovelace, Belford strikes the cruelest blow of all: "I had rather part with all the friends I have in the world, than with this lady: I never knew what a virtuous, a holy friendship, as I may call mine to her, was before. . . . Thank Heaven, I lose her not by MY OWN FAULT!" (1346).

As Belford elaborates Clarissa's trials with ever-increasing horror, ignoring Clarissa's refusal to help herself, accentuating her suffering, blaming Lovelace for the very suffering he so admires, Lovelace cannot help but rebel against Belford's enthusiasm for his role as biographer. "Thou runnest on with thy cursed nonsensical *reformado* rote, of dying, dying, dying, dying! and, having once got the word by the end, canst not help foisting it in at every period! The devil take me, if I don't think thou wouldst give her poison with thy own hands, rather than she should recover and rob thee of the merit of being a conjurer," he charges (1182). "Like Aesop's traveller, thou blowest hot and cold, life and death in the same breath, with a view no doubt to distract me. How familiarly dost thou use the words, DYING, DIMNESS, TREMOR? Never did any mortal ring so many changes on so few bells. Thy true father, I dare swear, was a butcher, or an undertaker, by the delight thou seemth to take in scenes of horror and death," he writes angrily. "Thy barbarous reflection that thou losest her not by thy own fault is never to be forgiven" (1346).

Belford, however, does his work well. Lovelace is never able to untangle himself from the combined stories of Clarissa the girl and Clarissa the saint. "Is death the NATURAL consequence of a rape?" he pleads, after Clarissa has died. "Upon the whole, Jack, had not the lady died, would there have been half so much said of it as there is? Was I the cause of her death? or could I help it? And have there not been, in a million of cases like this, nine hundred and ninety-nine thousand that have not ended as this has ended?—How hard, then, is my fate!" (1439).

Clarissa's death seals Lovelace's fate. Her story is told by a faithful biographer who is well aware of his own guilt and inferiority and proud of his ability to justify and revenge the saint he has helped to make. Lovelace's letters will be interpreted by Belford rather than by Clarissa herself because, as Jonathan Lamb explains, they represent "a chronicle of sufferings she doesn't understand."[39] It is a story that ensures that both Lovelace and both families will love her unconditionally, forever. It is an oppressive story, one that guarantees the perfection she has long agreed to exemplify, one that guarantees Lovelace's perdition.

Saint Clarissa's story is also Lovelace's. Her triumph over him and its perpetuation as legend are possible not because she is perfect and he is imperfect but because both are dualistic characters, as willing to mistrust themselves as others. Terrified that Clarissa's saintly vita will exonerate all her other persecutors at his expense, knowing that their shared language is a version of their story which only he can tell, Lovelace implores that he be allowed to tell the story himself. He pleads:

> I will take her papers. And as no one can do her memory justice equal to myself, and I will not spare myself, who can better show the world what she was, and what a villain he that could use her ill? And the world shall also see, what implacable and unworthy parents she had.
>
> All shall be set forth in words at length. No mincing of the matter. Names undisguised as well as facts. For as I shall make the worst figure in it myself, and have a right to treat myself as nobody else shall; who will control me? (1385)

Like Clarissa, Lovelace does not seem to realize that everyone around

111

him has assumed the "right" to interpret his story according to his or her own needs. He is denied this undertaking, although such a project might well allow him to confront therapeutically his guilt and, perhaps, to avoid the madness he faces.

Unafraid, at last, to allow Clarissa to usurp his place as an only and loved child, Lovelace offers to place her body "in my family vault between my own father and mother," the parents he never knew (1384). The rest of his family remain inappropriately united against him. They do not support the man who can now write: "When I consider all my actions by this angel of a woman, and in her the piety, the charity, the wit, the beauty I have *helped* to destroy, and the good to the world I have thereby been a means of frustrating, I can pronounce damnation upon myself. How then can I expect mercy anywhere else!" Rather, they exacerbate his guilt, "continually ringing charges in [his] ears" (1385).

"Faith and troth, Jack, I have had very hard usage, . . . to have such a plaguy ill name given me, pointed at, screamed out upon, run away from, as a mad dog would be; all my own friends ready to renounce me!" Lovelace laments. The narcissistic tendencies that once tortured him have now become a deeper madness; Mowbray discovers his brilliant and lively friend "silent in a corner, when he has tired himself with his mock-majesty and with his argumentation . . . teaching his shadow to make mouths against the wainscot" (1382–83).[40] Lovelace only escapes a deeper madness by accommodating the now accepted version of Clarissa's divinity. Predictably, he agrees to privilege the world's familiar tendency to judge him according to his reputation. Lovelace consents to remain as voiceless as the Lovelace in his dream, admitting, "Yet I think I deserve it all: for have I not been as ready to give up myself, as others are to condemn me? . . . Who will take the part of a man who condemns himself?—Who can?" (1437).

Because no one has yet tried to take Lovelace's part, or at least to understand it according to his own perspectives, both Clarissa and Lovelace (and often the men and women with whom they deal) have emerged from studies of their story in terms that often resemble Dinnerstein's mermaid and minotaur: "The treacherous mermaid, seductive and impenetrable female. . . . The fearsome minotaur, gigantic and eternally infantile . . . male representative of mindless, greedy power, [who] insatiably devours live human flesh." Both must appear "semi-human and monstrous" when the collaborations, accommodations, and intricacies of interaction between them are dismissed, rationalized, or polarized.[41]

Richardson's age was not unique in producing both unwanted and beloved children who are frustrated, miserable, destructive. The language of their hunger continues to dismay and divide literary scholars, psychologists, and historians, but it also intrigues us into investigating new ways of understanding the similarities between their world and our own. Our understanding of the past and its texts is surely as elusive and important as our understanding of ourselves.

Rachel Brownstein has called Clarissa "the spinach of heroines, served up for our own good."[42] Her story is a sort of food, more nourishing to others than to herself, but she has been taught to consider others' needs as her own and to use hunger as a language to address those needs. As Ellmann points out: "Food is the prototype of all exchanges with the other, be they verbal, financial, or erotic. . . . But there are many nuances of nothingness: and every hunger artist eats a different absence, speaks a different silence, and leaves a different kind of desolation."[43] Perhaps, some day in the future, when we understand the self-destructive behavior of young people as a learned and shared language, we will find a means of addressing the terror of their hunger.

4

A Historical Overview

It is Wednesday night, 22 March. Clarissa has been ordered to her room, no longer sees her parents, no longer eats with the family. No longer eats. Her lively friend Anna sends a consolatory letter containing an amusing portrait of the two men who pursue the prisoner as they might have been as boys at school. "Solmes I have imagined to be a little, sordid, pilfering rogue, who would purloin from everybody, and beg every boy's bread and butter from him; while, as I have heard a reptile brag, he would in a winter morning spit upon his thumbs, and spread his own with it, that he might keep it all to himself," she writes in delight. "Lovelace I have supposed a curl-pated villain, full of fire, fancy, and mischief; an orchard robber." The long-suffering Hickman, Anna's own disregarded beau, was undoubtedly teased and persecuted, a "great over-grown, lank-haired, chubby boy" (209–10).

In all three instances, we notice, the emphasis is on how the subject obtains and eats his food. Solmes hoards and defiles his stolen fare, Lovelace robs, and Hickman accommodates mistreatment and eats too much as well. Moreover, Anna maintains, "The same dispositions have grown up with them, and distinguish the men, with no very material alteration" (210). The Solmes who stole food and then made it repulsive so he would not have to share it is now a miser, deviously plotting for Clarissa's hand in order to gain another estate in proximity to his own. He is notorious for denying his immediate relatives, many of whom are in need, the benefits of his estate, although his title to it is suspect. He is short, squat, fat. Lovelace, the childishly adorable "orchard-robber," is handsome and debonair but a libertine. He considers himself a gourmet in his tastes in women and thinks little of seducing someone else's wife. He cannot be happy with what he has obtained and must always be searching for a better treat.[1]

Hickman is still persecuted, still overweight, still sober and slow.

The notion that food and eating habits are inextricably linked with human behavior and identity is certainly not new. Long before Jean Anthelme Brillat-Savarin's treatise on eating, *The Physiology of Taste*, declared, "Tell me what thou eatest, and I will tell thee what thou art," men and women were associating eating with personality.[2] Similarly, the eating practices of one's own society are typically regarded as natural, and unusual preferences are viewed as barbaric. Shakespeare's audience could safely regard the witches in *Macbeth* as evil solely because they had an unusual taste for soup enriched with "Eye of newt and toe of frog,/Wool of bat and tongue of dog,/Adder's fork and blindworm's sting,/Lizard's leg and howlet's wing."[3] The dramatist could rely on a predictably appalled response. Jonathan Swift relied on the same ability to shock his audience when he suggested cannibalism as a remedy to overpopulation in his satiric essay *A Modest Proposal*.

Anthropologists insist that, just as "cultural traits, social institutions, national histories, and individual attitudes cannot be entirely understood without an understanding also of how these have meshed with our varied and peculiar modes of eating," human behavior must be understood largely as "an interplay between eating behavior and cultural institutions."[4] Researchers of disordered eating have embraced the same assumptions. Clinical psychiatrist Howard Steiger explains:

> While investigations into the cultural practices that code asceticism may elucidate causes of AN [Anorexia Nervosa] in some cases, ultimately I think it necessary to assume that cultural ideals of many kinds (of slimness, of asceticism, of wealth, of power, of self-control, and so on) structure the development of this eating syndrome. AN, and perhaps all syndromes involving marked disturbances in "self" representations, will invariably reflect an interaction between cultural values (i.e., the maladaptive social pressures they can convey) and individuals' "self" structure.[5]

In order to understand this interplay researchers of eating behavior must attempt to investigate and combine both culturally imposed meanings of asceticism and the highly personal language of the individual—an often difficult task.

Behind the notion that "you are what you eat" lies the assumption that an individual can control identity and social status by controlling the amount and type of food which he or she eats—or does not eat. This seemingly simple idea is riddled with political implications. *To eat* is a powerful verb meaning "to consume, assimilate, become." Because food is the human's most fundamental resource and most basic need, and because eating is the only human behavior in which all people in every society engage several times a day, every day, it is perhaps the primary way of initiating and maintaining human relationships, of decreeing social status and sexual roles, and of defining identity. There are many reasons for this, but the most immediate concern economics.

Historically, human beings' most pressing and constant task has always been the production and distribution of food. Anthropologist Hortense Powdermaker relates that in preliterate societies the major part of all activity concerned agriculture, hunting, fishing, and food preparation. Despite arduous work on the part of everyone—men, women, and children alike—"Hunger was a common experience. Famines and periods of scarcity were not unusual. . . . It is, therefore, not difficult to understand that gluttony, one of the original sins in our society, was an accepted and valued practice for these tribal peoples whenever it was possible." In times of plenty, Powdermaker explains, the tribal members would joyously, and quite seriously, eat until they vomited, a practice later copied, although for different reasons, by the Romans.[6]

Changing attitudes toward gluttony seem to have accompanied a change in the social distribution of wealth. In noncommunal societies in which food was scarce and only a privileged few could obtain a sufficiency, being well nourished, or even obese, was considered a sign of power and distinction. Royalty and prosperous families were carried in litters and exercised very little. Plumpness was considered beautiful in young, marriageable girls, perhaps because, as eating disorder specialist Hilde Bruch points out, "Many girls were so under-nourished, scrawny, and skinny that it took this special preparation and indulgence to get them ready for adult life, pregnancy, and motherhood."[7] A massive body implied control of one's body, circumstances, perhaps of others, rather than a lack of control over one's eating habits.[8]

This attitude toward gluttony changed dramatically as societies became more communal. In the Middle Ages eating became a powerful religious symbol, the basic motif of Christianity. In the eucharistic meal, at

116

which God became bread and wine, Christian joined with Christian in one symbolic meal. To fast, to deny oneself earthly food, was simultaneously to feed Christ's body, the Church, and to nourish oneself spiritually. Bynum notes:

> When the medieval authors Bernard of Clairvaux, Mechtild of Magdeburg, Hadewijch, and John Tauler spoke of eating and being eaten by God, their language echoed words voiced centuries before. Augustine of Hippo (d. 430) and Hilary of Poitiers (d. 367) had said that we are all present in the sacrifice and Resurrection of the cross, that Christ, in dying, digests and assimilates us, making us new flesh in his flesh. When Alan of Lille (d. 1203) wrote in his *Summa* for preachers that a faster "must take little food at meals so that part can go to the needs of his neighbor," he was repeating in less resonant and expansive language Leo the Great's exhortation to Christians ["Let the abstinence of the faithful become the nourishment of the poor"] to couple abstinence with almsgiving. When Thomas Aquinas (d. 1274) discussed fasting and abstinence in his *Summa Theologiae,* he carefully examined the patristic notion that humankind fell from paradise through the sin of gluttony.[9]

Within Christian society, with its emphasis on divine recognition of earthly sacrifice, the ability to give away food increasingly entitled one to the status of patriarch; gluttony became a deadly sin and fasting a supreme sacrifice of social as well as of religious significance. "For the hungry, food forces itself forward as an insistent fact, an insistent symbol," explains Bynum.[10] A consideration of this all-encompassing approach to the evils of gluttony may help to explain the enthusiasm with which Richardson's readers embraced Clarissa's self-denial, suffering, and charitable service.

The last volume of Richardson's novel contains constant references to Clarissa's "fasts" and to their effect on others as she is metamorphosed from a girl who does not eat to a saint who does not eat. In keeping with Christian tradition, Clarissa's abstinence nurtures the poor. What she denies herself becomes a fund. Carol Flynn calls this communal self-abnegation "putting on the Christian," pointing out that Clarissa's family can never find relief from her "charity":

Exerting her "will" posthumously, Clarissa punished the family that had punished her in life. We remember "the times they were accustomed to meet together in the family way," times to judge Clarissa and determine new ways to punish, times to force the odious Solmes upon her. Breakfast, tea time, and dinner—all became nightmares for Clarissa. Now, wearing the Christ-like mask of forgiveness, Clarissa can make such occasions nightmares for her family.[11]

If modern critics have suspected the sincerity of Clarissa's virtue, it may well be because her virtuous austerity is grounded on her reputation as a wealthy woman; her contemporaries would probably have celebrated her virtue for precisely these reasons.

Throughout the eighteenth century physicians warned aristocrats that they were particularly prone to the evils of gluttony, evils that would affect not only their own bodies and souls but the course of the nation. Samuel Richardson may well have had such warnings in mind when he wrote *Clarissa* and thus celebrated the virtue of a wealthy woman who controls her circumstances by denying herself both the wealth she has inherited and her meals. Failure in self-control is no less than "self-murder," wrote George Cheyne, advisor and personal physician to Samuel Johnson, John Wesley, David Hume, Alexander Pope, and Samuel Richardson.[12] Although Cheyne's own weight at times approached 450 pounds, he spent his life advocating a regimen of self-denial and was successful in imposing his rather Spartan measures on many of his patients as well. From 1733 on, Richardson undertook not only the laborious business of editing and printing Cheyne's publications (*The English Malady* [1733], *An Essay on Regimen* [1740], *The Natural Method of Cureing* [1742]), but also the more dubious task of following the doctor's advice.[13]

Richardson's willingness to adhere to a strict diet and daily purges for years suggests his apparent appreciation of the rationale behind Cheyne's prescriptions. In his *Essay on Health and Long Life*, printed in 1724 by Richardson's brother-in-law James Leake, the physician pleads, "To cut off our days by intemperance, indiscretion, and guilty passions, to live miserably for the sake of gratifying a sweet tooth, or a brutal itch; to die martyrs to our luxury and wantonness, is equally beneath the dignity of human nature, and contrary to the homage we own the Author of our beings."[14]

Cheyne suggested the existence of a culturally conditioned malady, a distemper particularly associated with the climate and customs of Britain. Of greatest consequence, he maintained, were the dangers of appetite and love of luxury prevalent among the "rich, lazy, and voluptuous" English upper classes and rapidly spreading to the trade classes.[15] Although Cheyne does not specify the point at which gratification becomes indulgence, or comfort becomes luxury, he is clear on one issue: self-denial is to be regarded not only as a matter of personal health but also as a doctrine of national consequence, social responsibility, Christian duty.[16]

In Richardson's *Clarissa,* the equation of power with gluttony is almost immediately apparent.[17] Angry at the encroaching ways of men, Clarissa's friend Anna uses a metaphor of consumption to support a theory of polarity between victims and oppressors. She relates:

> All the animals in the creation are more or less in a state of hostility with each other. The wolf, that runs away from a lion, will devour a lamb the next moment. I remember that I was once so enraged at a game-chicken that was continually pecking at another (a poor humble one, as I thought him), that I had the offender caught, and without more ado, in a pet of humanity, wrung his neck off. What followed this execution?— Why that other grew insolent, as soon as *his* insulter was gone, and was continually pecking at one or two under *him.* Peck and be hanged, said I—I might as well have preserved the first; for I see it is the *nature of the beast.* (487)

The polarity within Anna's metaphor is hard to sustain and cannot quite serve her purpose. According to the story, Anna's humble chicken is never humble to begin with; his insolence is natural. When opportunity presents him with the perception of his potential to oppress, this insolence immediately expresses itself in his behavior to others. One might also argue, however, that the humble chicken is indeed naturally humble and that not until he is elevated from his original circumstances and differentiated from his peers does he "grow" insolent and assume a disposition that corresponds to his new position. Applied to humans, Cheyne's theory of "natural aggression" thus reveals the impossibility of separating individual motivations from culturally conditioned ones in the investigation of eating behavior. For this reason modern therapists embrace a more complex acceptance of the constant interplay of these two considerations.

Clarissa is never able fully to examine this interplay in her dealings with her family and Lovelace because she is enmeshed within it; rather, there is a rigid Cheynien pattern to Clarissa's moral and economic worldview which reveals itself in both her letters and her eating behavior, frustrating her ability to make sense of the power structures and interpersonal dynamics around her. One particularly fascinating episode occurs early in Clarissa's adventures and has been strangely ignored by critics. In order to pass the time while she is confined to her room and prohibited from dining with the family, Clarissa proposes to amuse herself and Miss Howe by relating a bit of a conversation with her sister's saucy maid. "As she attended me at dinner," Clarissa writes,

> she took notice that nature is satisfied with a very little nourishment: and thus she complimentally proved it—For, miss, said she, you eat nothing, yet never looked more charmingly in your life.
>
> As to the former part of your speech, Betty, said I, you observe well; and I have often thought, when I have seen how healthy the children of the labouring poor *look*, and *are*, with empty stomachs and hardly a good meal in a week, that Providence is very kind to its creatures in this respect as well as in all others, in making *much* not necessary to the support of life; when three parts in four of its creatures, if it were, would not know how to obtain it. It puts me in mind of two proverbial sentences which are full of admirable meaning.
>
> What, pray, miss, are they? I love to hear you talk when you are so sedate as you seem now to be.
>
> The one is to the purpose we are speaking of; *poverty is the mother of health;* and let me tell you, Betty, if I had a better appetite and were to encourage it, with so little rest, and so much distress and persecution, I don't think I should be able to preserve my reason.
>
> *There's no inconvenience but has its convenience,* said Betty, giving me proverb for proverb. But what is the other, madam?

> That the *pleasures of the mighty are obtained by the tears of the poor.* It is but reaonable [*sic*] therefore, methinks, that the plenty of the one should be followed by distempers; and that the indigence of the other should be attended with that health which makes all its other discomforts light on the comparison. (263–64)

Clarissa's reasoning suggests that, if needs have been tempered by providence according to human beings' ability to meet them, appetite may signal a destructive desire far more often than actual need. If hunger is less a biological signal of the body's needs than a barometer of social aggression and immorality, lack of appetite should indicate gentleness and moral refinement, qualities that Clarissa wishes to attribute to the well-bred, well-born individual yet apparently associates with the poor and uncorrupted.

This theory of health as a natural result of poverty and of ill health as a divine punishment for the "natural" gluttony of the rich provides an interesting explanation for Clarissa's insistence that she does not need to eat. Lovelace further reinforces the notion of a character naturally above need and out of place in her class by suggesting that Clarissa has circumvented the natural propensities of the rich and has acquired her ability to abstain by abstaining: "She loves to use herself hardily (by which means, and by a temperance truly exemplary, she is allowed to have given high health and vigour to an originally tender constitution)" (400).

If gluttony is a distemper associated with the rich, Clarissa has remained healthy because she is a Cinderella character, a member of a rich family and prone to its taint yet actually enjoying the disposition of a servant, willing to serve, eager to please. This reputation will be of real value to an aristocratic woman whose sufferings and fasts confirm the saintliness that guarantees her "God-like" ability to bestow charitably the wealth she herself rejects.[18]

Clarissa's "fasting," her ability to live solely on the Eucharist, however, is not only a rejection of food but a denying of her company. Clarissa's desire to absent herself from others is a choice that carries both a symbolic weight and a personal message. While the Eucharist may have been the central act of the Church within early communal societies, it was not a feast but, rather, a frugal repast. The emphasis on Christ's body and blood bound all who partook of it in a common human bond. As anthropologist Gillian Feeley-Harnik points out, the early Christians not only "took over Jewish notions of food as the embodiment of God's wisdom" but also continued a tradition of commensality. "From the Christian passover—no longer a private, domestic meal—none was excluded. Rich and poor, Jew and Gentile, coward and hero, all celebrated together. Eating Christ's body was an inclusive act, one that created community."[19]

In all societies eating together is considered a primary way of establishing relationships, of confirming affection, trust, respect, and elaborate meals often become the means of celebrating special family occasions; it is not uncharacteristic, then, that the core of Christian unity should be a symbolic meal or that denying a meal should represent rejection and expulsion from the community. As Maud Ellmann explains:

> It is through the act of eating that the ego establishes its own domain, distinguishing its inside from its outside. But it is also in this act that the frontiers of subjectivity are most precarious. Food, like language, is originally vested in the other, and traces of that otherness remain in every mouthful that one speaks—or chews. From the beginning one eats for the other, from the other, with the other: and for this reason eating comes to represent the prototype of all transactions with the other, and food the prototype of every object of exchange.[20]

Embracing this assumption, some critics have maintained that Clarissa's asceticism is an attempt to cast off her body and to embrace spirituality at the expense of her social interactions.[21] Castle exemplifies this approach to interpreting food refusal, arguing that the heroine's unwillingness to eat suggests a "repudiation of the world of signs and interpretation":

> Having already misread, dreadfully, the signs of edibility, she now refrains from having to make any semantic decisions. ... Betrayed once [by the drug hidden in her tea], ... she saves herself, in this grotesque and perversely self-denying manner, from the task of deciphering. Paradoxically, she would rather starve herself it now seems, than trust her own readings. Those substances looking, smelling, and tasting like food have poisoned her; no food is better than nonfood.[22]

Contemporary feminist research has further complicated the notion that food refusal suggests women's frustration at being "embodied," or inextricably bound up with their bodies.[23] The starving girl, argues Palazzoli, labors under a dualistic logic; she believes that the body and the mind are separate appendages (the former an object she *owns*, the latter what she *is*). To reject the body, then, "is at one and the same time a rejection of sociability, human solidarity and responsibility." Contempt for her body, her rejection of it as an object, is "not the spiritual choice it purports to be, but a purely materialistic escape mechanism reflecting a kind of social 'absenteeism,' and a refusal to become committed to any kind of interhuman relationship."[24] Clarissa, writes Margaret Doody, in a related stance, "is revolted by the suggestion that she become a commodity, and a property.... [She] prefers dying in Covent Garden to going to Pennsylvania."[25]

Differing interpretations of cultural attitudes toward women have thus allowed Clarissa's food-related behavior to be interpreted as both communal and antisocial, self-destructive and empowering. Fasting women have long puzzled and worried physicians and the clergy, precisely because they represent a threat to the concept of community and social solidarity. "Today's anorectic," writes Joan Brumberg, "is one of a long line of women and girls throughout history who have used control of appetite, food, and the body as a focus of their symbolic language." "Historical, anthropological, and psychological studies suggest that women use appetite as a form of expression more often than men."[26] Eating and appetite control, she argues, are powerful social and cultural symbols that lie at the core of debates concerning gender, identity, and class struggles.[27]

While fashion is often blamed for the slimness and pale complexions that have characterized so many unhealthy women from the eighteenth century through modern times, class struggles are often the ground for these ideals. William Law's popular eighteenth-century handbook on child-rearing techniques recounts the story of a mother who insisted that her daughters be tightly laced, denied food, and given constant purges and enemas so that they might retain a fashionably pallid complexion. All became ill, and the eldest died at twenty.[28] Although such misguided practices were universally condemned by doctors and philosophers, they were imposed by loving parents who believed that their daughters' chances in the marriage market depended on an emaciated body and pallid complexion. As historian Lawrence Stone explains: "The importance attached to these matters was a direct result of the decline of money and the rise of personal choice as the most important factor in the selection of a marriage partner. Girls were now competing with one another in an open market, for success in which physical and personal attributes had to a considerable degree taken over the role previously played by the size of the dowry."[29]

By 1792 even aristocratic women were positing a want of appetite as proof of an "exquisite sensibility," and many aristocratic women were making themselves "sickly" in an attempt to compete with women of less privileged classes. Mary Wollstonecraft complained that "false notions of female excellence make [women] proud of this delicacy."[30]

Feminists such as Susie Orbach, Marlene Boskin-Lodahl, and Susan Bordo argue that, in generally prosperous communities, female eating disorders constitute women's response to a misogynistic society that objectifies women's bodies and devalues their emotions. The thin, fragile, subordinate female body is valued within such a society both for aesthetic reasons and because it exemplifies an inherent logic of patriarchal capitalism. In deferring to others, they maintain, a woman comes to hide her needs from herself; in making herself desirable to others, created in another's image, she may end up losing herself completely.[31] Sandra Gilbert and Susan Gubar claim, "Patriarchal socialization literally makes women sick, both physically and mentally." "Learning to become a beautiful object, the girl learns anxiety about—perhaps even loathing of—her own flesh."[32]

In *Fat Is a Feminist Issue* Orbach maintains that "anorexia reflects an ambivalence about femininity, a rebellion against feminization that in its particular form expresses both a reflection and an exaggeration of the image."[33] She elaborates further in *Hunger Strike,* explaining: "Whenever woman's spirit has been threatened, she has taken the control of her body as an avenue of self expression. The anorectic refusal of food is only the latest in a series of women's attempts at self-assertion which at some point have descended directly upon her body. If woman's body is the site of her protest, then equally the body is the ground on which the attempt for control is fought."[34]

Such contemporary feminist analysis has been valuable for its emphasis on the interrelationship between culture, gender, and food, but it assumes that women who refuse food control their refusal in protest of an oppressive system. Maud Ellmann summarizes this attitude, insisting that "*self-inflicted* hunger is a struggle to release the body from all contexts, even from the context of embodiment itself. It de-historicizes, de-socializes, and even de-genders the body."[35] In opposition to such views, I wish to argue that, if hunger is considered a form of discourse, it can no longer be regarded merely as a response to a power system but, rather, must be seen as an interaction—even a collaboration—with an accepted system of understanding. Such a discourse need not be gender specific nor specific to a particular period or society, but it must always be interactive. Eating behavior does not reduce easily to a single cause but exists as part of the interaction between broad cultural, social, and biological forces; any attempt to investigate eating imagery as a vehicle to social commentary must embrace this interactive model. As Hilde Bruch maintains:

> the very organization of awareness of hunger and other bodily needs is the outcome of reciprocal transactional processes within the interpersonal field, and not something inherent in the individual organism. . . . Hunger is not innate knowledge; learning is necessary for its organization into recognizable patterns. . . . Put another way, even when an illness is organic, being sick is a social act.[36]

Contemporary feminist analyses of eating disorders as protests against patriarchy follow centuries of interpretations by men which have categorized female refusal of food as deviant social behavior, typical of women. Just as food preferences and the organization of meals are culturally fixed (although they seem "natural"), self-denial constitutes a behavior peripheral to what society considers normal, and so starving girls have been classified by such thinkers as Freud and Foucault as "hysterical" and "melancholic," even though they appear to exhibit an unusual amount of sagacity and prudence.[37] The malady of "hysteria" took its name from the Greek word for "womb" (*hyster*) because it was thought to be caused by the female reproductive system. Freudian theory was revolutionary, however, in connecting a profound disgust for food with an expression of the sexual drive. In 1895 Freud wrote, "The famous anorexia nervosa of . . . young girls seems to me . . . to be a melancholia where sexuality is undeveloped."[38]

Eleven years later Pierre Janet, director of the psychology laboratory at Salpetriere Clinic in Paris, gave a series of lectures at Harvard Medical School. He declared that anorexia nervosa was due to a "deep psychological disturbance of which the refusal of food is but the outer expression."

Although he differed from Freud in his belief that the anorectic consciously controlled her appetite rather than experienced a complete lack of it, Janet reinforced the notion that such behavior was tied to repressed sexuality.[39] One major result of their approach was that it ensured that the patient had to be spoken with, had to tell her story in her own words, rather than simply be treated for malnutrition. No one had ever before asked the patient why she did not eat.

Repressed sexuality was only one explanation for the baffling disease that allowed seemingly fragile women who barely touched their food to bustle about in a frantic and inexplicable manner. Physical and mental hyperactivity were not only considered conspicuous symptoms of anorexia nervosa but were largely blamed as its cause, at least in the case of women, who were considered too delicate for physical or mental exertion. Early accounts of eating disorders in women stressed the destructive role of mental exertion. In 1645 the governor of the Massachusetts Bay Colony, John Winthrop, laments in his journal that Anne Hopkins "has fallen into a sad infirmity, the loss of her understanding and reason, . . . by occasion of her giving herself wholly to reading and writing, . . . if she had attended her household affairs, and such things as belong to women . . . she had kept her wits."[40] In 1873 Dr. E. H. Clarke, of Harvard University, published *Sex in Education*, which maintains that intense mental effort by women damages their reproductive capacities and that higher education for women thus endangers the species.[41] Wendy Martin records that in the nineteenth century "a thinking woman was considered such a breach of nature that a Harvard doctor reported that during his autopsy on a Radcliffe undergraduate he discovered that her uterus had shrivelled to the size of a pea."[42] It is perhaps no mere coincidence that Jane Eyre learns Hindustani, and in *Middlemarch* Dorothea learns Greek, from men who desire them to become asexual, sterile amanuenses. Jocelyn Harris's argument that Samuel Richardson accepted the reasoning of Locke and Mary Astell and advocated unlimited education for women as a way of reshaping the world would, perhaps, be suspect in its enthusiasm, if viewed within this historical framework.

Richardson surely enjoyed the company of educated women and advocated intellectual endeavors for the "gentle sex," yet the context of his heroine's activities is by no means gloriously subversive. Clarissa has undertaken the study of Latin, but there can be little doubt that Anna Howe's abhorrence of the "man-woman" is meant to be taken seriously:

Were indeed the mistress of the family, like the wonderful young lady I so MUCH and so JUSTLY admire, to know how to confine herself within her own respectable rounds of the needle, the pen, the housekeeper's bills, the dairy, for her amusement; to see the poor fed from superfluities WOULD otherwise be wasted; and exert herself in all the really useful branches of domestic management; then would she move in her proper sphere; then would she render herself AMIABLY useful and RESPECTABLY necessary . . . and everybody would love her. (476)

Clarissa finds a way to subvert the limits of her "proper sphere" without seeming to do so, merely by manipulating the only resources in her power—her body and its demands.

Anna's letter supports Bynum's contention that food is "particularly a woman-controlled resource," a resource that women can manipulate more easily than anything else.[43] Women have traditionally been responsible for preparing and serving meals, so much so, in fact, that medieval men found the female control over sustenance threatening and resented women's power to poison or manipulate them by adding potions to their food. From the story of Eve and the apple through countless folktales and legends to the novels of such current writers as Kaye Gibbons, Clyde Edgerton, and Fanny Flagg, food in the hands of women has been presented as both natural and suspect. Ian Watt equates the rise of the novel itself in part to the increased leisure afforded women who no longer needed to attend to the traditional household duties: "spinning and weaving, making bread, beer, candles and soap"; he is quick to point out, however, that "in the rural areas further from London the economy changed much more slowly, and women certainly continued to devote themselves almost entirely to the multifarious duties of a household that was still largely self-supporting."[44] Clarissa, we are told, inherits from her grandfather an estate that she calls her "dairy-house." Richardson notes:

Her grandfather, in order to invite her to him as often as her other friends would spare her, indulged her in erecting and fitting-up a dairy-house in her own taste. When finished, it was so much admired for its elegant simplicity and convenience that the whole seat, before of old time from its situation called THE GROVE, was generally known by the name of

THE DAIRY-HOUSE. Her grandfather, particularly, was fond of having it so called. (41)

While Clarissa's stock of chickens afford her more amusement than nourishment, the country dairy to which she flees with Lovelace in the first days of her journey to London is obviously self-supporting. When Lovelace suggests inviting one of the young daughters of the family to accompany Clarissa to London, her response reflects an understanding of the girls' value to the dairy: "It were a pity to break in upon that usefulness which the whole family were of to each other: each having her proper part, and performing it with an agreeable alacrity" (442). Clarissa's choice of pronouns and adjectives when she declares that each member of a family consisting of men and women has "her" *proper* part is indicative of what she considers the *proper* roles of men and women. Later, in London, she is poisoned by women—to whom Lovelace has unquestioningly permitted the task of administering a potion in her tea, her beer, her water. When she notices the "odd" taste of the mixture, the prostitutes Lovelace has hired to impersonate his relatives explain that she is drinking "LONDON MILK; far short of goodness of what they were accustomed to from their own dairies" (1008). Clarissa accepts their judgment without question.

"Why, Miss, you have eat nothing at all," exclaims her maid, as she attends Clarissa in the earliest days of her trials at home (264). There can be no question that Clarissa spends most of the last nine months of her life not eating. Clarissa's death has frustrated readers for several centuries precisely because starvation continues to be a most terrifying and confusing language. Hunger has always been a powerful metaphor of suffering and desire. Fear of hunger is so universal that, throughout the centuries, voluntary starvation has been a particularly effective means of impressing and manipulating others. Bruch relates that in ancient Japan a man could effectively humiliate his enemy by "starving against him."[45] In India Ghandi undertook seventeen fasts "to the death" against British colonial rule.[46] The hunger strikes of British suffragettes and of Irish political prisoners are well documented.[47] As Bruch and Ellmann have pointed out, however, "Fasting as a means of coercion is effective only in relation to a responsive partner and in areas where food is abundant and its refusal can be considerably disruptive." Bruch notes that "it is inconceivable that noneating political prisoners in Nazi Germany would have been granted their freedom, or been given any other special consideration."[48]

Once Clarissa's attempt to use food as an analogue to self is placed within the context of her interactions with others, the polarities that have been introduced by two centuries of critics become as questionable as Cheyne's rigid polarities between the classes. If we assume that Clarissa and Lovelace use hunger as a language that both have been taught to respect, then we must also assume that their food-related behavior can function as a discourse only within a supportive community, a community they must either accommodate willingly or create for themselves. Tortured by too many forms of hunger, both children learn to manipulate very dangerous forms of self-definition and discourse. The process by which they learn to participate in these destructive patterns, a process that has been set forth by Richardson with meticulous care, is, to me, just as terrifying as its fatal results.

We know that a linear cause-effect relationship does not exist between societal risk factors and eating disorders (otherwise, as Jane White points out, all females in societies that stress a slender physique or perfectionism would develop these disorders).[49] Profiles of particular family dynamics or personality traits which seem often interrelated with these disorders have been identified, however, and we now know that the developmental issues of autonomy and control which adolescents must face are compounded when they occur within families that are enmeshed, triangulated, and do not possess adequate strategies for addressing conflict. When the developing child attempts to resolve identity issues, body image concerns, or the process of separation-individuation through dieting, an eating disorder is well on its way.

"The threat of eating disorders to women's health today is without question," White insists, and psychiatrists worldwide are agreeing. In a society that is achievement and perfection oriented, women are particularly at risk because women "consider their performance across the *many* domains of their lives (rather than a circumscribed number of domains) to be central to their self definition."[50] Because eating behavior is always an interplay between sociocultural factors and personal motivations, education is an essential strategy in helping to understand the risk factors surrounding young people. This study is based not only on a respect for (and love of) Richardson's fascinating novel but also on my belief that reading the stories of hunger in current and classic literature as instances of discourse can provide one further step in the complex process of decoding the frightening language of hunger.

Notes

INTRODUCTION

1. For an excellent overview, see Vincenzo F. DiNicola, "Anorexia Multiforme: Self-Starvation in Historical and Cultural Context," *Transcultural Psychiatric Research Review* 27 (1990): 165–96.

2. Although my treatment of language differs substantially from Ellmann's fascinating study, we agree on several key assumptions. Most important among them is that "speech is necessarily a dialogue whose meanings do not end with the intention of the speaker but depend upon the understanding of the interlocutor" (*The Hunger Artists: Starving, Writing, and Imprisonment* [Cambridge: Harvard University Press, 1993], 3). The basis of this study is also indebted to Deborah Tannen's work, especially her recent book *Gender and Discourse* (Oxford: Oxford University Press, 1994). As Tannen explains, "Fundamental principles of interactional sociolinguistics include the convictions that (1) roles are not given but are created in interaction; (2) nothing that occurs in interaction is the sole doing of one party but rather is a 'joint production,' the result of the interaction of individuals' ways of speaking" (10).

3. There are many excellent studies in this area. See Kim Chernim, *The Hungry Self: Women, Eating and Identity* (New York: Harper and Row, 1985), for a discussion of food as metaphoric expression of the desire for autonomy. Becky W. Thompson, in *A Hunger So Wide and So Deep: American Women Speak Out on Eating Problems* (Minneapolis: University of Minnesota Press, 1994), challenges the popular notion that eating problems occur only among white, upper-class women. She interviews African-American, Latina, and lesbian women to address the effects of race, poverty, and sexual preference on women's eating patterns. Susan Bordo's book *Unbearable Weight: Feminism, Western Culture, and the Body* (Berkeley: University of California Press, 1993), discusses women's eating habits as conditioned responses to complex cultural messages involving the containment of female hunger, desire, and power.

4. Helena Michie's book *The Word Made Flesh* (Oxford: Oxford University Press, 1987) provides a good bibliography of literary treatments of nineteenth-century hungry heroines and a general summary of their arguments.

5. See Katharine M. Rogers, "Sensitive Feminism vs. Conventional Sympathy: Richardson and Fielding on Women," *Novel* 9, no. 3 (Spring 1976): 257.

6. DiNicola, "Anorexia Multiforme," 179. For a good discussion of the history of the term, see W. Vandereycken and R. Van Deth, "Who Was the First to Describe Anorexia Nervosa: Gull or Lasegue?" *Psychological Medicine* 19 (1989): 837–45.

7. See the American Psychiatric Association, *Diagnostic and Statistical Manual of Mental Disorders*, vol. 69, 3d rev. ed. (Washington, D.C.: APA, 1987).

8. Howard Steiger, "Anorexia Nervosa: Is It the Syndrome or the Theorist That Is Culture- and Gender-Bound?" *Transcultural Psychiatric Research Review* 30 (1993): 352, 350.

9. Di Nicola, "Anorexia multiforme," 179; W. L. Parry-Jones, "Archival Exploration of Anorexia Nervosa," *Journal of Psychiatric Research* 19 (1985): 100; and M. Selvini Palazzoli, *Self-Starvation: From Individual to Family Therapy in the Treatment of Anorexia Nervosa*, trans. A. Pomerans (New York: Jason Aronson, 1974), 3.

10. A. Lipton has outlined a general systems approach to the study of literature for this purpose, in which the reader "observes the interpersonal interactions and makes note of systems data that emerge from close observations of the [literary] family. These systems data reveal the family's differentiation patterns, triangling situations, dimensions of loyalty and autonomy, issues regarding separation and individuation, and extra familial, cultural factors that affect a family's functioning" ("'Death of a Salesman': A Family Systems Point of View," *The Family* 11 [1984]: 60).

11. DiNicola, "Anorexia Multiforme," 177.

12. Jane H. White, "Women and Eating Disorders, Part I: Significance and Sociocultural Risk Factors"; and "Part II: Developmental, Familial, and Biological Risk Factors," *Health Care for Women International* 13 (1992): 351–62, 363–73.

13. Maurice Funke argues that Clarissa's wasting away demonstrates "her total rejection of sexuality and the will to live" (*From Saint to Psychotic: The Crisis of Human Identity in the Late Eighteenth Century* [New York: Peter Lang, 1983], 181). John Dussinger portrays Clarissa's fasting after the rape as a "mortification of the flesh" ("Love and Consanguinity in Richardson's Novels," *Studies in English Literature* 24 [1984]: 519); in "Conscience and the Pattern of Christian perfection in Clarissa" (*PMLA* 81, no. 3 [June 1966]: 243–44) he calls her death by starvation a "complete renunciation of the world, flesh, and devil." Leo Braudy discusses Clarissa's "refusal of physicality," in "Penetration and Impenetrability in Clarissa," in *New Approaches to Eighteenth-Century Literature*, ed. Phillip Harth (New York: Columbia University Press, 1974), 189–97. Ellmann claims that Clarissa fasts to "disembody herself" (*Hunger Artists,* 72). Patricia Meyer Spacks discusses Clarissa's "self-division" in primarily spiritual terms: "Her spiritual self, yearning for translation to another mode of being, would reject the burden of her earthly nature" ("The Grand Misleader: Self-Love and Self-Division in Clarissa," *Studies in the Literary Imagination* 28, no. 1 [Spring 1995]: 17).

14. Terry Castle, *Clarissa's Ciphers: Meaning and Disruption in Richardson's "Clarissa"* (Ithaca: Cornell University Press, 1982), 124–25. Castle and William Warner argue that *Clarissa* thematizes interpretation. Their acrimonious debate over the role of language in the novel has been widely discussed. See Quentin Kraft, "On Character in the Novel: William Beatty Warner versus Samuel Richardson and the Humanists," *College English* 50, no. 1 (January 1988): 32–47; and Warner's reply to Castle in "Reading Rape: Marxist-Feminist Figurations of the Literal," *Diacritics* (Winter 1983): 12–32.

15. Focusing on the character of the conventional eighteenth-century rake, John Carroll argues that Lovelace is "manacled to convention" ("Lovelace as Tragic Hero," *University of Toronto Quarterly* 42, no. 1 [Fall 1972]: 24). See also Penelope Biggs, "Hunt, Conquest, Trial: Lovelace and the Metaphors of the Rake," *Studies in Eighteenth-Century Culture*, ed. Harry C. Payne, 2 (1982): 51–64. Tom Keymer argues that Lovelace is portrayed as "the archetypal enemy of society" in his recent book *Richardson's "Clarissa" and the Eighteenth-Century Reader* (Cambridge: Cambridge University Press, 1992), 157. Lois Beuler offers that *Clarissa* weaves three fairly stereotypical plot structures with recognizable precedents in Christian mythology, drama, and classical ethics (*"Clarissa"'s Plots* [Newark: University of Delaware Press, 1994]). See Tassie Gwilliam's discussion of gender ideology in *Clarissa* and of Lovelace as a character with "cross-gender identifications" (*Samuel Richardson's Fictions of Gender* [Stanford: Stanford University Press, 1993], 51–110). See also John Dussinger, "*Clarissa*, Jacobitism, and the 'Spirit of the University,'" *Studies in the Literary Imagination* 28, no. 1 (Spring 1995): 55–65.

16. Contemporary figures show that self-starvation is still a particularly female experience, but it is by no means gender restrictive. Reports indicate that perhaps 5 to 10 percent of patients treated for AN are male. See D. J. Carlat and C. A. Camargo Jr., "A Review of Bulimia Nervosa in Males," *American Journal of Psychiatry* 148, no. 7 (1991): 831–43; W. Vandereycken and A. Van Den Broucke, "Anorexia Nervosa in Males: A Comparative Study of 107 Cases Reported in the Literature (1970–1980)," *Acta Psychiatrica Scandinavica* 70 (1984): 447–54; and H. Steiger, "Anorexia Nervosa and Bulimia in Males: Lessons from a Low Risk Population," *Canadian Journal of Psychiatry* 34 (1989): 419–24.

17. Tannen, *Gender and Discourse,* 13.

18. Critical approaches to *Clarissa* have commonly characterized Richardson, his writing, and his time as "divided" or "dual." Variations of this stance include Eagleton's view of the author as "a contradictory figure" (*The Rape of Clarissa* [Minneapolis: University of Minnesota Press, 1982], 101); Flynn's argument that "Richardson himself held a double view of himself and his writing" (*Samuel Richardson: A Man of Letters* [Princeton: Princeton University Press, 1982], ix, xii, x); Fiedler's argument that the conflict between the characters represents "a psychological division in the soul of the man itself" (*Love and Death in the American Novel* [New York: Stein and Day, 1960], 29–42); Golden's affirmation that there is "a split that goes through his life and all of his writings" (*Richardson's Characters* [Ann Arbor: University of Michigan Press, 1963], 192); and Izubuchi's argument that "there are indeed two Richardsons," the Richardson of theory and the Richardson of practice ("Subversive or Not? Anna Howe's Function in *Clarissa,*" in *Samuel Richardson: Passion and Prudence,* ed. Valerie Grosvenor Myer [London: Vision Press, 1986], 89). In a discussion of William Warner's portrayal of the authors Quentin Kraft celebrates Warner's elucidation of "the tensions between the two Richardsons," explaining, "Warner finds Richardson divided between two opposed principles of being. It is as if Richardson were at once two quite distinct men, each with his own motive for writing. While Warner opposes the aims of Richardson the critic, he defends the interests of Richardson the novelist." He con-

cludes, "The struggle between the two critics, Warner and Richardson, is as well a struggle between two versions of Richardson: the creator and novelist versus the interpreter and critic" (Kraft, *Reading "Clarissa"* [New Haven: Yale University Press, 1979], 32).

19. See Deborah Tannen, *You Just Don't Understand: Women and Men in Conversation* (New York: William Morrow, 1990), 18.

20. Tannen, *Gender and Discourse*, 7–8.

21. Dorothy Dinnerstein, *The Mermaid and the Minotaur: Sexual Arrangements and Human Malaise* (New York: Harper and Row, 1976), 3.

22. Jane Tompkins, "Me and My Shadow," *New Literary History* 19 (1987–88): 169–78.

23. Rachel Mayer Brownstein, "'An Examplar to Her Sex': Richardson's Clarissa," *Yale Review* 67 (1977): 39–40.

24. For example, I quote from Alice Miller's book, *The Drama of the Gifted Child,* trans. Ruth Ward (New York: Basic Books, 1981); Maclean accuses Miller of "depoliticizing women's anger" ("Citing the Subject," in *Gender and Theory: Dialogues on Feminist Criticism,* ed. Linda Kauffman [Oxford: Basil Blackwell, 1989], 148).

25. Nancy J. Chodorow, *Feminism and Psychoanalytic Theory* (New Haven and London: Yale University Press, 1989), 94.

26. Ellmann, *Hunger Artists,* 16.

CHAPTER 1: HUNGER AT HOME

1. Samuel Richardson, *Clarissa,* ed. Angus Ross (New York: Penguin Books, 1985), 39. All further references are to this edition and are cited within the text. Although the AMS 1751 edition is generally considered preferable for scholarly purposes, I have chosen to use the Ross edition because it is the most accessible to students.

2. For an interesting discussion of this letter's possible effect on the reader in terms of Anna's "hunger for knowledge," see Patricia Meyer Spacks, "The Novel as Ethical Paradigm," *Novel* 21, nos. 2–3 (Winter–Spring 1988): 181–88.

3. Clarissa's memory of a happy childhood has fueled critical debates. Stevenson accepts her perceptions, explaining: "If we look at the prehistory (that is, the time before page one) of the Harlowes, the picture that emerges is that of a household dominated by Clarissa . . . she is the constant center of attention . . . it is this period of personal adulation that Clarissa recalls throughout the novel like some lost golden age of perfect family harmony" ("The Courtship of the Family: Clarissa and the Harlowes Once More," *ELH* 48 [1981]: 771). Doody argues that Clarissa must discover "that her view of her childhood and her always-loved place in the family was a fiction" because "the fictions of each individual about personal iden-

tity (of self and others) are inevitably inadequate" ("Disguise and Personality in Richardson's *Clarissa*," *Studies in the 18th Century*, ed. Jocelyn Harris, 12, no. 2 [May 1988]: 28–29). This position is not unlike Castle's argument that Clarissa is guilty of a "failure of insight" in not realizing that "'being a sister' is purely conventional—part of a sentimental ideology of kinship. The Harlowes expose familial obligation itself as a fictional construct—to Clarissa's distress" (*Clarissa's Ciphers*, 74).

4. For a Lacanian analysis of this dilemma, see Katharine Cummings, "Clarissa's 'Life with Father,'" *Literature and Psychology* 32, no. 4 (1986): 30–36. See also Stevenson, "Courtship of the Family," in which he discusses the family's adulation of their youngest daughter and her remembrance of the "golden age of perfect family harmony" as an insidious form of family self-definition. Stevenson cleverly argues that the Harlowes exploit both Clarissa and Solmes, urging them toward a marriage that would allow Clarissa to remain a family possession.

5. Alice Miller, *The Drama of the Gifted Child: The Search for the True Self,* trans. Ruth Ward (New York: Basic Books, 1981), 74–75. As Linda Kauffmann writes: "Clarissa does not maintain that she is a paragon of virtue. . . . The word *possession* reverberates through the novel because of its sexual and proprietary overtones and because *self-possession* is what everyone denies Clarissa" (*Discourses of Desire*, 133, 135).

6. In "The Trauma of Eventlessness," *Psychoanalysis and Women: Contributions to New Theory and Therapy,* ed. Jean Baker Miller, M.D. (New York: Brunner/Mazel, 1973), Dr. Robert Seidenberg insists that it is crucial that we consider the contrasting destinies of sibling rivals. The "hopelessness" of an overlooked sibling must not be simplified as "pent-up sexualized or deneutralized aggression" (362). Discussions of Clarissa's siblings do, however, tend to rely on these formulas. In *Clarissa's Ciphers* Castle argues that the Harlowes' treatment of Clarissa is conditioned by "ill will alone" (67). Stevenson calls the novel a Cinderella story about sibling rivalry ("Courtship of the Family," 773). Janet Todd describes Arabella as "physically [*sic*] ill-favored . . . soured into a jealous and rancorous sister" (*Women's Friendship in Literature* [New York: Columbia University Press, 1980], 26). For Todd, Arabella is the victim of a "patriarchal sisterhood . . . where women must compete through waiting for men," but Todd does not allow this to excuse the "physical, mental, and spiritual inequality between [Arabella] and her sister." Her Arabella is naturally and irredeemably "the ugly-stepsister . . . indolent, envious, spiteful, and unrelenting . . . cruel like a man, even bloodthirsty" (31–33). Lilian Furst also refers to Clarissa's mother, sister, and aunt as "older, socially conditioned women siding with the masculine established phalanx" but suggests that Clarissa's "unrecognized and uncontrolled emotions" contribute substantially to her sufferings ("The Man of Sensibility and the Woman of Sense," *Jahrbuch fur Internationale Germanistik* 14, no. 1 [1982]: 14–15).

7. Counseling psychologists exploring the separation-individuation process in adolescence from both psychodynamic and systems perspectives agree that "it involves a gradual resolution of the conflict between maintaining a feeling of con-

nectedness in family relationships and the establishment of autonomous ego functioning in the individual" (Sandra L. Perosa and Linda M. Perosa, "Relationships among Minuchin's Structural Family Model, Identity Achievement, and Coping Style," *Journal of Counseling Psychology* 40, no. 4 [1993]: 479). Family therapist Andolfi writes, "Disturbed behavior is a signal that needs for autonomy and differentiation have been sacrificed to maintain dysfunctional family relationships" (*Family Therapy: An Interactional Approach,* trans. H. C. Cassin [New York: Plenum, 1979], 11). See also P. Blos, *On Adolescence: A Psychoanalytic Perspective* (New York: Free Press of Glencoe, 1962); C. Cooper, H. Grotevant, and S. Condon, "Individuality and Connectedness in the Family as a Context for Adolescent Identity Formation and Role-Taking Skill," in *New Directions in Child Development,* vol. 22: *Adolescent Development in the Family,* ed. R. H. Grotevant and C. Cooper (W. Damon, ser. ed.) (San Francisco: Jossey-Bass, 1983), 43–49; H. Grotevant and C. Cooper, "Patterns of Interaction in Family Relationships and the Development of Identity Exploration in Adolescents," *Child Development* 56 (1985): 425–28; D. Harvey and J. Bray, "Evaluation of an Intergenerational Theory of Personal Development: Family Process Determinants of Psychological and Health Distress," *Journal of Family Psychology* 4 (1991): 298–325; R. Josselson, "Ego Development in Adolescence," in *Handbook of Adolescent Psychology,* ed. J. Adelson (New York: Wiley, 1980), 188–210; and also "The Embedded Self: I and Thou Revisited," in *Self, Ego, and Identity: Integrative Approaches,* ed. D. K. Lapsley and F. C. Power (New York: Springer, 1988), 91–108; and S. Quintana and J. Kerr, "Relational Needs in Late Adolescent Separation-Individuation," *Journal of Counseling and Development* 71 (1993): 349–54.

8. Alan Macfarlane. *Marriage and Love in England: Modes of Reproduction, 1300–1840* (Oxford: Basil Blackwell, 1986), 61.

9. See Randolph Trumbach's argument that the change in the death rate was not due to a lessening in disease or to improvements in nutrition but, rather, to the quality of care aristocratic children were now receiving from their mothers. Until mid-century aristocratic women had generally been discouraged from accepting the intimate care of their children, yet Trumbach notes that cultural changes in the family structure were shifting at this time to allow women far more say in the raising of their children. He claims, "above all children require for their psychological well-being that they forge a strong bond of attachment to a single mothering figure, and it is very likely that a child who has forged such a bond will not only be happier but healthier as well, and more likely to live" (*The Rise of the Egalitarian Family: Aristocratic Kinship and Domestic Relations in Eighteenth-Century England* [New York: Academic Press, 1978], 187–88). Trumbach derives his account of attachment theory from John Bowlby, *Attachment and Loss,* 2 vols. (London: Hogarth Press, 1969–73); Marion J. Levy et al., *Aspects of the Analysis of Family Structure* (Princeton: Princeton University Press, 1965); and Lionel Tiger and Robin Fox, *The Imperial Animal* (New York: Holt, Rinehart and Winston, 1971), 56–68.

10. Lawrence Stone, *The Family, Sex and Marriage in England, 1500–1800* (New York: Harper and Row, 1977), 435–36.

11. See Lady Mary Wortley Montagu, *The Letters of Lady Mary Wortley Montagu,* ed. Wharncliffe (Lord), 3 vols. (London: R. Bentley, 1837), ii, 414.

12. While this child-oriented century saw its share of indulged children and devoted parents, affectionate parents did not feel that their identities depended on their children. Far more common were complaints that indulged children had become demanding and undisciplined by Clarissa's age or that they openly resent and resist the submission of the will required by authoritarian parents who consider them prodigies. See Stone's account of Mrs. Thrale's ambitious forced promotion of her children, a story he calls "atypical" but "firmly embedded in the culture of her time and her class" (Stone, *Family, Sex and Marriage,* 458–63).

13. See Bruch, *Eating Disorders,* chap. 5, 66–86.

14. Sofie Lazarsfeld points out the necessity of keeping in mind the difference between "the sound striving for perfection and the neurotic wanting to be perfect." She notes: "In every human being there is a striving to grow, to improve, a striving for perfection. . . . It is a healthy and necessary attribute as long as it manifests itself within the range of common sense and with social interest. . . . In perfectionism the fiction of perfection takes the place of real achievement and this facade then has to be maintained at all cost, whatever may happen" ("The Courage for Imperfection," *Individual Psychology* 47, no. 1 [March 1991]: 93). In his discussion of perfectionism Adler argued, "To reach a neurotic goal, no expense will seem too high" (*The Individual Psychology of Alfred Adler* [New York: Basic Books, 1956], 266). See also Adler, *Superiority and Social Interest* (Evanston, Ill.: Northwestern University Press, 1964); and Arnold Rothstein's "On Some Relationships between Fantasies of Perfection and the Calamities of Childhood," *International Journal of Psycho-Analysis* 72 [1991]: 313–23.

15. Avis Rumney, *Dying to Please* (Jefferson and London: McFarland and Company, 1983), 2, 6. It is interesting to note Rumney's use of the gender-specific term *mothering* to describe the giving of warmth and encouragement. W. R. D. Fairbairn also relates conditional love to the development of the schizoid personality; he writes, "disturbed development results when the mother does not succeed in making the child feel she loves him for his own sake and as a person in his own right" (qtd. in Harry Guntrip, *Personality Structure and Human Interaction* [New York: International Universities Press, 1961], 284).

16. In her reading of the novel Rachel Brownstein perfectly captures the nightmarish confusion that surrounds the individuals caught in dysfunctional roles:

> The characters who besiege and torment Clarissa Harlowe have clear motives, coherent natures, identifiable voices; they are differentiated, well drawn, the creations of a fine novelist; yet they have the lurid common coloration of figures in a delusion. One feels the people in the novel are compelled to be what they are, that they do not choose to be themselves. Both events and character seem to be determined, half-willingly undertaken or assumed, confining. The heroine's character and her destiny are on the one hand remarkable, chosen by a strong, tenacious will, and on the other hand inevitable, helplessly submitted to. (*Becoming a Heroine,* 41)

She does attempt to account for this duality. Although she acknowledges that the exemplar "is not born but made," she does not examine the process (43).

17. Bruch, *Eating Disorders,* 262.

18. Hilde Bruch, *The Golden Cage* (New York: Random House, 1978), 59.

19. In an interesting discussion of this incident Janet Butler claims that "Clarissa *chooses*—but her consciousness will not admit it. Instead, she dissociates from herself and for the single time in the novel speaks of herself, as of another person ('the fool'), in the third person. With more psychological insight than he knew, Richardson depicted what happens to the mind when an idea, inadmissible to the conscious self, splits off." Butler suggests that Richardson so worried that Clarissa's duality at this point might be construed as conscious complicity in her elopement that he changed the wording of the incident in the 1751 edition to stress her lack of volition ("The Garden," 540–42).

20. For a very different discussion of Clarissa's self-splitting, see Spacks, "Grand Misleader."

21. Studies in the history of family relations and early childhood education point to the mid-eighteenth century as a time when self-determination was generally advocated as a goal in child-rearing practices—to the point, often, of overt permissiveness. Rousseau's *Emile* was widely read in England, and most writings on child-rearing practices recognized that the child has a unique individual personality that can best be developed through happiness and relaxed self-enrichment. Rigid control over a child's expression of his or her needs was neither recommended nor condoned. For an interesting summary of writings from the time, see Stone, *Family, Sex and Marriage,* 403–15. Stone concludes, "Eighteenth-century noblewomen, and even noblemen, wanted themselves to be remembered—as affectionate, even doting, mothers and fathers—and in many cases . . . the reality approximated the ideal" (412). Lower classes took their lead from the nobles.

22. See Bruch on dysfunctional families (*Eating Disorders,* 67–104).

23. While studies suggest that the process of separation-individuation from the mother is more difficult for girls and that these conflicts persist longer in females, Clarissa's complete internalization of her mother's needs is decidedly unhealthy. See H. J. Beattie, "Eating Disorders and the Mother-Daughter Relationship," *International Journal of Eating Disorders* 7 [1988]: 453–57.

24. James Andrew Hogg and Mary Lou Frank, "Toward an Interpersonal Model of Codependence and Contradependence," *Journal of Counseling and Development* 70 [1992]: 371.

25. Harriet Goldhor Lerner, *The Dance of Anger* (New York: Harper and Row, 1985), 188. While Chodorow believes that "when a mother's whole life and sense of self depends on rearing 'good' or 'successful' children, this must produce anxiety over performance and over-identification with children" (*Feminism,* 41–42), Lerner maintains that this anxiety may be more likely to occur in the child; the destruc-

tive demands on self and other thus become a vicious circle as mother and child interact. See also Phyllis Greenacre, *Emotional Growth: Psychoanalytic Studies of the Gifted and a Great Variety of Other Individuals* (New York: International Universities Press, 1971). Greenacre posits that the gifted infant has a greater sensitivity to sensory stimulation and therefore becomes more intensely involved with early personal objects. For such a child there is always a fantasy audience; this may be the reason the gifted child often shows artistic capacities, although his or her personality may tend to become split into a "creative" self and a conventional, social self (490–98). For the exemplar these two become merged.

26. Miller, *Drama of the Gifted Child,* 8, 22, 28, 32, 35, 46, 85.

27. This inappropriate mirroring/merging should not be confused with the "double identification," which may occur when "a woman identifies with her own mother and, through identification with her child, she (re)experiences herself as a cared-for child" (Chodorow, *Feminism,* 48). See Melanie Klein and Joan Riviere, *Love, Hate and Reparation* (New York: W. W. Norton, 1964); and Helene Deutsch, *The Psychology of Women* (New York: Grune and Stratton, 1944 and 1945): "In relation to her own child, woman repeats her own mother-child history" (1:205); both are quoted in Chodorow, *Feminism,* 48–49. Nor am I referring to the preoedipal symbiosis that might occur for a daughter whose mother prolongs the period of mother-infant attachment. See chapter 9 (on *The Reproduction of Mothering*) in Hester Eisenstein's discussion of the mother's tendency to see the infant as coextensive with herself (*Contemporary Feminist Thought,* 90–91).

28. Bruch, *Eating Disorders,* 56. In *Toward a New Psychology of Women* Jean Baker Miller points out that women have traditionally been encouraged to come to see their needs as identical to the perceived needs of others (usually men or children) (19). This sort of transference is vastly complicated in Clarissa's case because she is expected to internalize the needs of a very troubled mother, to sacrifice herself sexually to save her mother's marriage. Clarissa's desire not to cause contention between her parents (a typical wish of any child) is thus exploited, making her compliance far more complex than mere boundary confusion. A study of boundary confusion between mothers and daughters is discussed at length in Deutsch, *Psychology of Women.* See also Philip Slater, "Toward a Dualistic Theory of Identification," *Merrill-Palmer Quarterly of Behavior and Development* 7 (1961): 113–26. Carol Gilligan's study *In a Different Voice: Psychological Theory and Women's Development* (Cambridge: Harvard University Press, 1982) argues that women tend to delineate themselves in terms of relationships.

29. S. Minuchin, B. Montalvo, B. G. Guerney Jr., B. L. Rosman, and F. Schumer, *Families of the Slums: An Exploration of Their Structure and Treatment* (New York: Basic Books, 1967), 221.

30. Richardson would seem to have had an appreciation for submissiveness in wives. His first major exercise, *Letters Written to and for Particular Friends, on the Most Important Occasions Directing Not Only the Requisite Style and Forms to Be*

Observed in Writing Familiar Letters; But How to Think and Act Justly and Pru-
dently, in the "Common Concerns of Human Life," was published in 1741, when he
was fifty-two years old. Of the one hundred and seventy-three letters almost half
concern love and marriage; included are a letter admonishing a daughter not to talk
back to her husband even if he is wrong, a reproof to a wife who scolds her servants
and insists on absolute cleanliness in housekeeping at the expense of her husband's
domestic peace, and a warning to a daughter not to show her jealousy of her husband whether founded or not. (See discussion of Richardson's views on marriage in
Eaves and Kimple, *Samuel Richardson: A Biography* [Oxford: Clarendon Press, 1971],
94–95). His correspondence with Lady Bradshaigh during 1751–52 involves a raging
dispute over the issue of wifely subjection and fear. He writes, "I am sorry to say it,
but I have too often observed that fear, as well as love, is necessary, on the lady's part,
to make wedlock happy" (*Correspondence of Samuel Richardson,* intro. Anna Laetitia
Barbauld, 6 vols. [1804; reprint, New York: AMS Press, 1966], iv, 129). One must,
however, balance these professions against the author's reputation as a quiet and
gentle friend to numerous women and his own admission to Miss Mulso that "I was
always a meek husband; but now I am quite a tame one" (*Correspondence,* 3:234).

31. Henry Home Kanes, *Loose Hints upon Education* (Edinburgh: Bell, Robinson,
and Murray, 1782), 228–29; qtd. in Willystine Goodsell, *A History of Marriage and
the Family,* rev. ed. (New York: Macmillan, 1934), 322.

32. Mary Astell, *Some Reflections upon Marriage* (1730; reprint, New York: Source
Book Press, 1970), 43. William Cobbett echoes these sentiments when he reminds
young girls what they give up on their wedding days: "[The bride] makes a surrender, an absolute surrender, of her liberty, of the joint lives of the parties: she gives
the husband the absolute right of causing her to live in what place, and in what
manner and what society, he pleases; she gives him the power to take from her,
and to use, for his own purposes, all her goods, unless reserved by some legal
instrument; and, above all, she surrenders to him her *person.*" See William Cobbett,
Advice to Young Men (1829), ed. H. Morley (London, 1887), 167–68; qtd. in
Macfarlane, *Marriage and Love,* 149.

33. See Stone's extensive study (*Family, Sex and Marriage,* 405–78).

34. Stone notes, "Mrs. Boswell was far from unique" when in 1778 she was "unable
to think herself happy without her children and so allowed her philandering husband to go to London without her" (See J. Boswell, *Life of Samel Boswell LLD,*
Everyman edition [London, 1906], 2:160; qtd. in Stone, *Family, Sex and Marriage,*
456). Lady Sarah Lennox attributed her closeness to her children to their recognizing her as "the object of their father's tender love and care, seeing me at the
same time holding a high place in his estimation as his friend and companion"
(*Life and Letters of Lady Sarah Lennox, 1745–1826,* ed. Countess of Ilchester and
Lord Stavordale [London,1902], 599). Such testimonies were widespread and vastly
at odds with Mrs. Harlowe's subservience to her husband and manipulation of
her daughter for his sake.

35. *Letters,* 3:23; 1:174–75.

36. Brownstein, *Becoming a Heroine*, 41, 45, 77. In "'An Examplar to Her Sex': Richardson's Clarissa" she is more forthright, insisting that Clarissa's oppression has less to do with her gender than with her excellence: "the Examplar is a Puritan version or adaptation of the cliche that a woman is a goddess, a convention of courtship, literature, and polite society which ... serves in fact to oppress women.... the chastity for which she is celebrated endows her with value as a commodity: because she is unworldly, the Examplar is desired and imitated and besieged by the world" (35).

37. Concentrating on Fauchery's claim that the destiny of any eighteenth-century heroine depended on defloweration, Nancy Miller accepts as conventional the Harlowes' sudden transformation from a family proud of their little girl to a family brutally aware of her sexual value as a marriageable woman. See "The Exquisite Cadavers: Women in Eighteenth-Century Fiction," *Diacritics* (Winter 1975): 37–43. In his fascinating essay "The Courtship of the Family: Clarissa and the Harlowes Once More" John Stevenson twists this insight, arguing that, when the heroine achieves sexual maturity, her family members join in an insidiously incestuous plot to possess their exemplary daughter forever, yet he, too, explains their behavior by assuming that marriage as exchange and incestuous desire are cultural universals (*ELH* 48 [1981]: 757–77). In a similarly complicated and enjoyable discussion of triangular desire (*ressentiment*), James H. Maddox Jr. develops the idea that the family's desire for the exemplary Clarissa is both envious and incestuous ("Lovelace and the World of Ressentiment in *Clarissa*," *Texas Studies in Literature and Language* 24, no. 3 [Fall 1982]: 271–92). Janet Todd and Terry Castle also assume that all Clarissa's sufferings are the result of the patriarchal system, suggesting that even the women who oppress the heroine have been ruined by its contagion. They cannot explain, though, how the angelic heroine has managed to escape the fate of her peers. See Castle, *Clarissa's Ciphers;* and Todd, *Women's Friendship in Literature.*

38. As Maurice Funke points out: "Avarice is simply not developed as a motive sufficiently strong for the father to curse his daughter, the mother to ban her and the entire family to reject her even when she is on the verge of death. However, if we view the Harlowe family as a symbol of society as a whole, the author's intentions become clear" (*From Saint to Psychotic*, 55). Jocelyn Harris advises that *Clarissa* is, at best, a vehicle for the author's political voice: "Domestic relations, at that time, reflected for political theorists like Filmer and Locke the social relations of the state; while conversely, in the edgy amorous civil warfare of Restoration plays, characters very much like Richardson's bandied about the risky terminology of usurpation, tyranny, slavery, rebellion, liberty and birthright. . . . Whenever Richardson wrote of relationships, . . . he inevitably wrote of politics" (*Samuel Richardson* [Cambridge: Cambridge University Press, 1987], 33).

See also Nancy Armstrong's correlation of the household as a "counterimage" of the political world (*Desire and Domestic Fiction: A Political History of the Novel* [Oxford: Oxford University Press, 1987]); and Kay's contention that Richardson used domestic debates to comment on political institutions through the influence of public opinion (*Political Constructions: Defoe, Richardson, and Sterne in Relation to Hobbes, Hume, and Burke* [Ithaca and London: Cornell University Press, 1988]).

Pointing out that both Clarissa's father and Lord M. are weak authority figures, Florian Stuber argues that *Clarissa* is about the partly illusory nature of authority and the heroine's attempts to imitate an idealized image of the commitments of paternity ("On Fathers and Authority in *Clarissa,*" *SEL* 25 [1985]: 557–73).

Not unpredictably, many feminist critics have discussed the politics of paternity so apparent in the novel in terms of what Furst calls "the male urge to dominate and the female tendency to submit" ("Man of Sensibility," 15). Janet Todd argues persuasively that Clarissa suffers at the hands of men within patriarchy and women "who have assimilated its views and become its implements" (35–43). Judith Wilt maintains that Lovelace has lost his "feminine" virtue through the machinations of the depraved "patriarchal" whores ("He Could Go No Farther: A Modest Proposal about Lovelace and Clarissa," *PMLA* 92, no. 1 [1977]: 19–32). See also Brian McCrea's essay "Clarissa's Pregnancy and the Fate of Patriarchal Power," *Eighteenth-Century Fiction* 9, no. 2 [January 1997]: 125–48).

39. Trumbach notes that after 1720, and certainly by 1753, enforced marriages had become generally unacceptable, and mercenary marriages were especially condemned (97–113). In 1779 Boswell maintained that a father had no right to control the inclination of his daughter in marriage (see George Birkbeck Hill, ed., *Boswell's Life of Johnson,* 6 vols. [Oxford: Clarendon Press, 1887], 3:377). Macfarlane writes: "There was an . . . old and vocal tradition of criticizing those parents who took too much power into their own hands. The warnings were widespread in the eighteenth century" (*Marriage and Love,* 133). William Buchan warned: "The first thing which parents ought to consult in disposing their children in marriage, is certainly their inclinations. Were due regard always paid to these, there would be fewer unhappy couples, and parents would not have so often cause to repent the severity of their conduct, after a ruined constitution, a lost character, or a distracted mind, has shewn them their mistake" (*Domestic Medicine,* 11th ed. [Hartford: Nathaniel Patten, 1789], 119–20; qtd. in Macfarlane, *Marriage and Love,* 133).

40. T. R. Malthus, *An Essay on Population,* 2 vols., Everyman Library (n.d.; reprint, London: Dent, 1933), 2:184.

41. Richard Allestree, *The New Whole Duty of Man,* 24th ed. (London, 1792), 202–3; qtd. in Stone, 412.

42. *Letters,* 1:19; 2:77.

43. *The Spirit of the Laws,* 2 vols., trans. Thomas Nugent (New York: Hafner Publishing, 1975), 2:6; qtd. in Macfarlane, *Marriage and Love,* 125.

44. See Macfarlane's discussion (*Marriage and Love,* 126–28), in which he writes: In the eighteenth century, Richard Burn pointed out that by "civil" law (that is, Roman law), men under the age of 25 and women under 20 could not marry without parental consent. (Richard Burn, *Ecclesiastical Law,* 4 vols., 15th Edn, 1788., ii, 403) . . . [But] in only one part of Europe—England—did Roman law never reassert itself. There the common law, equally based on old Germanic custom, instead of stifling the canon law, lent it support in emphasizing that marriage was

solely a contract between the two parties. To be valid, like all contracts, it needed their consent; but it was not, ultimately, a contract that required any other parties' agreement. (Macfarlane, *Marriage and Love,* 126)

45. Macfarlane, *Marriage and Love,* 128. See also P. M. Bromley, *Family Law,* 4th ed. (London: Butterworth, 1971), 24–25.

46. Macfarlane, *Marriage and Love,* 129.

47. Qtd. in Macfarlane, *Marriage and Love,* 129. Perhaps because of this notion of freedom in consent, the ideal of the companionate marriage flourished during the eighteenth century according to principles set forth by such writers as John Locke, who maintained that marriage "draws with it mutual support and assistance, and a communion of interests too" (*The Second Treatise of Government,* ed. J. W. Gough, 3d ed. [Oxford: Basil Blackwell, 1966], 40). Macfarlane points out that throughout the century numerous editions of the enormously popular book *The New Whole Duty of Man* professed love as an essential prerequisite of Christian marriage and promoted the primacy of the husband-wife relationship: "No law obliges a man to marry; but he is obliged to love the woman whom he has taken in marriage" (*New Whole Duty,* 227). Macfarlane points out that the marriage ceremony itself suggests that a wife need only obey if the husband be loving: "The husband first promises to love his wife, before she promises to obey him: and consequently his love is the condition of her obedience" (176). Robert Brain notes that the ideology of romantic love as a necessary bond in the conjugal relationship continues to subvert the arranged marriage systems it encounters around the world because "the power of the ideology is unquestioned" (*Friends and Lovers* [New York: Basic Books, 1976], 245–48).

48. Buchan, *Domestic Medicine,* 120. qtd. in Macfarlane, 137.

49. Macfarlane, *Marriage and Love,* 138–39.

50. Janet Todd rightly notes that Mrs. Harlowe's dutiful passivity actually reduces her husband at the same time it nullifies her will, thus problematizing its merit (*Women's Friendship,* 28).

51. Chodorow states that "most psychoanalytic and social theorists claim that the mother inevitably represents to her daughter (and son) regression, passivity, dependence, and lack of orientation to reality." Because she never establishes adequate ego boundaries, the mother indirectly encourages the growing child to break the psychological unity by projecting what she sees as a "bad" dependence onto the mother (*Feminism,* 59–64). I find Clarissa's insight of her mother's active passivity far more mature than a girlish oedipal rejection of her mother. It is more along the lines of the "essential female tragedy" Adrienne Rich describes when she protests: "Many daughters live in rage at their mothers for having accepted, too readily and passively, 'whatever comes.' A mother's victimization does not merely humiliate her, it mutilates the daughter who watches her for clues as to what it means to be a woman" (*Of Woman Born: Motherhood as Experience and Institution* [New York: W. W. Norton, 1976], 237, 243). In Clarissa's case, however, there

is a recognition that her mother is actively collaborating with her oppressors, offering Clarissa as a hostage to buy her own peace.

52. Castle calls this scene with the mother a "surreal dialogue," an "archetypal" demonstration of the "instability in human sign systems [which] makes possible the abusive situation in Harlowe-Place" (*Clarissa's Ciphers*, 70–72). While she maintains that distortions in communication cause this family to be dysfunctional, I believe that distorted communication is a symptom of the dysfunctional family, not its cause.

53. Miller, *Drama of the Gifted Child*, 6.

54. It is interesting to note here that Lovelace, too, is expected to be accommodating. He obliges a family whose members have an "appetite" for his stories of debauchery even when he has come to hate them himself. At a time when he is most inclined to honest affection for Clarissa, he is forced to play the rake for a hypocritical peer (1023–25).

55. Rachel Brownstein discusses this tendency in terms of the threatening recesses of Gothic houses, images that function as a metaphor for the heroine because "part of herself makes another part its victim" (see *Becoming a Heroine*, 58; and "'An Examplar to Her Sex,'" 30).

56. See Miller, *Drama of the Gifted Child*, 12–13.

57. See Stuber's analysis of the dreams in *Clarissa* in "*Clarissa:* A Religious Novel?" *Studies in the Literary Imagination* 28, no. 1 (Spring 1995): 105–24.

58. In this sense Clarissa is indeed the "hermeneutic casualty" Castle portrays in *Clarissa's Ciphers* (16). Our studies differ, though, in several important ways. What I believe to be a structured pattern of destructive behavior typified by indirect communication, she describes as "license" and "a kind of hermeneutic libertinage" inherent in language itself (54–55). In maintaining that Clarissa is powerless and silenced, she shows that the heroine is compelled to accept ideas of herself, but she does not recognize Clarissa's willing accommodation of this compulsion, blaming it, instead, on Lovelace (164).

59. Studies show that lack of family cohesiveness, parental inequality of treatment of siblings, and family conflict during discussion of sibling problems can lead to highly aggressive behavior between siblings. See E. Mark Cummings, "Marital Conflict and Children's Functioning," *Social Development* 3, no.1 [1994]: 16–36; G. H. Brody, Z. Stoneman, and M. Burke, "Family System and Individual Child Correlates of Sibling Behavior," *American Journal of Orthopsychiatry* 57 [1987]: 561–69; and G. H. Brody, Z. Stoneman, J. K. McCoy and R. Forehand, "Contemporaneous and Longitudinal Associations of Sibling Conflict with Family Relationship Assessments and Family Discussions about Sibling Problems," *Child Development* 63 [1992]: 391–400.

60. John A. Sours, *Starving to Death in a Sea of Objects* (New York: Jason Aronson, 1980), 319.

61. Sours, *Starving to Death*, 329. In their study of suicidal adolescents Mary Mitchell and David Rosenthal argue that the management of hostility in the families of such children is often a covert process: "The triangulation of the child is adaptive serving" and functions as a "solution in the management of spousal conflict," often related to role orientation and disagreements over child rearing. There are often no clear boundaries surrounding the marital dyad in such families, and yet they present a superficially healthy appearance that effectively masks the child's problems with familial rigidity and enmeshment ("Suicidal Adolescents: Family Dynamics and the Effects of Lethality and Hopelessness," *Journal of Youth and Adolescence* 21, no. 1 [1992]: 32). While there is no indication that Clarissa is suicidal at this point, her family uncannily fits this profile. Clarissa often laments during her confinement at home that she did not die of a childhood fever and in fact dies of apparent self-starvation only months later.

62. Hardwick's comment that Clarissa's parents "have not reached the point of trusting the sentiments" is oversimplified in view of these distortions in feeling (*Seduction*, 207).

63. There have been many critical attempts to analyze the distorted intercourse between various members of the Harlowe hierarchy. Christopher Hill explains these odd transfers of authority in terms of plans for family aggrandizement in a patriarchal society in which all members of the family must jealously guard family interests (which become synonymous with James's interests). His solution is inviting and supportable, yet the struggle between the Harlowes, their inability to communicate at all, seems far more complex than mere family interest would explain ("Clarissa Harlowe and Her Times," *Essays in Criticism* 5 [1955]: 315).

64. Castle relates the lack of authority in this family to the rhetorical "death of the author" (*Clarissa's Ciphers*, 170). Lack of authority seems to me less of a problem than the fact that it has been suspended or transferred inappropriately. As Rachel Brownstein points out, the heroine has a "surplus of fathers" because of the family's collusion (*Becoming a Heroine*, 51). Linda Kauffman also notes that Clarissa is "surfeited with father figures" (*Discourses of Desire*, 132).

65. A phrase coined by Harriet Lerner (*Dance of Anger*) to describe the intricate and repetitive steps followed by participants in triangular relationships.

66. Lerner, *Dance of Anger*, 123–24, 140–42. This notion of collusion is a complication of Jean Baker Miller's argument that women transform their needs into those of their families (*Toward a New Psychology*, 19–20). This concept of mediated desires can be compared to critical theorist Rene Girard's discussions of triangular desire in narrative, but in this case characters are not victims of mediation but, rather, active participants in the pattern (see Girard, *Deceit, Desire, and the Novel: Self and Other in Literary Structure*, trans. Yvonne Freccero [Baltimore: Johns Hopkins University Press, 1965]).

67. Lerner, *Dance of Anger*, 155–56.

68. Many critics have argued that the epistolary form is actually responsible for the indirect communication and mediation in Clarissa's world. Castle claims that

"the novel in letters constantly reminds the reader of the problem of origins" which makes any direct communication possible (*Clarissa's Ciphers*, 152). In *Epistolarity: Approaches to a Form* (Columbus: Ohio State University Press, 1982) Janet Altman similarly argues that letter writing, from the beginning, "serves a mediatory function" and emphasizes the circuitous communications between characters: "frequently . . . one character 'comes into the presence' of another by letter only, and not necessarily through a letter addressed to that person. . . . When she writes her mother, her Uncle John responds for the mother; Clarissa then writes her Uncle John, but her Uncle Antony replies for him; when Clarissa writes her Uncle Antony, her sister answers brutally." While Altman and I agree that "the use of letters in *Clarissa* serves to emphasize the estrangement and isolation of the title character, such an indirect device being emblematic of the psychological and physical barriers separating her from her family, Lovelace, and friends," she immediately theologizes this insight, claiming that letters emphasize the "moral distance" between heaven, the world, and hell within Richardson's "moral landscape," as Clarissa undertakes a mythic pilgrimage from the Eden of Harlowe Place to the world of Sinclair's and then to paradise. Mediation thus becomes confused with intercession between the sacred and the profane (22–26).

69. Bruch, *Eating Disorders*, 49.

70. For an interesting discussion of systemic family therapy and social psychological theory of interaction involving eating disorders, see F. Kroger, A. Drinkmann, W. Herzog, and E. Petzold, "Family Diagnostics: Object Representation in Families with Eating Disorders," *Small Group Research* 22, no. 1 [February 1991]: 99–114.

71. M. Dadds, M. Morrison, M. Rebgetz, and M. Sanders, "Childhood Depression and Conduct Disorder: II. An Analysis of Family Interaction Patterns in the Home," *Journal of Abnormal Psychology* 101, no. 3 [1992]: 506. See also, M. R. Dadds, M. R. Behrens, and J. E. James, "Marital Discord and Child Behavior Problems: A Description of Family Interactions during Treatment," *Journal of Clinical Child Psychology* 16 [1987]: 192–203.

72. Rumney, *Dying to Please*, 2.

73. Dare, Eisler, Russell, and Szmulker write, "The presence of such distinctive qualities as enmeshment, poor intergenerational boundaries, rigidity and problems in conflict resolution defines the structure of the anoretic famil[y]" ("The Clinical and Theoretical Impact of a Controlled Trial of Family Therapy in Anorexia Nervosa," *Journal of Marital and Family Therapy* 16 [1990]: 53).

74. Sours, *Starving to Death*, 320.

Chapter 2: The Hungry Lover

1. The increasingly accepted eighteenth-century view of companionate marriage as a commitment that privileges the husband-wife rather than the parent-child

relationship as the most important psychological and social bond may help to justify Lovelace's insistence that Clarissa prefer him to her family before he can marry her. Stone explains such an ideology as a product of changing views toward marriage: "The shift along the continuum from arranged marriage to individual choice has implications for demographic features because it alters the balance within the family. The romantic-love ideology justifies children in breaking away from family control. They marry for 'love' and can now put their conjugal relationship first, above their ties to parents and siblings" (Stone, *Family, Sex and Marriage*, 122).

2. John Dussinger notes: "To some extent [Lovelace] may be genuinely sympathetic with Clarissa's rebelliousness. Both begin as allies against the patriarchal tyranny, and, however different their destinies, both rely on their psychic resources to confront a system ostensibly unchangeable" ("Love and Consanguinity," 520).

3. Kay, *Political Construction*, 187.

4. Stevenson, "Courtship of the Family," 763–64.

5. Lovelace's reference to this explosive family meeting as a "comedy" has enraged many critics. Few give him credit for what might be painful sarcasm. Although he manages to tease his relatives and tries to appear casually confident, a real undercurrent of discomfort runs through his account of his "trial."

6. Arranged economic marriages were rapidly becoming archaic in Richardson's time, and his correspondence shows that he did not accept or advocate them; as the title page to *Clarissa* states, these forced arrangements constituted "misconduct" on the part of both parents and children.

7. These considerations include not only the economic well-being of their households but the extent to which each might remain a welcome child of that household.

8. Brownstein notes, "When the two are together, their reports back to the hostile camps of their allegiance exacerbate their opposition" (*Becoming a Heroine*, 64).

9. William Warner argues that "one factor that makes Clarissa's story complex is the evidence that Clarissa is raped by a man she loves, and Lovelace rapes a woman he loves." He refers to this as an instance of the "vexed ambivalence of human desire" ("Reading Rape: Marxist-Feminist Figurations of the Literal," *Diacritics* [Winter 1983]: 22, 28). I see it more as an instance of the distorting effect of triangular anger on love.

10. Of Clarissa, Brownstein comments, "It is not megalomaniacal to want to be significant; it is only human" (*Becoming a Heroine*, xv). This truth can surely apply to Lovelace as well.

11. Margaret Anne Doody and Florian Stuber's statement that "fear of Clarissa's superiority is one of the motives for the rape" is surely true if Lovelace's fear is considered as part of a conditioned insecurity ("Clarissa Censored," *SEL* 29 [1988]: 85).

12. Harris, *Samuel Richardson*, 71. Linda Kauffman elaborates: "By dismissing Clarissa's pain after the rape as a 'mere notional violation,' Lovelace negates the body, holding rigidly to dichotomies in which mind can triumph over matter, intellect over the senses. But in lamenting that Lovelace 'killed her head,' Clarissa is asserting that intellect cannot be separated from the body. Her mind is devastated when her maidenhead is destroyed; both are united in unspeakable pain that is well-nigh unbearable precisely because it is both psychic and physical" (*Discourses of Desire*, 142).

13. See Richetti's interesting discussion of Lovelace as a divided character and of the constructed nature of his rakish personality. Richetti rightly notes that even such constructions require reciprocity and are collusive in nature ("Lovelace Goes Shopping at Smith's: Power, Play, and Class Privilege in *Clarissa*," *Studies in the Literary Imagination* 28, no. 1 [Spring 1995]: 23–34.)

14. These protestations have unfortunately led numerous critics to accuse Clarissa of hypocrisy and complicity in her own rape. Elizabeth Hardwick writes, "[Lovelace] at last rapes [Clarissa], since she will not have it otherwise" (*Seduction and Betrayal: Women and Literature* [New York: Vintage Books, 1975], 208). In a similar vein Dorothy Van Ghent forwards V. S. Pritchett's suggestion that Clarissa "'represents that extreme of puritanism which desires to be raped.' In a sense, she keeps her cake while eating it" (V. S. Pritchett, *The Living Novel* [New York: Reynal and Hitchcock, 1947], 28; qtd. in Van Ghent, *The English Novel: Form and Function* [New York: Harper and Row, 1961], 61). Rachel Brownstein protests such approaches: "It is oversimplification to call Clarissa a hypocrite—to read *Clarissa* as a novel about repressed sexuality is to reduce it to banality" ("Examplar," 36).

15. Harris, *Samuel Richardson*, 63.

16. In opposition to critics such as Hardwick, who calls Lovelace "a monomaniac who seeks life through sex" (*Seduction and Betrayal*, 208), Carol Kay feels that Richardson is not at all convincing in his claims of Lovelace's insatiable sexual appetite because there is only one sex act in the book and "he shows no attraction to any other woman" (*Political Constructions*, 176). While this statement is admittedly problematized in the third edition, in which Lovelace's previous affairs (many ending in paternity) are detailed, his relationship to Clarissa is never one of sexual debauchery (as he constantly reminds her). Were Lovelace really a lust-crazed fiend, surely he would have raped Clarissa on their first night at St. Albans instead of offering a sincere proposal of marriage. Zomchick calls Lovelace "a mere slave to lust" but concedes, "Even though his imagination provides him with ways of aping, baffling, and circumventing the law, it cannot provide him with alternatives to the distorted human relationships generated by the very structures he opposes" ("Tame Spirits," 100–101, 111).

17. This view of Richardson's characters is popular. Carol Flynn argues that Richardson used the fantastic/romantic to lure his reader into a consideration of conventional morality. Flynn's interpretation of the novel rests on the supposition that Richardson was exploring point of view. Lovelace is not really the monster he

seems to be, she argues, in an interesting twist, but, "since we see and experience what Clarissa does, we also see him as a monster, as terrible as any that ever stalked a fairy tale." This approach is engaging, but it does not question why Clarissa should see Lovelace as a monster, why she should accommodate or resist the views of others, how she might resist or lament her perceptions (*Samuel Richardson,* 146–47, 149).

18. Flynn, *Samuel Richardson,* 248–49. See also Spacks, "Grand Misleader."

19. I feel that the application of modern psychology to literary characters is not only possible but important if literature is to help us understand ourselves and our world. For a defense of this view, see Heinz Kohut, "Psychoanalysis and the Interpretation of Literature: A Correspondence with Erich Heller," *Critical Inquiry* 4 (1978): 433–50. See also Bernard Paris, *A Psychological Approach to Fiction* (Bloomington: Indiana University Press, 1974), in which the author argues that motivations and behavior of literary figures may be observed and analyzed as though they were real persons. Paris relies on the methodology of Karen Horney combined with close textual analysis. For an intriguing application of Paris's work to *Clarissa,* see Patricia Eldredge's unpublished doctoral dissertation "Samuel Richardson's 'Clarissa': A Psychological Study" (Michigan State University, 1983). Eldredge uses Horney's approach to provide a convincing account of Lovelace's narcissism. See also Maud Ellmann's fascinating comparison of *Clarissa* and Irish hunger strikers (in *Hunger Artists*).

Psychologists seem to lack the compunctions that characterize literary historians when it comes to examining fictional portrayals of behavior which exemplify theoretical psychological concepts and illuminate patients' behaviors. Two related studies include Arthur Robbins's examination of the behavior exhibited by Dickens's character Harold Skimpole in *Bleak House* in relation to descriptions of grandiosity set forth by W. Bonime and I. Alger in "*Grandiosity:* An Overview," *Psychotherapy-Patient* 5, nos. 3–4 (1989): 17–26; and Scott Johnson's study of family enmeshment, parentified children, coalitions and triangles, and disordered eating in "Structural Elements in Franz Kafka's 'The Metamorphosis,'" *Journal of Marital and Family Therapy* 19, no. 2 (April 1993): 149–57.

20. Richardson's deliberate attempts to blacken Lovelace's character in subsequent editions reinforce a psychological approach to this character. For example, Lovelace's wild scheme to kidnap both Anna and Mrs. Howe and to rape them at sea carries his grandiose and narcissistic tendencies to an extreme. Psychologists maintain that these "male" fantasies can be especially common for boys in households in which the father is conspicuously absent (see Alexander Mitscherlich, *Society without the Father* [New York: Schocken Books, 1970]). Roger Burton and John W. M. Whiting argue that "father-absence" may lead to gang behavior, including "strong denial of anything feminine, with corresponding emphasis on masculinity—on risk and daring, sexual prowess, rejection of home life, and physical violence . . . as requirements of gang membership" ("The Absent Father and Cross-Sex Identity," *Merrill-Palmer Quarterly of Behavior and Development* 7 [1961]: 90–91; qtd. in Chodorow, *Feminism,* 39). Lovelace's "confraternity" of rakes, most of whom do not have homes and claim to despise marriage and women, might be considered as just such a gang. Seen as typical gang behavior, Lovelace's scheme,

combined with his original mistrust of himself, combine to portray a remarkably disturbed young man.

21. "Grandiosity: An Overview," *Psychotherapy-Patient* 5, nos. 3–4 (1989): 21.

22. "Narcissistic Pathology of Everyday Life: The Denial of Remorse and Gratitude," *Contemporary Psychoanalysis* 26, no. 3 (1990): 439.

23. In *The Analysis of the Self* (New York: International Universities Press, 1971) Heinz Kohut argues, "The equilibrium of primary narcissism is disturbed by the unavoidable shortcomings of maternal care, but the child replaces the previous perfection (a) by establishing a grandiose and exhibitionistic image of the self: *the grandiose self;* and (b) by giving over the previous perfection to an admired, omnipotent (transitional) self-object: *the idealized parent imago*" (25). If Lovelace narcissistically perceives Clarissa as a self-object, he will be dependent on her and experience her as a missing part of himself. Melanie Klein argues that such idealization involves "fantasies of merging of the self with good, unrealistically idealized objects." See Otto Kernberg's discussion of Klein in *Internal World and External Reality: Object Relations Theory Applied* (New York and London: Jason Aronson, 1980), 32–33.

24. "Grandiosity: The Shadow of Shame," *Men Healing Shame,* ed. Roy U. Schenk (New York: Springer, 1995), 208.

25. "If the King Feels Grandiose, He Thinks He Is a God," *Psychotherapy-Patient* 5, nos. 3–4 (1989): 181. Carl Goldberg notes, "Grandiosity is a fantasized reconstruction of self, which excludes the importance of real people and the hard work of maintaining caring and equitable interpersonal relationships in the development of selfhood" ("'Mirror of Your Eyes,'" *Psychotherapy-Patient* 5, nos. 3–4 [1989]: 197).

26. Miller, *Drama of the Gifted Child,* 33.

27. For an early study of healthy narcissism, see Kohut, "Forms and Transformations of Narcissism," *Journal of American Psychoanalytic Association* 14 (1966): 243–72. Many critics argue that the oedipal phase, rather than preoedipal separation, is responsible for insecurity in boys. Margaret Mead maintains that a boy's training is different from a girl's in that it involves no identification of the self with the mother: "His upbringing . . . is characterized by its conditional nature . . . love and approval are dependent upon success" (*Male and Female* [New York: William Morrow, 1949], 295); Karen Horney relates this anxiety toward the mother to the adult male's "dread of women," arguing that the tendency to glorify or to debase women may be a response to this oedipal fear ("The Dread of Women," *International Journal of Psychoanalysis* 13 [1982]: 351). Chodorow suggests that because a boy is encouraged to define masculinity in negative terms, "as that which is not feminine," he is forced to denigrate whatever he perceives to be feminine both inside himself and in the outside world. All his action, therefore, is an expression of insecurity (*Feminism,* 44, 51). Dinnerstein blames the early relationship of the male child with his mother on men's need to dominate women and their fear of female autonomy (*Mermaid,* 91).

28. M. Mahler, *On Human Symbiosis and the Vicissitudes of Individuation* (New York: International Universities Press, 1968); qtd. in Miller, "Depression and Grandiosity as Related Forms of Narcissistic Disturbances," *International Review of Psycho-Analysis* 6, no. 61 (1979): 63.

29. Miller, *Drama of the Gifted Child,* 17, 21. There is much controversy among psychoanalytic theorists of narcissism about whether it is an attempt to recover a lost experience of perfection—a state of primary narcissism lost during childhood—or, rather, an exaggerated attempt to achieve the perfection all humans naturally seek. Arnold Rothstein discusses the variety of perspectives and theoretical frameworks associated with the term in "An Exploration of the Diagnostic Term 'Narcissistic Personality Disorder,'" *International Journal of Psycho-Analysis* 72, no. 2 (1991): 313–23. See Alford's discussion of Daniel Stern's highly contested view that "at no time is the infant so cognitively and emotionally undeveloped that it experiences itself as fused with the mother and the world, an experience that for many theorists is the paradigm of narcissistic wholeness and bliss. Rather, this notion is an elaborate secondary construction, albeit an enormously powerful one" (*Narcissism: Socrates, the Frankfurt School, and Psychoanalytic Theory* [New Haven: Yale University Press, 1988], 8; discussing Daniel Stern, *The Interpersonal World of the Infant: A View from Psychoanalysis and Developmental Psychology* [New York: Basic Books, 1985]).

For an interesting review of the implications of Alice Miller's theories of narcissism as self-object loss for clinical psychology, see David Kitron's "Depression and Grandiosity: Clinical and Theoretical Issues in the Treatment of Narcissistic Disturbances," *Journal of Contemporary Psychotherapy* 24, no. 3 (1994): 203–11.

30. Harris, *Samuel Richardson,* 76.

31. Miller, *Drama of the Gifted Child,* 15. Psychoanalysts have long been fascinated by the tendency of narcissistic patients to develop grandiose fantasies; most point to inadequate early parental care as the usual cause of such personality disorders. Writing of Heinz Kohut's theories in *Narcissism and the Text: Studies in Literature and the Psychology of Self* (New York and London: New York University Press, 1986), editors Lynne Layton and Barbara Ann Schapiro explain, "the persistence of archaic grandiosity is often due to an unempathetic parent (usually the mother), who can neither recognize the child's in-phase needs for merger-mirror-approval nor gradually discourage out-of-phase demands of the child's grandiose self" (5). For Melanie Klein, Harry Guntrip, and W. R. D. Fairbairn grandiosity is distinctly related to preoedipal disappointment. Guntrip asserts that personality disorders develop as a defense against "the more serious dangers of the earlier psychotic conditions" (*Personality Structure and Human Interaction* [New York: International Universities Press, 1961], 311). Jacobson also stresses the importance of the early mother-child relationship, claiming that proper individuation cannot occur without help from a mature and empathetic parent (Edith Jacobson, *The Self and the Object World* [New York: International Universities Press, 1964]). See also D. W. Winnicott's concept of "good-enough mothering" as that ability of the parent to "[meet] the omnipotence of the infant and to some extent [make] sense of it" so that his or her infantile grandiosity will be tamed and not cause a sense of despair

in adulthood (*The Maturational Processes and the Facilitating Environment: Studies in the Theory of Emotional Development* [New York: International Universities Press, 1965], 145.

32. Referring to his inability to engage Clarissa in a healthy way, Zomchick declares that Lovelace's heart "can neither receive nor return fellow-feeling," that he is "a mere slave to lust" ("Tame Spirits, Brave Fellows, and the Web of the Law: Robert Lovelace's Legalistic Conscience," *ELH* 53, no. 1 [Spring 1986]: 111–12). D. C. Rain is frightened at the "extent of evil" that exists in the heart of this man ("Richardson's *Clarissa*," review essay in the *Explicator* 47, no. 1 [Fall 1988]: 12–15). Castle calls him a "Male-Delinquent" playing with "his 'bauble' Clarissa" (*Clarissa's Ciphers*, 26). Kay writes of his "lack of desire to appear in a consistent character" but does not pursue her insight that "Lovelace does not claim for himself the expression of an authentic, inner self any more than Clarissa does" (*Political Constructions*, 178). "He is so self-alienated that he feels nothing at all," Linda Kauffman decides (*Discourses of Desire*, 153).

33. Qtd. in Guntrip, *Personality Structure*, 287. In "*Clarissa* and Ritual Cannibalism" (*PMLA* 105, no. 5 [October 1990]: 1083–94) Raymond F. Hilliard argues that object-relations theory provides an insight into Lovelace's "peculiar mixture of aggression and affection" for Clarissa. In attempting to tie all orality in the novel to ritual cannibalism, however, he oversimplifies his approach, insisting that Lovelace rapes Clarissa out of preoedipal "infantile rage."

34. The obsession with the unattainable object has been discussed by many theorists. The chronic feeling of emptiness, of blankness, which Lovelace associates with the loss of Clarissa is discussed by Kernberg as a characteristic of narcissistic personality structure, in *Borderline Conditions and Pathological Narcissism* (New York: Aronson, 1975). Guntrip uses a metaphor of consumption to describe the tortured dependence of the infantile narcissist, for whom relationships are "both a mutual swallowing and a mutual merging, and the patient is never quite sure at any given moment whether he feels most as if he is being swallowed or doing the swallowing. . . . Thus the patient in a state of marked infantile dependence is always both inordinately possessive towards the love-object and yet feels helplessly dependent and loses personality to the love-object (*Personality Structure*, 315–16). Fairbairn's theory of the terror of object relations is perhaps the most expressive: "The more the need to love is frustrated, the more intense does it become and the unhappy person oscillates between an overpowering need to find good objects and a compulsive flight into detachment from all objects, under pressure mainly of the terror of exploiting them to the point of destruction" (qtd. in Guntrip, *Personality Structure*, 287). Penelope Biggs suggests this theory when she writes of Lovelace: "He might even be compared to the child going round and round the block, who explains that he is running away from home but not allowed to cross the street" ("Hunt, Conquest, Trial," 55–56).

35. Olga Cheselka, "Strategies of Interpersonal Power," *Contemporary Psycho-Analysis* 27, no. 4 (October 1991): 705–6.

36. Cheselka, "Strategies," 318.

37. Cheselka, "Strategies," 708.

38. Miller, *Drama of the Gifted Child*, 15, 89–90.

39. "The Golden Fantasy: A Regressive Reaction to Separation Anxiety," *International Journal of Psycho-Analysis* 58 (1977): 314.

40. Miller, *Drama of the Gifted Child*, 38. Winnicott also believes that overintellectualization may become a defense for gifted persons with disturbed personalities. Such frustrated individuals may develop the intellect into a "false self" that either suppresses the "true" (inner or feeling) self or forces it to live a secret life, denying it integration with the social self that masks it (see *Maturational Processes*). Tompkins's article "Me and My Shadow" discusses in similar fashion the discomfort many professional women feel when the demands of their work force them to perceive themselves as two such separate beings, completely dissociated. "The healthiest relation," write Layton and Schapiro, occurs when one is able to form "a compromise between the compliant, false self, and the true self" (*Narcissism and the Text*, 13).

41. Quentin Kraft confuses this duality with self-delusion when he writes that, although Lovelace may see himself as a hero, "whenever it suits his purposes, he thinks of himself in quite a different way, indeed in an opposing way. And when he does, he thinks that he is a being distinct from his actions and totally independent of them. Such a way of thinking enables him to tell himself that the rape of Clarissa does not much affect what he is [because] . . . he is still a 'gentleman.'" Kraft maintains that "as we do, so *in effect* we are" ("On Character in the Novel: William Beatty Warner versus Samuel Richardson and the Humanists," *College English* 50, no. 1 [January 1988]: 44).

42. Harris, *Samuel Richardson*, 52.

43. Smith, "Golden Fantasy," 311. At the center of grandiose fantasies there is always a wish for respect, attention, unconditional acceptance. Miller explains,

For example: I am in the center, my parents are taking notice of me and are ignoring their own wishes (fantasy: I am the princess attended by my servants); my parents understand when I try to express my feelings and do not laugh at me (fantasy: I am a famous artist, and everyone takes me seriously, even those who don't understand me); my parents are rich in talents and courage and not dependent on my achievements; they do not need my comfort nor my smile (they are king and queen). This would mean for the child: I can be sad or happy whenever anything makes me sad or happy; I don't have to look cheerful for someone else, and I don't have to suppress my distress or anxiety to fit other people's needs. I can be angry and no one will die or get a headache because of it. I can rage and smash things without losing my parents. (16)

44. D. W. Winnicott, "The Use of an Object," *International Journal of Psychoanalysis* 50:700, 716; qtd. in Miller, *Drama of the Gifted Child*, 16.

45. Lovelace's parents died when he was young; we know little of them, beyond the

fact that Clarissa considers the father "a man of honour" and the mother one "who deserved a better son" (912). During Lovelace's "trial" Lord M. exclaims, "How would my sister Lovelace have reproached herself for all her indulgent folly to this favourite boy of hers, had she lived till now," revealing (through the term *folly* more than *indulgent*) a conflict that may well have existed between the parental figures in this extended family during the boy's youth (1036). Lovelace attempts to rationalize his frustrating duality by blaming his parents, but his attempt is weak and generalized: "I have seen parents (perhaps my own did so) who delighted in those very qualities in their children, while young, the natural consequences of which (too much indulged and encouraged) made them, as they grew up, the plague of their hearts" (789). From this mention of "those very qualities" one does get the sense, however, that Lovelace was also taught to perceive himself as a gifted, "special" child.

46. Miller, *Drama of the Gifted Child*, 42.

47. "You will allow, that in both [matrimony and dancing], man has the advantage of choice, woman only the power of refusal" (Jane Austen, *Northanger Abbey* [New York: Penguin Books, 1972], 95).

48. "Truth to tell, Anna *is* Lovelace's rival," argues James Maddox ("Lovelace," 283). For a fascinating view of this triangle as an erotic one, see Todd, *Women's Friendship*, 56–60; see also Pettit, "Wit, Satire, and Comedy."

Chapter 3: Saintly Hunger

1. T. C. Duncan Eaves and Ben D. Kimpel, *Samuel Richardson: A Biography* (Oxford: Clarendon Press, 1971), 282.

2. Kinkead-Weekes, *Samuel Richardson*, 271.

3. A. O. J. Cockshut, *Man and Woman: A Study of Love and the Novel, 1740–1940* (New York: Oxford University Press, 1978), 35.

4. Stuber suggests, "In its essence, *Clarissa* is a psychological analysis of moral phenomena; the literary imagination which created it is informed by a secular humanism which may be justified by, but which is not dependent upon, the Christian system" ("*Clarissa*: A Religious Novel?" 122).

5. Cockshut, *Man and Woman*, 42. Mullen agrees, "*Clarissa* stages a virtue which soars as it renounces practical involvement in the world" (*Sentiment and Sociability*, 66). In an intriguing essay Janet Aikens questions whether Richardson scholarship might have taken a different view of the heroine's accomplishments had more women contributed to it ("*Clarissa* and the New Woman: Contexts for Richardson Scholarship," *Studies in the Literary Imagination* 28, no. 1 [Spring 1995]: 67–86).

6. Cockshut, *Man and Woman*, 43. Anne Robinson Taylor argues, "[Richardson] manages to create a mythic figure, yes, but one who is surely terrible and frightening" (*Male Novelists and Their Female Voices: Literary Masquerades* [Troy, N.Y.:

Whitston Publishing, 1981], 58). Pursuing this theme, Margaret Anne Doody writes that both Clarissa and Lovelace are "immoderate people in a world which counsels a debased moderation [and so] they find themselves solitary in a society which has little to say to them. . . . Clarissa is . . . without knowing it, a martyr for her faith." She concludes, "The eighteenth century, hardly less than the twentieth, finds martyrdom displeasing" (*A Natural Passion: A Study of the Novels of Samuel Richardson* [Oxford: Clarendon Press, 1974], 102–5).

While "excellence is in itself a kind of mortal illness . . . not native to the world, nor can it flourish there," as Doody notes, it is also a worldly aspiration. Her argument is an intriguing and complex portrayal of Clarissa and Lovelace as "curiously parallel," equally desperate for freedom, equally dangerous to society and to themselves; however, she does not examine the interaction between society and the self but, rather, assumes the "personal imperial principle manifested in Lovelace's will and [in] Clarissa's Christian morality." How parallel desires for freedom might result in such distinctly opposed behaviors is an equally fascinating consideration (172, 125). See also Spacks's argument that Lovelace's self-division and self-aggrandizement represent a "spiritual muddle" ("Grand Misleader," 18).

7. Terry Eagleton, *The Rape of Clarissa* (Minneapolis: University of Minnesota Press, 1982), 82.

8. Ruth Perry, *Women, Letters, and the Novel* (New York: AMS Press, 1980), 3. Historical critics have often found the relationship between Richardson and his age highly ambivalent if not actually hostile. "*Clarissa* is an extremely odd novel, noticeably different from the dominant fiction of Richardson's own day," writes Margaret Doody. "Coming upon Richardson's tragic novel in the midst of all the social-minded fiction of the 1740's, the student may well feel startled, as if he had stumbled into a dark labyrinth beneath a cheerful Georgian square. One wonders how the author was able to conceive of such characters, such a kind of action" (*Natural Passion,* 106).

Critics of the previous century, a century less removed from the author's own, were no less perplexed: Coleridge came to the conclusion that Richardson was simply not, after all, the individual of "nice" tastes he pretended to be. His uneasy judgment has been often quoted: "I confess that it has cost, and still costs, my philosophy some exertion not to be vexed that I must admire, aye, greatly admire, Richardson. His mind is so very vile a mind, so oozy, so hypocritical, praise-mad, canting, envious, concupiscent!" (*Anima Poetoe,* ed. Ernest Hartley Coleridge [London, 1895], 166).

9. As Carol Kay points out, "Casting himself as the reforming student of Clarissa's virtue is especially frustrating to Lovelace's sovereign imagination since it authorizes her as his teacher . . . especially because he has actually become the willing pupil he pretends to be" (*Political Constructions,* 179).

10. This agonized confession complicates Kauffman's contention that Clarissa's "role is to hold the mirror up not to nature but to Lovelace, to let him luxuriate in narcissism; . . . he is still obsessively defining her either as a heavenly mediator or as perversely self-destructive" (*Discourses of Desire,* 133). Kauffman quotes Castle's similarly polarized view: "Here again, . . . those who can define are the masters,

and the male once again defines himself as the arbiter of reason, speech, and discourse, while the female is relegated to madness, silence, self-destruction" (Castle, *Clarissa's Ciphers,* 89–90; qtd. in Kauffman, *Discourses of Desire,* 145). Both Castle and Kauffman ignore the extent to which Clarissa's silence and self-destruction have always been accommodated and potentially powerful.

11. Lovelace insists on approaching his reformation in this triangular (and manipulative) way until Clarissa's death. As she is expiring, he writes, "Tell her, Oh tell her, Belford, that her prayers and wishes, her superlatively generous prayers and wishes, shall *not* be in vain: that I *can,* and *do,* repent—and *long* have repented—Tell her of my frequent deep remorses—It was impossible that such remorse should not at last produce *effectual* remorses—Yet she must not leave me— she must live, if she would wish to have my contrition perfect—for what can despair produce?" (1344). Belford never reads this letter to Clarissa.

12. Even critics seem to love Clarissa the more for her sufferings. Hardwick writes, "her saintly suffering [is] the apotheosis of degradation which truly ennobles her, like a salvation finally achieved" (*Seduction and Betrayal,* 209).

13. Critical attempts to place these visions into a framework of linear antagonisms often ignore what they can tell us of the characters' perceptions in favor of what they can reveal about the characters' adversarial roles in the novel. Maurice Funke writes, "The influence of the divine on Lovelace's private life is shown in his subconscious premonition of perdition, i.e., the nightmare which reveals his fate" (*From Saint to Psychotic,* 179). Altman realizes that "the dream sequence typifies the thematic emphasis on mediation and intercession in this novel" but notes only that this functions to reinforce the mediating property of the epistolary form (*Epistolarity,* 25–26). William Warner maintains that the two dreams delineate the "stark alternatives" of Clarissa's world, forcing the characters into a neatly balanced struggle. Warner's commentary treats Lovelace's dream as though it were Clarissa's, not her tormented lover's (*Reading "Clarissa,"* 16–17).
    Carol Flynn also approaches the two dreams as disconnected halves of one vision. She argues that Clarissa must suffer in order to embrace the comfort of her savior. While Flynn's discussion concerning Clarissa is interesting, it gives no attention to Lovelace. In focusing on Richardson's fascination with his saint's purification through suffering, a process in which she perceives Lovelace as an instrument, she disregards the question of why Lovelace should dream this dream.
    Margaret Doody points out that "the dream of falling is a well-known phenomenon, a sufficiently horrible symbol of failure and fear," but maintains that Lovelace's dream is a revelation of a neatly polarized moral schism between the divine Clarissa and her literally damned lover: "Clarissa has always been elevated; Lovelace has felt her superiority to him. Lovelace has always been 'base,' 'low,' a 'devil'" Their true relationship is expressed once and for all." For Doody, Lovelace's dream is a well-timed message from the author (see *A Natural Passion,* 237–28). For an intriguing discussion of Richardson's views concerning dreams, see Murray L. Brown, "Conflicting Dreams: Lovelace and the Oneirocritical Reader," *Eighteenth-Century Life* 19, no. 3 [November 1995]: 1–21).

14. As Florian Stuber justly notes, it is an "anxiety dream" ("*Clarissa:* A Religious Novel?" 112).

15. In his dream Lovelace actually becomes Castle's Clarissa: "that voice which repeatedly fails to make itself heard" (*Clarissa's Ciphers,* 22).

16. Ellmann, *Hunger Artists,* 70.

17. "Clarissa's illness (probably galloping consumption) is certainly a trifle mysterious," writes Margaret Doody (*Natural Passion,* 175). Brophy opts for a less biological cause of death, insisting, "Clarissa judges herself more harshly than anyone else would, and in losing self-respect she loses her will to live" (*Samuel Richardson: The Triumph of Craft* [Boston: Twayne Publishers, 1987], 107). Castle calls the death "a methodical self-expulsion from the realm of signification," a "progressive movement away from systems of linguistic exchange" (*Clarissa's Ciphers,* 109, 110). Terry Eagleton politicizes Clarissa's depression, treating it as a "performance," and argues, "the public nature of Clarissa's death is the whole point: her dying is in a profound sense a political gesture, a shocking, surreal act of resignation from a society whose power system she has seen in part for what it is. It would be considerably too convenient for the ruling class to make of her death a hole-in-the-corner affair. The death is a properly collective event, a complex, material business, a negation of society . . . an exemplary liturgical action whose end is to involve and transform others" (73–74).

18. Doody, *Natural Passion,* 179.

19. For reviews of recent literature linking self-starvation and religious/ascetic ideals, see Howard Steiger, "Anorexia Nervosa: Is It the Syndrome or the Theorist That Is Culture- and Gender-Bound?" *Transcultural Psychiatric Research Review* 30, no. 4 (1993): 347–58; and Caroline G. Banks, "'Culture' in Culture-Bound Syndromes: The Case of Anorexia Nervosa," *Social Science and Medicine* 34, no. 8 (April 1992): 867–84.

20. Benedict XIV, *De servorum Dei beatificatione et beatorum canonizatione,* bk. 4, pt. 1, chap. 26, and app. by J. B. Beccari to bk. 4, pt. 1 (new ed., Naples: Johannis-Franciscus Pacus, 1773–75), 8:219–29 and 15:89–127. See Caroline Walker Bynum's discussion in *Holy Feast and Holy Fast: The Religious Significance of Food to Medieval Women* (Berkeley: University of California Press, 1987), 74–75.

21. Bynum, *Holy Feast,* 23, 73.

22. When Terry Castle worries that "those elements of significance [in Clarissa's 'Story'] readers normally search for in fiction (transparent cause-effect relations, the resolution of ambiguities) . . . are either lacking, or mysteriously inconclusive," she fails to realize that this very ambiguity is crucial to the saint's "Story" (*Clarissa's Ciphers,* 36).

23. Bynum, *Holy Feast,* 206–7.

24. Bynum, *Holy Feast,* 212.

25. Bynum, *Holy Feast,* 245.

26. Bynum, *Holy Feast,* 250.

27. Bynum, *Holy Feast,* 251, 253.

28. Bynum, *Holy Feast,* 151.

29. See Bynum's discussion on hunger, mystical craving, and desire (*Holy Feast,* 150–86), in which she reprints the following poem by Saint Hadewijch:

> Inseparable satiety and hunger
> Are the appanage of lavish Love
> . . . .
> Satiety: for Love comes, and they cannot bear her;
> Hunger: for she withdraws, and they complain.
> . . . .
> How does Love's coming satiate?
> Filled with wonder, we taste what she is,
> She grants possessing of her sublime throne:
> She imparts the great treasure of her riches.
> How does Love's refusal create hunger?
> Because we cannot come at what we wish to know
> Or enjoy what we desire:
> That increases our hunger over and over.
> . . . .
> May new light give you new ardor;
> New works, new delights to the full;
> New assaults of Love, new hunger so vast
> That new Love may devour new eternity!

See also Hadewijch, *Mengeldichten,* ed. J. Van Mierlo, Leuvense Studien en Tekstuitgaven (Antwerp: N. V. Standaard Boekhandel, 1954); Poems in Stanzas, poem 33, trans. Columba Hart, *Hadewijch: The Complete Works* (New York: Paulist Press, 1980), 221–23.

30. For this reason I disagree with Castle's suggestion that "Clarissa's 'Story' is . . . without social and material force . . . a futile utterance" (*Clarissa's Ciphers,* 25). I think it functions as a story of tremendous power, even before her death.

31. Bynum, *Holy Feast,* 233–34.

32. Bynum, *Holy Feast,* 233.

33. McKeon calls them "nothing more substantial than the posthumous requital of one's persecutors" (*Origins,* 380).

34. See Rudolph Bell, *Holy Anorexia* (Chicago: University of Chicago Press, 1985).

35. Bynum, *Holy Feast,* 140, 149.

36. Warner, *Reading "Clarissa,"* 44.

37. See Bynum's comparison of these intriguing saints (*Holy Feast,* 95–102).

38. At this point Lovelace once again becomes the equivalent of Castle's Clarissa, insisting that the significance of human actions inhere in the actions themselves, not in the self-serving constructions others place on them. See Castle, *Clarissa's Ciphers,* 20–21.

39. Jonathan Lamb, "The Fragmentation of Originals and *Clarissa,*" *Studies in English Literature* 28 (1988): 443–59.

40. Some critics object to Lovelace's levity after Clarissa's death as proof that his madness (and reformation) is short-lived. In an interview that Belford finds genuine and moving, Lovelace confesses, "'Whatever airs I give myself, this charming creature has fast hold of me *here* (clapping his hand upon his heart); and I must either appear what you see me, or be what I so lately was—Oh the divine creature!'" (1463).

41. Dinnerstein, *Mermaid,* 5.

42. Brownstein, "Examplar," 42.

43. Ellmann, *Hunger Artists,* 112–13.

Chapter 4: A Historical Overview

1. The orchard-robber metaphor has been discussed by a number of critics, although none have concentrated on the importance of food-related behavior itself. Janet Butler discusses the apple metaphor in an article in which she maintains that "the image of the garden works subliminally on readers to suggest willing disobedience on Clarissa's part and, therefore, Richardson's ultimate responsibility for that image and all its resonances" ("The Garden: Early Symbol of Clarissa's Complicity," *Studies in English Literature* 24 [1984]: 528, 534). Linda Kauffman points out that "*Newelty* means novelty, newness, but it also connotes food that is a delicacy. . . . In one sense Clarissa is a delicacy Lovelace would like to consume . . . this is his doom: since he so freely indulges his appetite for women, he is constantly looking for some delicate morsel to refresh his surfeited palate" (*Discourses of Desire,* 136–37). Lovelace the orchard-robber is similarly described by Elizabeth Hardwick as "never satisfied, never resting, mythically hungry" (*Seduction and Betrayal,* 185) and by Rachel Brownstein as "a glutton for girls" (*Becoming a Heroine,* 47). See also Alexander Pettit's interesting discussion of Anna Howe as a dangerously inexpert satirist ("Wit, Satire, and Comedy," 35–54).

2. Jean Anthelme Brillat-Savarin, *The Physiology of Taste* (New York: Liveright Publishing, 1948), xxxiii; qtd. in Peter Farb and George Armelagos, *Consuming Passions: The Anthropology of Eating* (Boston: Houghton Mifflin, 1980), 3.

3. Shakespeare, *Macbeth,* 4.1.14–17.

4. Farb and Armelagos, *Consuming Passions,* 4. Castle elaborates on this idea, noting: "Food taboos provide a classic illustration [of naturalized social construc-

tions], for as any cross-cultural study shows, societies make different decisions about what is edible and what is not. Though the food taboo is perceived as coming from Nature, it models a cultural, rather than a natural category" (*Clarissa's Ciphers*, 53).

5. Qtd. in Steiger's interesting review of two articles by anthropologists which suggest that psychiatric formulations of anorexia nervosa should reassess their cultural and gender-specific assumptions ("Anorexia Nervosa," 352).

6. Hortense Powdermaker, *An Anthropological Approach to the Problem of Obesity* (New York: Academy of Medicine, Bull, 1960): 36, 286–95.

7. Bruch, *Eating Disorders*, 15.

8. Nancy Chodorow notes that involvement in food production may well be responsible for the determination of characteristics classified as male or female within a given culture. In her discussion of a study by anthropologists Herbert Barry III, Irvin L. Child, and Margaret K. Bacon ("Relation of Child Training to Subsistence Economy," *American Anthropologist* 61 [1959]: 51–63), she writes that children may learn gender expectations as they learn the work expected of them according to means of food production. Girls tend to have much more regular and controlled behavior as the variations in their work are small; "men's and boys' work . . . can be more radically different than women's and girls' work. Men may *either* hunt, or fish, or farm, or herd" (*Feminism,* 24–27). Chodorow emphasizes that this cross-cultural research suggests that there are no "biologically derived .. . psychological or personality characteristics which universally differentiate men and women" (23). See also Chodorow, *The Reproduction of Mothering: Psychoanalysis and the Sociology of Gender* (Berkeley: University of California Press, 1978), 11–30.

9. J. P. Migne, ed., *Patrologiae cursus completus: series graeca*, 221 vols. (Paris: Migne, 1841–64), hereafter referred to as PL. Augustine, *City of God*, bk. 10, chap. 6, PL 41, col. 284C; Hilary, *Tractatus in CXXV psalmum*, para. 6, PL 9, col. 688B–C; Hilary, *De Trinitate*, bk. 8, chaps. 13–14, PL 10, cols. 246–47; Alan of Lille, *Summa de arte praedicatoria*, chap. 34: *De jejunio*, PL 210, col. 177D; Pope Leo the Great, sermon 20, Ninth Sermon for the December Fast, para. 2–3, PL 54, cols. 189–90. Aquinas, *Summa Theologiae*, Blackfriars ed., 61 vols. (New York: McGraw-Hill, 1964–81), II, IIae, q. 148: *De gula,* 3, vol, 43, pp. 122–24; qtd. in Bynum, *Holy Feast,* 31–32.

10. Bynum, *Holy Feast,* 1.

11. Flynn, *Samuel Richardson,* 45. Michael McKeon describes *Clarissa* as "manifest discursive and imaginative empowerment, whose material register consists in nothing more substantial than the posthumous requital of one's persecutors" (see *The Origins of the English Novel, 1600–1740* [Baltimore: Johns Hopkins University Press, 1987], 380).

12. George Cheyne, *The English Malady* (New York: Scholars' Facsimiles and Reprints, 1976), xi.

13. Always disturbed by the author's stoutness and sedentary life, Cheyne advocated a strict diet, frequent vomiting, cold baths, and purging by means of "a Tea Spoonful or two of the Tincture of Soot and Assa Foetida made on [*sic*] Peony Water in a cold Infusion" to be drunk in peppermint water in order to make Richardson "break Wind plentifully" (George Cheyne, Letter to Samuel Richardson, 1 July 1739, *The Letters of Doctor George Cheyne to Samuel Richardson (1733–1743)*, ed. Charles Mullett v18, no. 1(Columbia, Mo.: University of Missouri Press, 1943).

14. George Cheyne, *An Essay on Health and Long Life* (London: G. Strahan and J. Leake, 1724), 4.

15. See Eric T. Carlson's discussion of the implications of this suggestion in his introduction to *The English Malady* (New York: Scholars' Facsimiles and Reprints, 1976), x–xii.

16. See Ellmann's discussion of gluttonous eating practices as symbolic of a lack of patriotism (*Hunger Artists,* 7–11).

17. It is interesting to note that, in keeping with the rationale of this equation of appetite with inclination to avarice, most of the characters described as wealthy and acquisitive in the novel are also plump. "The poor Bella has, you know, a plump, high-fed face, if I may be allowed the expression," Clarissa tells Anna, reinforcing the correlation between greed and corpulence (60). The miserly Uncle Antony is oddly described as a "plump-hearted soul" (70). Both the intemperate Lord M. and Clarissa's cruel father suffer from gout. "A man of £8000 a year to prefer his appetite to his health!—He deserves to die!" Lovelace declares of his uncle (931). Mother Sinclair, the infamous brothel keeper, sports a "horse-mouth, stiff hams," and "fat arms" (537). Clarissa's aristocratic mother, naturally generous and caught between the demands of her family and those of her conscience, suffers from related disorders. Margaret Doody points out, "The stress of family warfare and of her own efforts to do well by all takes its toll in nervousness and (psychologically well observed) in afflictions of the digestive system" (*Natural Passion,* 103).

18. As she takes leave of her physicians for the last time, Clarissa prays, "[I] beg of God . . . that it may be in the power of you and yours to the end of time, to confer benefits, rather than to be obliged to receive them. This is a god-like power, gentlemen" (1248).

19. Gillian Feeley-Harnik, *The Lord's Table: Eucharist and Passover in Early Christianity* (Philadelphia: University of Pennsylvania Press, 1981), 139–64; qtd. in Bynum, *Holy Feast,* 49.

20. Ellmann, *Hunger Artists,* 53.

21. Funke argues that Clarissa's wasting away is simply "her total rejection of sexuality and the will to live" (*From Saint to Psychotic,* 181). John Dussinger argues that references to food and sexual appetite are inextricable in the novel; therefore, Clarissa's fasting after the rape must surely be a "mortification of the flesh" ("Love and Consanguinity," 519). In "Conscience and the Pattern of Christian Perfection

in *Clarissa*" he calls her death by starvation "complete renunciation of the world, flesh, and devil" (243–44).

22. Castle, *Clarissa's Ciphers,* 124–25. See also Leo Braudy's discussion of Clarissa's "refusal of physicality" ("Penetration," 189–97).

23. See Brumberg's excellent *Fasting Girls: The Emergence of Anorexia Nervosa as a Modern Disease* (Cambridge: Harvard University Press, 1988).

24. Mara Selvini Palazzoli, *Self-Starvation,* trans. Arnold Pomerans (New York: Jason Aronson, 1981), 152.

25. Margaret Anne Doody, "The Man-Made World of Clarissa Harlowe and Robert Lovelace," in *Samuel Richardson: Passion and Prudence,* ed. Valerie Myer (London: Vision Press, 1986), 69, 74.

26. According to researchers, the prevalence of eating disorders is increasing, and women are affected more than men by a 10:1 ratio. See White, "Women and Eating Disorders, Part I," 359.

27. Brumberg, *Fasting Girls,* 2, 5–6.

28. W. Law, *A Serious Call to a Devout and Holy Life* (London, 1729), 354. Law's handbook was so widely read that it ran to ten editions between 1729 and 1772.

29. Stone, *Family, Sex and Marriage,* 446.

30. M. A. Wollstonecraft, *A Vindication of the Rights of Woman* (1972), (1792), ed. Carol H. Poston, Norton edition (London: W.W. Norton, 1988), 43–49, 44.

31. Susie Orbach, *Fat Is a Feminist Issue: The Anti-Diet Guide to Permanent Weight Loss* (New York: Berkley Publishing, 1978); *Hunger Strike: The Anorectic's Struggle as a Metaphor for Our Age* (London: Faber and Faber, 1986); see also Carole M. Counihan, "What Does It Mean to Be Fat, Thin, and Female in the United States? A Review Essay," *Food and Foodways* 1 (1985): 77–94; Marlene Boskin-Lodahl, "Cinderella's Stepsisters: A Feminist Perspective on Anorexia and Bulimia," *Signs* 2 (1976): 342–56; Susan Bordo, "Anorexia Nervosa: Psychopathology as a Crystallization of Culture," *Philosophical Forum* 17 (Winter 1985–86): 73–104. See also Bordo, *Unbearable Weight: Feminism, Western Culture, and the Body* (Berkeley: University of California Press, 1993); and Leslie Heywood, *Dedication to Hunger: The Anorexic Aesthetic in Modern Culture* (Berkeley: University of California Press, 1996).

32. Sandra Gilbert and Susan Gubar, *The Madwoman in the Attic* (New Haven: Yale University Press, 1979), 53–54.

33. Orbach, *Fat Is a Feminist Issue,* 169.

34. Orbach, *Hunger Strike,* 19. Compare Elaine Showalter, *The Female Malady: Women, Madness and English Culture, 1830–1980* (New York: Pantheon Books, 1985), writing of the suffragists in 1912: "The hunger strikes of militant women prisoners brilliantly put the symptomatology of anorexia nervosa to work in the service of a feminist cause" (162).

35. Ellmann, *Hunger Artists*, 14.

36. Bruch, *Eating Disorders*, 5.

37. See Michel Foucault, *Madness and Civilization: A History of Insanity in the Age of Reason*, trans. Richard Howard (New York: Random House, 1965); and *The Standard Edition of the Complete Psychological Works of Sigmund Freud*, ed. and trans. James Strachey, vol. 1: *Pre-Psychoanalytic Publications and Unpublished Drafts* (London: Hogarth Press, 1966).

38. Freud, 200–201.

39. Pierre Janet, *The Major Symptoms of Hysteria* (New York: Macmillan, 1907), 233–37. See Brumberg's discussion of Freud and Janet on sexuality (*Fasting Girls*, 213–17). See also DiNicola's historical overview of AN and controversies surrounding its causes and possible treatment.

40. John Winthrop, *The History of New England from 1630 to 1649*, ed. James Savage (Boston, Phelps and Farnham, 1826), 2:216. Available on microfilm from the Massachusetts Historical Society (1976); qtd. in Gilbert and Gubar, *Madwoman*, 56.

41. See Edward Hammond Clarke, *Sex in Education: A Fair Chance for the Girls* (Boston: J. R. Osgood and Company, 1873).

42. Wendy Martin, "Anne Bradstreet's Poetry: A Study of Subversive Piety," in Gilbert and Gubar, *Shakespeare's Sisters*, 19–31; qtd. in Gilbert and Gubar, *Madwoman*, 56.

43. Bynum, *Holy Feast*, 189.

44. Ian Watt, *The Rise of The Novel: Studies in Defoe, Richardson and Fielding* (Berkeley: University of California Press, 1957), 44–45.

45. Bruch, *Eating Disorders*, 12–13.

46. E. H. Erikson, *Gandhi's Truth* (New York: W. W. Norton, 1969). See Bruch's discussion (*Eating Disorders*, 12).

47. See discussion in Showalter, *Female Malady*, 162; and Ellmann, *Hunger Artists*.

48. Bruch, *Eating Disorders*, 12–13.

49. White, "Women and Eating Disorders, Part II," 369.

50. White, "Women and Eating Disorders, Part I," 357.

Works Cited

Adler, A. *The Individual Psychology of Alfred Adler.* New York: Basic Books, 1956.
———. *Superiority and Social Interest.* Evanston, Ill.: Northwestern University Press, 1964.
Aikens, Janet E. "*Clarissa* and the New Woman: Contexts for Richardson Scholarship." *Studies in the Literary Imagination* 28, no. 1 (Spring 1995): 67–86.
Alford, Fred C. *Narcissism: Socrates, the Frankfurt School, and Psychoanalytic Theory.* New Haven: Yale University Press, 1988.
Alkon, Paul. "Recent Studies in the Restoration and Eighteenth Century." *Studies in English Literature* 29 (1988): 579–81.
Allestree, Richard. *The New Whole Duty of Man,* 24th ed. London, 1792.
Altman, Janet Gurkin. *Epistolarity: Approaches to a Form.* Columbus: Ohio State University Press, 1982.
American Psychiatric Association. *Diagnostic and Statistical Manual of Mental Disorders.* 3d rev. ed. Washington, D.C.: APA, 1987.
Andolfi, M. *Family Therapy: An Interactional Approach.* Trans. H. C. Cassin. New York: Plenum, 1979.
Armstrong, Nancy. *Desire and Domestic Fiction: A Political History of the Novel.* Oxford: Oxford University Press, 1987.
Astell, Mary. *Some Reflections upon Marriage.* 1730. Reprint. New York: Source Book Press, 1970.
Austen, Jane. *Northanger Abbey.* New York: Penguin Books, 1972.
Barry, Herbert III, Irvin L. Child, and Margaret K. Bacon. "Relation of Child Training to Subsistence Economy." *American Anthropologist* 61 (1951): 51–63.
Battestin, Martin C. Introduction to *Joseph Andrews.* Riverside edition. Boston: Houghton Mifflin, 1961.
Beattie, H. J. "Eating Disorders and the Mother-Daughter Relationship." *International Journal of Eating Disorders* 7 (1988): 453–57.
Bell, Rudolph, M. *Holy Anorexia.* Chicago: University of Chicago Press, 1985.
Benedict XIV. *De Servorum Dei beatificatione et beatorum canonizatione.* New ed. Naples: Johannis-Franciscus Pacus, 1773–75.
Beuler, Lois. *Clarissa's Plots.* Newark: University of Delaware Press, 1994.
Biggs, Penelope. "Hunt, Conquest, Trial: Lovelace and the Metaphors of the Rake." *Studies in 18th-Century Culture,* ed. Harry C. Payne, 2 (1982): 51–64.
Blos, P. *On Adolescence: A Psycholanalytic Perspective.* New York: Free Press of Glencoe, 1962.
Bordo, Susan. "Anorexia Nervosa: Psychopathology as a Crystallization of Culture." *Philosophical Forum* 17 (Winter 1985–86): 73–104.
———. *Unbearable Weight: Feminism, Western Culture, and the Body.* Berkeley: University of California Press, 1993.
Boskin-Lodahl, Marlene. "Cinderella's Stepsisters: A Feminist Perspective on Anorexia and Bulimia." *Signs* 2 (1976): 342–56.

Boswell, James. *Boswell's Life of Johnson*. ed. George Birkbeck Hill. Oxford: Clarendon Press, 1887.

Bowlby, John. *Attachment and Loss*. 2 vols. London: Hogarth Press, 1969–73.

Brain, Robert. *Friends and Lovers*. New York: Basic Books, 1976.

Braudy, Leo. "Penetration and Impenetrability in *Clarissa*." In *New Approaches to Eighteenth-Century Literature*, ed. Phillip Harth, 189–97. New York: Columbia University Press, 1974.

Brillat-Savarin, Jean Anthelme. *The Physiology of Taste*. New York: Liveright Publishing, 1948.

Brodsky, Claudia. "Narrative Representation and Criticism: 'Crossing the Rubicon' in *Clarissa*." In *Reading Narrative: Form, Ethics, Ideology*, ed. James Phelan, 201–19. Columbus: Ohio State University Press, 1989.

Brody, G. H., Z. Stoneman, and M. Burke. "Family System and Individual Child Correlates of Sibling Behavior." *American Journal of Orthopsychiatry* 57 (1987): 561–69.

Brody, G. H., Z. Stoneman, J. K. McCoy, and R. Forehand. "Contemporaneous and Longitudinal Associations of Sibling Conflict with Family Relationship Assessments and Family Discussions about Sibling Problems." *Child Development* 63 (1992): 391–400.

Bromley, P.M., *Family Law*. 4th ed. London: Butterworth, 1971.

Brophy, Elizabeth Bergen. *Samuel Richardson*. Boston: Twayne Publishers, 1987.

Brown, Murray L. "Conflicting Dreams: Lovelace and the Oneirocritical Reader." *Eighteenth-Century Life* 19, no. 3 (November 1995): 1–21.

Brownstein, Rachel Mayer. "'An Examplar to Her Sex': Richardson's Clarissa." *Yale Review* 67 (1977): 30–47.

———. *Becoming a Heroine: Reading about Women in Novels*. New York: Viking Press, 1982.

Bruch, *Eating Disorders: Obesity, Anorexia Nervosa, and the Person Within*. New York: Basic Books, 1973.

———. *The Golden Cage*. New York: Random House, 1978.

Brumberg, Joan Jacobs. *Fasting Girls: The Emergence of Anorexia Nervosa as a Modern Disease*. Cambridge: Harvard University Press, 1988.

Buchan, William. Domestic Medicine: or, The Family physician. Hartford: S. Andrus, 1849.

Butler, Janet. "The Garden: Early Symbol of Clarissa's Complicity." *Studies in English Literature* 24 (1984): 527–44.

Bynum, Caroline Walker. *Holy Feast and Holy Fast: The Religious Significance of Food to Medieval Women*. Berkeley: University of California Press, 1987.

Carlat, D. J., and C. A. Camargo Jr. "A Review of Bulimia Nervosa in Males." *American Journal of Psychiatry* 148, no. 7 (1991): 831–43.

Carroll, John. "Lovelace as Tragic Hero." *University of Toronto Quarterly* 42, no. 1 (Fall 1972): 14–25.

Castle, Terry. *Clarissa's Ciphers: Meaning and Disruption in Richardson's "Clarissa."* Ithaca: Cornell University Press, 1982.

———. "Lovelace's Dream." In *Studies in 18th Century Culture*, ed. O. M. Brack Jr., 13:29–42. Madison: University of Wisconsin Press, 1984.

Chernim, Kim. *The Hungry Self: Women, Eating and Identity.* New York: Harper and Row, 1985.

Cheselka, Olga. "Strategies of Interpersonal Power." *Contemporary Psycho-Analysis* 27, no. 4 (October 1991): 702–19.

Cheyne, George. *The Letters of Doctor George Cheyne to Samuel Richardson (1733–1743),* ed. Charles Mullet. Columbia: University of Missouri Press, 1943.

Chodorow, Nancy. *The Reproduction of Mothering: Psychoanalysis and the Sociology of Gender.* Berkeley: University of California Press, 1978.

————. *Feminism and Psychoanalytic Theory.* New Haven and London: Yale University Press, 1989.

Clarke, Edward Hammond. *Sex in Education: A Fair Chance for the Girls.* Boston: J. R. Osgood and Company, 1873.

Cockshut, A. O. J. *Man and Woman: A Study of Love and the Novel, 1740–1940.* New York: Oxford University Press, 1978.

Coleridge, Samuel Taylor. *Anima Poetoe,* ed. Ernest Hartley Coleridge. London, 1895.

Cooper, C., H. Grotevant, and S. Condon. "Individuality and Connectedness in the Family as a Context for Adolescent Identity Formation and Role-taking Skill. In *New Directions in Child Development,* vol. 22: *Adolescent Development in the Family,* ed. R. H. Grotevant and C. Cooper, 43–59. W. Damon, ser. ed. San Francisco: Jossey-Bass, 1983.

Counihan, Carole M. "What Does It Mean to Be Fat, Thin, and Female in the United States? A Review Essay." *Food and Foodways* 1 (1985): 77–94.

Cummings, Katherine. "Clarissa's 'Life with Father.'" *Literature and Psychology* 32, no. 4 (1986): 30–36.

Cummings, Mark E. "Marital Conflict and Children's Functioning." *Social Development* 3, no. 1 (1994): 16–36.

Dadds, M. R., M. R. Sander, B. C. Behrens, and J. E. James. "Marital Discord and Child Behavior Problems: A Description of Family Interactions during Treatment." *Journal of Clinical Child Psychology* 16 (1987): 192–203.

Dadds, M. R., M. R. Sanders, M. Morrison, and M. Rebgetz. "Childhood Depression and Conduct Disorder. II: An Analysis of Family Interaction Patterns in the Home." *Journal of Abnormal Psychology* 101, no. 3 (1992): 505–13.

Dare, C., I. Eisler, G. F. M. Russell, and G. I. Szmukler. "The Clinical and Theoretical Impact of a Controlled Trial of Family Therapy in Anorexia Nervosa." *Journal of Marital and Family Therapy* 16 (1990): 39–57.

Deutsch, Helene. *The Psychology of Women.* Vol 1. New York: Grune and Stratton, 1944–45.

DiNicola, Vincenzo F. "Anorexia Multiforme: Self-Starvation in Historical and Cultural Context." *Transcultural Psychiatric Research Review* 27 (1990): 165–96.

Dinnerstein, Dorothy. *The Mermaid and the Minotaur: Sexual Arrangements and Human Malaise.* New York: Harper and Row, 1976.

Doederlein, Sue Warwick. "*Clarissa* in the Hands of the Critics." *Eighteenth Century Studies* 16 (1983): 401–14.

Doody, Margaret Anne. *A Natural Passion: A Study of the Novels of Samuel Richardson.* Oxford: Clarendon Press, 1974.

———. "The Man-Made World of Clarissa Harlowe and Robert Lovelace." In *Samuel Richardson: Passion and Prudence*, ed. Valerie Grosvenor Myer, 52–77. London: Vision Press, 1986.

———. "Disguise and Personality in Richardson's *Clarissa*." *Studies in the 18th-Century*, ed. Jocelyn Harris, 12, no. 2 (May 1988): 18–39.

Doody, Margaret Anne, and Florian Stuber. "*Clarissa* Censored." *Modern Language Studies* (Winter 1988): 74–88.

Dussinger, John. "Conscience and the Pattern of Christian Perfection in *Clarissa*." *PMLA* 81, no. 3 (June 1966): 236–45.

———. "Love and Consanguinity in Richardson's Novels." *Studies in English Literature* 24 (1984): 513–25.

———. "*Clarissa*, Jacobitism, and the 'Spirit of the University.'" *Studies in the Literary Imagination* 28, no. 1 (Spring 1995): 55–66.

Eagleton, Terry. *The Rape of Clarissa*. Minneapolis: University of Minnesota Press, 1982.

Eaves, T. C. Duncan, and Ben D. Kimpel. *Samuel Richardson: A Biography*. Oxford: Clarendon Press, 1971.

Eisenstein, Hester. *Contemporary Feminist Thought*. Boston: G. K. Hall, 1983.

Eldredge, Patricia, *Samuel Richardson's "Clarissa": A Psychological Study*. Ph.D. diss., Michigan State University, 1983.

Ellmann, Maud. *The Hunger Artists: Starving, Writing, and Imprisonment*. Cambridge: Harvard University Press, 1993.

Erikson, E. H. *Gandhi's Truth*. New York: W. W. Norton, 1969.

Fairbairn, W. R. D. *An Object-Relations Theory of the Personality*. New York: Basic Books, 1952.

Farb, Peter, and George Armelagos. *Consuming Passions: The Anthropology of Eating*. Boston: Houghton Mifflin, 1980.

Feeley-Harnik, Gillian. *The Lord's Table: Eucharist and Passover in Early Christianity*. Philadelphia: University of Pennsylvania Press, 1981.

Fiedler, Leslie. *Love and Death in the American Novel*. New York: Stein and Day, 1960.

Flynn, Carol Houlihan. *Samuel Richardson: A Man of Letters*. Princeton: Princeton University Press, 1982.

Foucault, Michel. *Madness and Civilization: A History of Insanity in the Age of Reason*. Trans. Richard Howard. New York: Random House, 1965.

Freud, Sigmund. *The Standard Edition of the Complete Psychological Works of Sigmund Freud*. Ed. and trans. James Strachey. London: Hogarth Press , 1966.

Funke, Maurice. *From Saint to Psychotic: The Crisis of Human Identity in the Late 18th Century*. New York: Peter Lang, 1983.

Furst, Lilian. "The Man of Sensibility and the Woman of Sense." *Jahrbuch für Internationale Germanistik* 14, no. 1 (1982): 13–26.

Gilbert, Sandra, and Susan Gubar. *The Madwoman in the Attic: The Woman Writer and the Nineteenth-Century Literary Imagination*. New Haven: Yale University Press, 1979.

Gilligan, Carol. *In a Different Voice: Psychological Theory and Women's Development*. Cambridge: Harvard University Press, 1982.

Goldberg, Carl. "'Mirror of Your Eyes.'" *Psychotherapy Patient* 5, nos. 3–4 (1989): 197–205.

Golden, Morris. *Richardson's Characters.* Ann Arbor: University of Michigan Press, 1963.

———. "Public Context and Imagining Self in *Clarissa.*" *Studies in English Literature* 25 (1985): 575–98.

Greenacre, Phyllis. *Emotional Growth: Psychoanalytic Studies of the Gifted and a Great Variety of Other Individuals.* New York: International Universities Press, 1971.

Grotevant, H., and C. Cooper. "Patterns of Interaction in Family Relationships and the Development of Identity Exploration in Adolescents." *Child Development* 56 (1985): 425–28.

Guntrip, Harry. *Personality Structure and Human Interaction.* New York: International Universities Press, 1961.

Gwilliam, Tassie. *Samuel Richardson's Fictions of Gender.* Stanford: Stanford University Press, 1993.

Hadewijch. *Mengeldichten.* Ed. J. Van Mierlo. Leuvense Studien en Tekstuitgaven. Antwerp: N. V. Standaard Boekhandel, 1954. Trans. Columba Hart. *Hadewijch: The Complete Works.* New York: Paulist Press, 1980.

Handwerk, Gary. *Irony and Ethics in Narrative from Schlegel to Lacan.* New Haven: Yale University Press, 1985.

Hardwick, Elizabeth. *Seduction and Betrayal: Women and Literature.* New York: Vintage Books, 1975.

Harris, Jocelyn. *Samuel Richardson.* Cambridge: Cambridge University Press, 1987.

Harvey, D., and J. Bray. "Evaluation of an Intergenerational Theory of Personal Development: Family Process Determinants of Psychological and Health Distress." *Journal of Family Psychology* 4 (1991): 298–325.

Heywood, Leslie. *Dedication to Hunger: The Anorexic Aesthetic in Modern Culture.* Berkeley: University of California Press, 1996.

Hill, Christopher. "Clarissa Harlowe and Her Times." *Essays in Criticism* 5 (1955): 315–40 .

Hilliard, Raymond. "*Clarissa* and Ritual Cannibalism." *PMLA* 105, no. 1 (October 1990): 1083–98.

Hogg, James Andrew, and Mary Lou Frank. "Toward an Interpersonal Model of Codependence and Contradependence." *Journal of Counseling and Development* 70 (1992): 371–75.

Horney, Karen. "The Dread of Women." *International Journal of Psychoanalysis* 13 (1982): 350–60.

Izubuchi, Keiko. "Subversive or Not? Anna Howe's Function in *Clarissa.*" In *Samuel Richardson: Passion and Prudence,* ed. Valerie Grosvenor Myer, 78–92. London: Vision Press, 1986.

Jacobson, Edith. *The Self and the Object World.* New York: International Universities Press, 1964.

Janet, Pierre. *The Major Symptoms of Hysteria.* New York: Macmillan, 1907.

Johnson, Scott. "Structural Elements in Franz Kafka's *The Metamorphosis.*" *Journal of Marital and Family Therapy* 19, no. 2 (1993): 149–57.

Josselson, R. "Ego Development in Adolescence." In *Handbook of Adolescent Psychology,* ed. J. Adelson, 188–210. New York: Wiley, 1980.

————. "The Embedded Self: I and Thou Revisited." In *Self, Ego, and Identity: Integrative Approaches,* ed. D. K. Lapsley and F. C. Power, 91–108. New York: Springer, 1988.

Kauffman, Linda. *Discourses of Desire: Gender, Genre, and Epistolary Fictions.* Ithaca and London: Cornell University Press, 1986.

Kay, Carol. *Political Constructions: Defoe, Richardson, and Sterne in Relation to Hobbes, Hume, and Burke.* Ithaca and London: Cornell University Press, 1988.

Kernberg, Otto. *Borderline Conditions and Pathological Narcissism.* New York: Aronson, 1975.

————. *Internal World and External Reality: Object Relations Theory Applied.* New York and London: Jason Aronson, 1980.

Keymer, Tom. *Richardson's "Clarissa" and the Eighteenth-Century Reader.* Cambridge: Cambridge University Press, 1992.

Kinkead-Weekes, Mark. "Clarissa Restored?" *Review of English Studies* 10, no. 38 (1959): 157–69.

————. Introduction to Everyman edition of *Pamela.* London: J.M. Dent, 1991.

————. *Samuel Richardson: Dramatic Novelist.* Ithaca: Cornell University Press, 1973.

Kitron, David G. "Depression and Grandiosity: Clinical and Theoretical Issues in the Treatment of Narcissistic Disturbances." *Journal of Contemporary Psychotherapy* 24, no. 3 (1994): 203–11.

Klein, Melanie, and Joan Riviere. *Love, Hate and Reparation.* New York: W. W. Norton, 1964.

Kohut, Heinz. "Forms and Transformations of Narcissism." *Journal of American Psychoanalytic Association* 14 (1966): 243–72.

————. *The Analysis of the Self.* New York: International Universities Press, 1971.

————. "Psychoanalysis and the Interpretation of Literature: A Correspondence with Erich Heller." *Critical Inquiry* 4 (1978): 433–50.

Kraft, Quentin. "On Character in the Novel: William Beatty Warner versus Samuel Richardson and the Humanists." *College English* 50, no. 1 (January 1988): 32–47.

Kroger, F., A. Drinkmann, W. Herzog, and E. Petzold. "Family Diagnostics: Object Representation in Families with Eating Disorders." *Small Group Research* 22, no. 1 (February 1991): 99–114.

Lamb, Jonathan. "The Fragmentation of Originals and *Clarissa.*" *Studies in English Literature* 28 (1988): 443–59.

Layton, Lynne, and Barbara Ann Schapiro. *Narcissism and the Text: Studies in Literature and the Psychology of Self.* New York and London: New York University Press, 1986.

Lazarsfeld, Sofie. "The Courage for Imperfection." *Individual Psychology* 47, no. 1 (March 1991): 93–96.

Lerner, Harriet Goldhor. *The Dance of Anger.* New York: Harper and Row, 1985.

Levy, Marion J., et al. *Aspects of the Analysis of Family Structure.* Princeton: Princeton University Press, 1965.

Lindgren, David L. "Grandiosity: The Shadow of Shame." In *Men Healing Shame,* ed. Roy U. Schenk, 201–10. New York: Springer, 1995.

Lipton, A. "' Death of a Salesman': A Family Systems Point of View." *The Family* 11(1984): 55–67.

Maclean, Gerald. "Citing the Subject." In *Gender and Theory: Dialogues on Feminist Criticism*, ed. Linda Kauffman, 140–57. Oxford: Basil Blackwell, 1989.

Macfarlane, Alan. *Marriage and Love in England: Modes of Reproduction, 1300–1840*. Oxford: Basil Blackwell, 1986.

Maddox, James H., Jr. "Lovelace and the World of Ressentiment in *Clarissa.*" *Texas Studies in Literature and Language* 24, no. 3 (Fall 1982): 271–92.

Mahler, M. *On Human Symbiosis and the Vicissitudes of Individuation*. New York: International University Press, 1968.

Malthus, T.R., *An Essay on Population*. 2 vols. Everyman Library. N.d. reprint. London: Dent, 1933.

Martin, Wendy. "Anne Bradstreet's Poetry: A Study of Subversive Piety." In *Shakespeare's Sisters: Feminist Essays on Women Poets*, ed. Sandra Gilbert and Susan Gubar. Bloomington: Indiana University Press, 1979.

McCrea, Brian. "Clarissa's Pregnancy and the Fate of Patriarchal Power." *Eighteenth-Century Fiction* 19, no. 2 (January 1997): 125–48.

McKeon, Michael. *The Origins of the English Novel, 1600–1740*. Baltimore: Johns Hopkins University Press, 1987.

McKillop, Alan Dugald. *The Early Masters of English Fiction*. Lawrence: University of Kansas Press, 1956.

McWilliams, Nancy, and Stanley Lependorf. "Narcissistic Pathology of Everyday Life: The Denial of Remorse and Gratitude." *Contemporary Psycho-Analysis* 26, no. 3 (1990): 430–51.

Mead, Margaret. *Male and Female*. New York: William Morrow, 1949.

Michie, Helena. *The Word Made Flesh*. Oxford: Oxford University Press, 1987.

Migne, J. P., ed. *Patrologiae cursus completus: series graeca*. 221 vols. Paris: Migne, 1841–64.

Miller, Alice. "Depression and Grandiosity as Related Forms of Narcissistic Disturbances." *International Review of Psycho-Analysis* 6, no. 61 (1979): 61–76.

———. *The Drama of the Gifted Child: The Search for the True Self*. Trans. Ruth Ward. New York: Basic Books, 1981.

Miller, J. Hillis. *The Ethics of Reading*. New York: Columbia University Press, 1987.

Miller, Jean Baker. *Towards a New Psychology of Women*, 2d ed. Boston: Beacon Press, 1986.

Miller, Nancy K. "The Exquisite Cadavers: Women in Eighteenth-Century Fiction." *Diacritics* 5, no. 4 (Winter 1975): 37–43.

Minuchin, S., B. Montalvo, B. G. Guerney Jr., B. L. Rosman, and F. Schumer. *Families of the Slums: An Exploration of Their Structure and Treatment*. New York: Basic Books, 1967.

Mitchell, Mary G., and David M. Rosenthal. "Suicidal Adolescents: Family Dynamics and the Effects of Lethality and Hopelessness." *Journal of Youth and Adolescence* 21, no. 1 (1992): 23–33.

Mitscherlich, Alexander. *Society without the Father*. New York: Schocken Books, 1970.

Montagu, Lady Mary Wortley. *The Letters of Lady Mary Wortley Montagu*. Ed. Wharncliffe, (Lord). 3 vols. London: R. Bentley, 1837.

Mullen, John. *Sentiment and Sociability: The Language of Feeling in the Eighteenth Century.* Oxford: Clarendon Press, 1988.

Myer, Valerie Grosvenor, ed. *Samuel Richardson: Passion and Prudence.* London: Vision Press Ltd., 1986.

Napier, Elizabeth. "'Tremble and Reform': The Inversion of Power in Richardson's *Clarissa.*" *EHL* 42 (1975): 214–23.

Orbach, Susie. *Fat Is a Feminist Issue: The Anti-Diet Guide to Permanent Weight Loss.* New York: Berkley Publishing, 1978.

———. *Hunger Strike: The Anorectic's Struggle as a Metaphor for Our Age.* London: Faber and Faber, 1986.

Palazzoli, Mara Selvini. *Self-Starvation: From Individual to Family Therapy in the Treatment of Anorexia Nervosa.* Trans. Arnold Pomerans. New York: Jason Aronson, 1981.

Paris, Bernard. *A Psychological Approach to Fiction.* Bloomington: Indiana University Press, 1974.

Parry-Jones, W. L. "Archival Exploration of Anorexia Nervosa." *Journal of Psychiatric Research* 19 (1985): 95–100.

Perosa, Sandra L., and Linda M. Perosa. "Relationships among Minuchin's Structural Family Model, Identity Achievement, and Coping Style." *Journal of Counseling Psychology* 40, no. 4 (1993): 479–89.

Perry, Ruth. *Women, Letters, and the Novel.* New York: AMS Press, 1980.

Pettit, Alexander. "Wit, Satire, and Comedy: *Clarissa* and the Problem of Literary Precedent." *Studies in the Literary Imagination* 28, no. 1 (Spring 1995): 35–44.

Powdermaker, Hortense. *An Anthropological Approach to the Problem of Obesity.* New York: Academy of Medicine, Bull, 1960.

Quintana, S., and J. Kerr. "Relational Needs in Late Adolescent Separation-Individuation." *Journal of Counseling and Development* 71 (1993): 349–54.

Rain, D. C. "Richardson's *Clarissa.*" Review essay in *The Explicator* 47, no. 1 (Fall 1988): 12–15.

Rich, Adrienne. *Of Woman Born: Motherhood as Experience and Institution.* New York: W. W. Norton, 1976.

Richardson, Samuel. *Clarissa.* Ed. Angus Ross. 1747–48. Reprint. Harmondsworth and New York: Penguin Books, 1985.

Richetti, John. "Lovelace Goes Shopping at Smith's: Power, Play, and Class Privilege in *Clarissa.*" *Studies in the Literary Imagination* 28, no. 1 (Spring 1995): 23–34.

Robbins, Arthur David. "Grandiosity: An Overview." *Psychotherapy Patient* 5, nos. 3–4 (1989): 17–26.

Rogers, Katherine M. "Sensitive Feminism vs. Conventional Sympathy: Richardson and Fielding on Women." *Novel* 9, no. 3 (Spring 1976): 256–70.

Rothstein, Arnold. "An Exploration of the Diagnostic Term Narcissistic Personality Disorder." In *Handbook of Character Studies: Psychoanalytic Explorations,* ed. F. Manfred et al., 303–18. Madison, Conn.: International Universities Press, 1991.

———. "On Some Relationships of Fantasies of Perfection to the Calamities of Childhood." *International Journal of Psycho-Analysis* 72, no. 2 (1991): 313–23.

Rumney, Avis. *Dying to Please*. Jefferson and London: McFarland and Company, 1983.

Sale, William. "From *Pamela* to *Clarissa*." In *Essays on the Eighteenth Century Novel*, ed. Robert D. Spector, 18–31. Bloomington: Indiana University Press, 1965.

Salvaggio, Ruth. *Enlightened Absence: Neoclassical Configurations of the Feminine*. Urbana and Chicago: University of Illinois Press, 1988.

Seidenberg, Robert. "The Trauma of Eventlessness." In *Psychoanalysis and Women: Contributions to New Theory and Therapy*, ed. Jean Baker Miller, 353–67. New York: Brunner/Mazel, 1973.

Shakespeare, William. *Macbeth*. In *The Complete Illustrated Shakespeare*, ed. Howard Staunton, 466–525. New York: Park Lane, 1979.

Showalter, Elaine. *The Female Malady: Women, Madness and English Culture, 1830–1980*. New York: Pantheon Books, 1985.

Slater, Philip. "Toward a Dualistic Theory of Identification." *Merrill-Palmer Quarterly of Behavior and Development* 7 (1961): 113–26.

Smith, Sydney. "The Golden Fantasy: A Regressive Reaction to Separation Anxiety." *International Journal of Psycho-Analysis* 58 (1977): 311–24.

Sours, John A. *Starving to Death in a Sea of Objects*. New York: Jason Aronson, 1980.

Spacks, Patricia Meyer. "The Novel as Ethical Paradigm." *Novel* 21, nos. 2–3 (Winter–Spring 1988): 181–88.

———. "The Grand Misleader: Self-Love and Self-Division in *Clarissa*." *Studies in the Literary Imagination* 28, no. 1 (Spring 1995): 7–22.

Steiger, Howard. "Anorexia Nervosa and Bulimia in Males: Lessons from a Low Risk Population." *Canadian Journal of Psychiatry* 34 (1989): 419–24.

———. "Anorexia Nervosa: Is It the Syndrome or the Theorist That Is Culture- and Gender-Bound?" *Transcultural Psychiatric Research Review* 30 (1993): 347–58.

Stern, Daniel N. *The Interpersonal World of the Infant: A View from Psychoanalysis and Developmental Psychology*. New York: Basic Books, 1985.

Stevenson, John Allen. "The Courtship of the Family: Clarissa and the Harlowes Once More." *ELH* 48 (1981): 757–77.

Stone, Lawrence. *The Family, Sex and Marriage in England, 1500–1800*. New York: Harper and Row, 1977.

Stuber, Florian. "On Fathers and Authority in *Clarissa*." *Studies in English Literature* 25 (1985): 557–73.

———. "On Original and Final Intentions, or Can There Be an Authoritive *Clarissa*?" In *TEXT: Transactions of the Society for Textual Scholarship*, ed. D. C. Greetham and W. Speed Hill, 2:229<N<44. New York: AMS Press, 1985.

———. "*Clarissa*: A Religious Novel?" *Studies in the Literary Imagination* 28, no. 1 (Spring 1995): 105–24.

Tabin, Johanna K. "If the King Feels Grandiose, He Thinks He Is a God." *Psychotherapy-Patient* 5, nos. 3–4 (1989): 181–95.

Tannen, Deborah. *You Just Don't Understand: Women and Men in Conversation*. New York: William Morrow, 1990.

———. *Gender and Discourse*. Oxford: Oxford University Press, 1994.

Taylor, Anne Robinson. *Male Novelists and Their Female Voices: Literary Masquerades*. Troy, N.Y.: Whitston Publishing, 1981.

Thompson, Becky W. *A Hunger So Wide and So Deep: American Women Speak Out on Eating Problems*. Minneapolis: University of Minnesota Press, 1994.

Tiger, Lionel, and Robin Fox. *The Imperial Animal*. New York: Holt, Rinehart and Winston, 1971.

Todd, Janet. *Women's Friendship in Literature*. New York: Columbia University Press, 1980.

Tompkins, Jane. "Me and My Shadow." *New Literary History* 19 (1987–88): 169–78.

Traugott, John. "Molesting Clarissa." Review essay in *Novel* 15, no. 2 (Winter 1982): 163–70.

Trumbach, Randolph. *The Rise of the Egalitarian Family: Aristocratic Kinship and Domestic Relations in Eighteenth-century England*. New York: Academic Press, 1978.

Van Ghent, Dorothy. *The English Novel: Form and Function*. New York: Harper and Row, 1961.

Vandereycken, W., and A. Van Den Broucke. "Anorexia Nervosa in Males: A Comparative Study of 107 Cases Reported in the Literature (1970–1980)." *Acta Psychiatrica Scandinavica* 70 (1984): 447–54.

Vandereychken, W., and R. Van Deth. "Who Was the First to Describe Anorexia Nervosa: Gull or Lasegue?" *Psychological Medicine* 19 (1989): 837–45.

Warner, William Beatty. *Reading "Clarissa."* New Haven: Yale University Press, 1979.

———. "Reading Rape: Marxist-Feminist Figurations of the Literal." *Diacritics* (Winter 1983): 12–32.

Watt, Ian. *The Rise of The Novel: Studies in Defoe, Richardson and Fielding*. Berkeley: University of California Press, 1957.

White, Jane H. "Women and Eating Disorders, Part I: Significance and Sociocultural Risk Factors." *Health Care for Women International* 13 (1992): 351–62.

———. "Women and Eating Disorders, Part II: Developmental, Familial, and Biological Risk Factors." *Health Care for Women International* 13 (1992): 363–73.

Wilt, Judith. "He Could Go No Further: A Modest Proposal about Lovelace and Clarissa." *PMLA* 92, no. 1 (1977): 19–32.

Winnicott, D. W. *The Maturational Processes and the Facilitating Environment: Studies in the Theory of Emotional Development*. New York: International Universities Press, 1965.

Winthrop, John. *The History of New England from 1630 to 1649*. Ed. James Savage. Boston: Phelps and Farnham, 1826.

Wolff, Cynthia Griffin. *Samuel Richardson and the Eighteenth Century Puritan Character*. Hamden, Conn.: Archon Books, 1972.

Zomchick, John P. "Tame Spirits, Brave Fellows, and the Web of the Law: Robert Lovelace's Legalistic Conscience." *EHL* 53, no. 1 (Spring 1986): 99–120.

Index

Entries in this index include the names of those secondary authors whose works are cited several times or at length in the text as part of a discussion of primary indexed topics.

anorexia multiforme, 3

anorexia nervosa (AN), 2–3, 115, 123–26, 129, 132n. 16, 159n. 5, 161n. 26, 161n. 34

Astell, Mary: *Some Reflections upon Marriage*, 23

attachment theory, 135n. 9

autonomy. *See* separation-individuation process

Belford: as biographer, 94–95, 104–12. *See also* saintly suffering, story of

boundary confusion. *See* Clarissa, relation with mother; mothering; perfect children, families of

Brownstein, Rachel Mayer, 6, 23, 113, 136–37n. 16, 143n. 55, 144n. 64, 146n. 8, 146n. 10, 147n. 14, 158n. 1

Bruch, Hilde, 13, 16, 38, 116, 125, 128

Brumberg, Joan Jacobs, 123

Bynum, Caroline Walker, 94–96, 98–99, 102–3, 105, 117, 127, 157n. 29, 158n. 37

cannibalism, 115, 151n. 33

Castle, Terry, 3–4, 122, 131n. 14, 134n. 3, 134n. 6, 140n. 37, 143n. 52, 143n. 58, 144n. 64, 150n. 32, 154–55n. 10, 156n. 15, 156n. 17, 156n. 22, 157n. 30, 158n. 4, 158n. 38

Cheyne, George, 118–20, 129, 160n. 13

child rearing, 12–13, 23, 123, 135n. 9, 136n. 12, 137n. 21. *See also* mothering

Chodorow, Nancy, 6, 137n. 25, 138n. 27, 142n. 51, 149n. 27, 159n. 8

Christianity. *See* Clarissa, as fasting saint, as mythic; Lovelace, as mythic; Richardson, as Christian writer; saintly suffering, story of

Clarissa, 5–7, 25, 82–83, 118–19, 133n. 1, 140–41n. 38, 146n. 6, 153nn. 4–5, 154n. 8; critical debates concerning, 1–2, 4–6, 23–24, 58, 118, 120, 132n. 18, 133–34n. 3, 153n. 5

Clarissa

asceticism of, 3, 82, 121–23, 160nn. 21–22

charity of, 100–102, 109–10, 160n. 18

death of, 83, 97–98, 101–4, 110–11, 128, 154n. 6, 155n. 11, 156n. 17, 157n. 30, 158n. 40, 160n. 21

as dreamer, 28–31, 33, 42, 92, 143n. 57

duality of, 6, 15–17, 37, 58, 137n. 16, 137nn. 19–20

as family possession, 11, 13, 15, 24, 28–30, 34, 38, 47, 50, 110, 133–34nn. 3–5, 140n. 37

as fasting saint, 82–83, 94–105, 108, 111, 117, 121, 131n. 13, 160–61n. 21

as mythic, 59–60, 145n. 68, 153n. 6, 155n. 13

passivity of, 7–10, 29–30, 32, 136–37n. 16, 143n. 58

and patriarchal power, 134n. 6, 141n. 38, 146n. 2

and prescribed perfection, 14–16, 20, 28, 31, 59–61, 71, 82–83, 106, 111

as public legend, 8–9, 11, 14–15, 45, 51, 69, 71, 101, 140n. 36

rape of, 16, 57, 69–70, 100, 146n. 9, 146n. 11, 147n. 12, 147n. 14